PRAXIS II
MATHEMATICS 0061

By: Sharon Wynne, M.S.

XAMonline, INC.
Boston

To obtain permission(s) to use the material from this work for any purpose including workshops or seminars, please submit a written request to:

XAMonline, Inc.
25 First Street, Suite 106
Cambridge, MA 02141
Toll Free 1-800-509-4128
Email: info@xamonline.com
Web: www.xamonline.com
Fax: 1-617-583-5552

Library of Congress Cataloging-in-Publication Data

Wynne, Sharon A.
    PRAXIS II Mathematics 0061 / Sharon A. Wynne. 4th ed
    ISBN 978-1-60787-324-2
    1. PRAXIS II Mathematics 0061
    2. Study Guides
    3. PRAXIS
    4. Teachers' Certification & Licensure
    5. Careers

Disclaimer:
The opinions expressed in this publication are the sole works of XAMonline and were created independently from the National Education Association, Educational Testing Service, or any State Department of Education, National Evaluation Systems or other testing affiliates.

Between the time of publication and printing, state specific standards as well as testing formats and Web site information may change and therefore would not be included in part or in whole within this product. Sample test questions are developed by XAMonline and reflect content similar to that on real tests; however, they are not former test questions. XAMonline assembles content that aligns with state standards but makes no claims nor guarantees teacher candidates a passing score. Numerical scores are determined by testing companies such as NES or ETS and then are compared with individual state standards. A passing score varies from state to state.

Printed in the United States of America   œ-1

PRAXIS II Mathematics 0061
ISBN: 978-1-60787-324-2

Table of Contents

DOMAIN I
ALGEBRA AND NUMBER THEORY 1

COMPETENCY 1
ALGEBRA AND NUMBER THEORY 3

Skill 1.1: Demonstrate an understanding of the structure of the natural, integer, rational, real, and complex number systems and the ability to perform basic operations ($+$, $-$, $\times$, and $\div$) on numbers in these systems 3

Skill 1.2: Compare and contrast properties *(e.g., closure, commutativity, associativity, distributivity)* **of number systems under various operations** 10

Skill 1.3: Demonstrate an understanding of the properties of counting numbers *(e.g., prime, composite, prime factorization, even, odd, factors, multiples)* 12

Skill 1.4: Solve ratio, proportion, percent, and average *(including arithmetic mean and weighted average)* **problems** 18

Skill 1.5: Work with algebraic expressions, formulas, and equations; add, subtract, multiply, and divide polynomials; add, subtract, multiply, and divide algebraic fractions; perform standard algebraic operations involving complex numbers, radicals, and exponents, including fractional and negative exponents 19

Skill 1.6: Solve and graph systems of equations and inequalities, including those involving absolute value 19

Skill 1.7: Interpret algebraic principles geometrically 27

Skill 1.8: Recognize and use algebraic representations of lines, planes, conic sections, and spheres 28

Skill 1.9: Solve problems in two and three dimensions *(e.g., find the distance between two points, find the coordinates of the midpoint of a line segment)* 34

DOMAIN II
MEASUREMENT, GEOMETRY, AND TRIGONOMETRY 35

COMPETENCY 2
MEASUREMENT 37

Skill 2.1: Make decisions about units and scales that are appropriate for problem situations involving measurement; use unit analysis 37

Skill 2.2: Analyze precision, accuracy, and approximate error in measurement situations 45

Skill 2.3: Apply informal concepts of successive approximation, upper and lower bounds, and limit in measurement situations 46

COMPETENCY 3
GEOMETRY 49

Skill 3.1: Solve problems using relationships of parts of geometric figures (*e.g., medians of triangles, inscribed angles in circles*) **and among geometric figures** (*e.g., congruence and similarity*) **in two and three dimensions** 49

Skill 3.2: Describe relationships among sets of special quadrilaterals, such as the square, rectangle, parallelogram, rhombus, and trapezoid 59

Skill 3.3: Solve problems using the properties of triangles, quadrilaterals, polygons, circles, and parallel and perpendicular lines 63

Skill 3.4: Solve problems using the properties of circles, including those involving inscribed angles, central angles, chords, radii, tangents, secants, arcs, and sectors 71

Skill 3.5: Understand and apply the Pythagorean Theorem and its converse 78

Skill 3.6: Compute and reason about perimeter, area/surface area, or volume of two- and three-dimensional figures or of regions or solids that are combinations of these figures. 80

Skill 3.7: Solve problems involving reflections, rotations, and translations of geometric figures in the plane 88

COMPETENCY 4
TRIGONOMETRY 94

Skill 4.1: Define and use the six basic trigonometric relations using degree or radian measure of angles; know their graphs and be able to identify their periods, amplitudes, phase displacements or shifts, and asymptotes 94

Skill 4.2: Apply the Law of Sines and the Law of Cosines 103

Skill 4.3: Apply the formulas for the trigonometric functions of $x/2$, $2x$, x, $x + y$, and $x − y$; prove trigonometric identities 104

Skill 4.4: Solve trigonometric equations and inequalities 109

Skill 4.5: Convert between rectangular and polar coordinate systems 111

DOMAIN III
FUNCTIONS AND CALCULUS 113

COMPETENCY 5
FUNCTIONS 115

Skill 5.1: Demonstrate an understanding of and the ability to work with functions in various representations (*e.g., graphs, tables, symbolic expressions, and verbal narratives*), **and the ability to convert flexibly among them** 115

Skill 5.2: Find an appropriate family of functions to model particular phenomena (*e.g., population growth, cooling, simple harmonic motion*) 116

Skill 5.3: Determine properties of a function such as domain, range, intercepts, symmetries, intervals of increase or decrease, discontinuities, and asymptotes 117

Skill 5.4: Use the properties of trigonometric, exponential, logarithmic, polynomial, and rational functions to solve problems 122

Skill 5.5: Determine the composition of two functions; find the inverse of a one-to-one function in simple cases and know why only one-to-one functions have inverses 133

Skill 5.6: Interpret representations of functions of two variables, such as three-dimensional graphs, level curves, and tables 135

COMPETENCY 6
CALCULUS

CALCULUS 137

Skill 6.1: **Demonstrate an understanding of what it means for a function to have a limit at a point; calculate limits of functions or determine that the limit does not exist; solve problems using the properties of limits** 138

Skill 6.2: **Understand the derivative of a function as a limit, as the slope of a curve, and as a rate of change** (e.g., velocity, acceleration, growth, decay) 141

Skill 6.3: **Show that a particular function is continuous; understand the relationship between continuity and differentiability** 143

Skill 6.4: **Numerically approximate derivatives and integrals** 148

Skill 6.5: **Use standard differentiation and integration techniques** 148

Skill 6.6: **Analyze the behavior of a function** (e.g., find relative maxima and minima, concavity); **solve problems involving related rates; solve applied minima-maxima problems** 153

Skill 6.7: **Demonstrate an understanding of and the ability to use the Mean Value Theorem and the Fundamental Theorem of Calculus** 161

Skill 6.8: **Demonstrate an intuitive understanding of integration as a limiting sum that can be used to compute area, volume, distance, or other accumulation processes** 163

Skill 6.9: **Determine the limits of sequences and simple infinite series** 179

DOMAIN IV
DATA ANALYSIS AND STATISTICS AND PROBABILITY 181

COMPETENCY 7
DATA ANALYSIS AND STATISTICS

DATA ANALYSIS AND STATISTICS 183

Skill 7.1: **Organize data into a suitable form** (e.g., construct a histogram and use it in the calculation of probabilities) 183

Skill 7.2: **Know and find the appropriate uses of common measures of central tendency** (e.g., population mean, sample mean, median, mode) **and dispersion** (e.g., range, population standard deviation, sample standard deviation, population variance, sample variance) 187

Skill 7.3: **Analyze data from specific situations to determine what type of function** (e.g., linear, quadratic, exponential) **would most likely model that particular phenomenon; use the regression feature of the calculator to determine curve of best fit; interpret the regression coefficients, correlation, and residuals in context** 192

Skill 7.4: **Understand and apply normal distributions and their characteristics** (mean, standard deviation) 196

Skill 7.5: **Understand how sample statistics reflect the values of population parameters, and use sampling distributions as the basis for informal inference** 199

Skill 7.6: **Understand the differences among various kinds of studies and which types of inferences can legitimately be drawn from each** 200

Skill 7.7: **Know the characteristics of well-defined studies, including the role of randomization in surveys and experiments** 200

COMPETENCY 8
PROBABILITY

PROBABILITY 202

Skill 8.1: **Understand the concepts of sample space and probability distribution, and construct sample spaces and distributions in simple cases** 202

Skill 8.2: Understand the concepts of conditional probability and independent events; understand how to compute the probability of a compound event..204

Skill 8.3: Compute and interpret the expected value of random variables in simple cases (e.g., fair coins, expected winnings, expected profit)..206

Skill 8.4: Use simulations to construct empirical probability distributions and to make informal inferences about the theoretical probability distribution 207

DOMAIN V
MATRIX ALGEBRA AND DISCRETE MATHEMATICS 209

COMPETENCY 9
MATRIX ALGEBRA 211

Skill 9.1: Understand vectors and matrices as systems that have some of the same properties as the real number system (e.g., identity, inverse, and commutativity under addition and multiplication)................................211

Skill 9.2: Scalar multiply, add, subtract, and multiply vectors and matrices; find inverses of matrices 212

Skill 9.3: Use matrix techniques to solve systems of linear equations 217

Skill 9.4: Use determinants to reason about inverses of matrices and solutions to systems of equations................219

Skill 9.5: Understand and represent translations, reflections, rotations, and dilations of objects in the plane by using sketches, coordinates, vectors, and matrices 220

COMPETENCY 10
DISCRETE MATHEMATICS 225

Skill 10.1: Solve basic problems that involve counting techniques, including the multiplication principle, permutations, and combinations; use counting techniques to understand various situations (e.g., number of ways to order a set of objects, to choose a subcommittee from a committee, to visit n cities) 225

Skill 10.2: Find values of functions defined recursively and understand how recursion can be used to model various phenomena; translate between recursive and closed-form expressions for a function................................231

Skill 10.3: Determine whether a binary relation on a set is reflexive, symmetric, or transitive; determine whether a relation is an equivalence relation 233

Skill 10.4: Use finite and infinite arithmetic and geometric sequences and series to model simple phenomena (e.g., compound interest, annuity, growth, decay) 234

Skill 10.5: Understand the relationship between discrete and continuous representations and how they can be used to model various phenomena 239

Skill 10.6: Use difference equations, vertex-edge graphs, trees, and networks to model and solve problems 241

SAMPLE TEST

Sample Test 244

Answer Key 260

Rigor Table 260

Sample Questions with Rationales 261

P R A X I S I I
MATHEMATICS 0061

SECTION 1

ABOUT XAMONLINE

XAMonline—A Specialty Teacher Certification Company

Created in 1996, XAMonline was the first company to publish study guides for state-specific teacher certification examinations. Founder Sharon Wynne found it frustrating that materials were not available for teacher certification preparation and decided to create the first single, state-specific guide. XAMonline has grown into a company of over 1,800 contributors and writers and offers over 300 titles for the entire PRAXIS series and every state examination. No matter what state you plan on teaching in, XAMonline has a unique teacher certification study guide just for you.

XAMonline—Value and Innovation

We are committed to providing value and innovation. Our print-on-demand technology allows us to be the first in the market to reflect changes in test standards and user feedback as they occur. Our guides are written by experienced teachers who are experts in their fields. And our content reflects the highest standards of quality. Comprehensive practice tests with varied levels of rigor means that your study experience will closely match the actual in-test experience.

To date, XAMonline has helped nearly 600,000 teachers pass their certification or licensing exams. Our commitment to preparation exceeds simply providing the proper material for study—it extends to helping teachers **gain mastery** of the subject matter, giving them the **tools** to become the most effective classroom leaders possible, and ushering today's students toward a **successful future**.

SECTION 2

ABOUT THIS STUDY GUIDE

Purpose of This Guide

Is there a little voice inside of you saying, "Am I ready?" Our goal is to replace that little voice and remove all doubt with a new voice that says, "I AM READY. **Bring it on!**" by offering the highest quality of teacher certification study guides.

Organization of Content

You will see that while every test may start with overlapping general topics, each is very unique in the skills they wish to test. Only XAMonline presents custom content that analyzes deeper than a title, a subarea, or an objective. Only XAMonline presents content and sample test assessments along with **focus statements**, the deepest-level rationale and interpretation of the skills that are unique to the exam.

Title and field number of test

∞Each exam has its own name and number. XAMonline's guides are written to give you the content you need to know for the specific exam you are taking. You can be confident when you buy our guide that it contains the information you need to study for the specific test you are taking.

Subareas

∞These are the major content categories found on the exam. XAMonline's guides are written to cover all of the subareas found in the test frameworks developed for the exam.

Objectives

∞These are standards that are unique to the exam and represent the main subcategories of the subareas/content categories. XAMonline's guides are written to address every specific objective required to pass the exam.

Focus statements

∞These are examples and interpretations of the objectives. You find them in parenthesis directly following the objective. They provide detailed examples of the range, type, and level of content that appear on the test questions. **Only XAMonline's guides drill down to this level.**

How Do We Compare with Our Competitors?

XAMonline—drills down to the focus statement level.
CliffsNotes and REA—organized at the objective level
Kaplan—provides only links to content
MoMedia—content not specific to the state test

Each subarea is divided into manageable sections that cover the specific skill areas. Explanations are easy to understand and thorough. You'll find that every test answer contains a rejoinder so if you need a refresher or further review after taking the test, you'll know exactly to which section you must return.

How to Use This Book

Our informal polls show that most people begin studying up to eight weeks prior to the test date, so start early. Then ask yourself some questions: How much do you really know? Are you coming to the test straight from your teacher-education program or are you having to review subjects you haven't considered in ten years? Either way, take a **diagnostic or assessment test** first. Also, spend time on sample tests so that you become accustomed to the way the actual test will appear.

This guide comes with an online diagnostic test of 30 questions found online at *www.XAMonline.com*. It is a little boot camp to get you up for the task and reveal things about your compendium of knowledge in general. Although this guide is structured to follow the order of the test, you are not required to study in that order. By finding a time-management and study plan that fits your life you will be more effective. The results of your diagnostic or self-assessment test can be a guide for how to manage your time and point you toward an area that needs more attention.

After taking the diagnostic exam, fill out the **Personalized Study Plan** page at the beginning of each chapter. Review the competencies and skills covered in that chapter and check the boxes that apply to your study needs. If there are sections you already know you can skip, check the "skip it" box. Taking this step will give you a study plan for each chapter.

Week	Activity
8 weeks prior to test	Take a diagnostic test found at www.XAMonline.com
7 weeks prior to test	Build your Personalized Study Plan for each chapter. Check the "skip it" box for sections you feel you are already strong in. ✘ SKIP IT ☐
6-3 weeks prior to test	For each of these four weeks, choose a content area to study. You don't have to go in the order of the book. It may be that you start with the content that needs the most review. Alternately, you may want to ease yourself into plan by starting with the most familiar material.
2 weeks prior to test	Take the sample test, score it, and create a review plan for the final week before the test.
1 week prior to test	Following your plan (which will likely be aligned with the areas that need the most review) go back and study the sections that align with the questions you may have gotten wrong. Then go back and study the sections related to the questions you answered correctly. If need be, create flashcards and drill yourself on any area that you makes you anxious.

SECTION 3
ABOUT THE PRAXIS EXAMS

What Is PRAXIS?

PRAXIS II tests measure the knowledge of specific content areas in K-12 education. The test is a way of insuring that educators are prepared to not only teach in a particular subject area, but also have the necessary teaching skills to be effective. The Educational Testing Service administers the test in most states and has worked with the states to develop the material so that it is appropriate for state standards.

PRAXIS Points

1. The PRAXIS Series comprises more than 140 different tests in over seventy different subject areas.

2. Over 90% of the PRAXIS tests measure subject area knowledge.

3. The purpose of the test is to measure whether the teacher candidate possesses a sufficient level of knowledge and skills to perform job duties effectively and responsibly.

4. Your state sets the acceptable passing score.

5. Any candidate, whether from a traditional teaching-preparation path or an alternative route, can seek to enter the teaching profession by taking a PRAXIS test.

6. PRAXIS tests are updated regularly to ensure current content.

Often **your own state's requirements** determine whether or not you should take any particular test. The most reliable source of information regarding this is either your state's Department of Education or the Educational Testing Service. Either resource should also have a complete list of testing centers and dates. Test dates vary by subject area and not all test dates necessarily include your particular test, so be sure to check carefully.

If you are in a teacher-education program, check with the Education Department or the Certification Officer for specific information for testing and testing time-lines. The Certification Office should have most of the information you need.

If you choose an alternative route to certification you can either rely on our Web site at *www.XAMonline.com* or on the resources provided by an alternative certification program. Many states now have specific agencies devoted to alternative certification and there are some national organizations as well:

National Center for Education Information
http://www.ncei.com/Alt-Teacher-Cert.htm

National Associate for Alternative Certification
http://www.alt-teachercert.org/index.asp

Interpreting Test Results

Contrary to what you may have heard, the results of a PRAXIS test are not based on time. More accurately, you will be scored on the raw number of points you earn in relation to the raw number of points available. Each question is worth one raw point. It is likely to your benefit to complete as many questions in the time allotted, but it will not necessarily work to your advantage if you hurry through the test.

Follow the guidelines provided by ETS for interpreting your score. The web site offers a sample test score sheet and clearly explains how the scores are scaled and what to expect if you have an essay portion on your test.

Scores are usually available by phone within a month of the test date and scores will be sent to your chosen institution(s) within six weeks. Additionally, ETS now makes online, downloadable reports available for 45 days from the reporting date.

It is **critical** that you be aware of your own state's passing score. Your raw score may qualify you to teach in some states, but not all. ETS administers the test and assigns a score, but the states make their own interpretations and, in some cases, consider combined scores if you are testing in more than one area.

What's on the Test?

PRAXIS tests vary from subject to subject and sometimes even within subject area. For PRAXIS Mathematics (0061), the test lasts for 2 hours and consists of approximately 50 multiple-choice questions. The use of a graphing calculator is required for this test. The breakdown of the questions is as follows:

Category	Approximate Number of Questions	Approximate Percentage of the test
I: Algebra and Number Theory	8	16%
II: Measurement	3	6%
-Geometry	5	10%
-Trigonometry	4	8%

Table continued on next page

Category	Approximate Number of Questions	Approximate Percentage of the test
III: Functions	8	16%
-Calculus	6	12%
IV: Data Analysis and Statistics	5-6	10-12%
-Probability	2-3	4-6%
V: Matrix Algebra	4-5	8-10%
-Discrete Mathematics	3-4	6-8%

The following process categories are distributed throughout the test questions in each category:
- Mathematical Problem Solving
- Mathematical Reasoning and Proof
- Mathematical Connections
- Mathematical Representation
- Use of Technology

This chart can be used to build a study plan. Sixteen percent may seem like a lot of time to spend on Algebra and Number Theory, but when you consider that amounts to about 4 out of 25 multiple choice questions, it might change your perspective.

Question Types

You're probably thinking, enough already, I want to study! Indulge us a little longer while we explain that there is actually more than one type of multiple-choice question. You can thank us later after you realize how well prepared you are for your exam.

1. Complete the Statement. The name says it all. In this question type you'll be asked to choose the correct completion of a given statement. For example:

> **The Dolch Basic Sight Words consist of a relatively short list of words that children should be able to:**
>
> A. Sound out
>
> B. Know the meaning of
>
> C. Recognize on sight
>
> D. Use in a sentence

The correct answer is C. In order to check your answer, test out the statement by adding the choices to the end of it.

2. Which of the Following. One way to test your answer choice for this type of question is to replace the phrase "which of the following" with your selection. Use this example:

> **Which of the following words is one of the twelve most frequently used in children's reading texts:**
>
> A. There
>
> B. This
>
> C. The
>
> D. An

Don't look! Test your answer. _____ is one of the twelve most frequently used in children's reading texts. Did you guess C? Then you guessed correctly.

3. Roman Numeral Choices. This question type is used when there is more than one possible correct answer. For example:

> **Which of the following two arguments accurately supports the use of cooperative learning as an effective method of instruction?**
> I.   Cooperative learning groups facilitate healthy competition between individuals in the group.
> II. Cooperative learning groups allow academic achievers to carry or cover for academic underachievers.
> III. Cooperative learning groups make each student in the group accountable for the success of the group.
> IV. Cooperative learning groups make it possible for students to reward other group members for achieving.
>
> A. I and II
>
> B. II and III
>
> C. I and III
>
> D. III and IV

Notice that the question states there are **two** possible answers. It's best to read all the possibilities first before looking at the answer choices. In this case, the correct answer is D.

4. Negative Questions. This type of question contains words such as "not," "least," and "except." Each correct answer will be the statement that does **not** fit the situation described in the question. Such as:

> **Multicultural education is not**
>
> A. An idea or concept
>
> B. A "tack-on" to the school curriculum
>
> C. An educational reform movement
>
> D. A process

Think to yourself that the statement could be anything but the correct answer. This question form is more open to interpretation than other types, so read carefully and don't forget that you're answering a negative statement.

5. Questions that Include Graphs, Tables, or Reading Passages. As always, read the question carefully. It likely asks for a very specific answer and not a broad interpretation of the visual. Here is a simple (though not statistically accurate) example of a graph question:

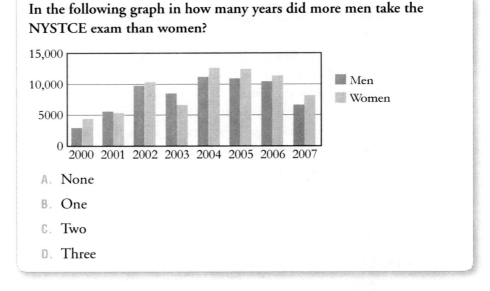

> **In the following graph in how many years did more men take the NYSTCE exam than women?**
>
> A. None
>
> B. One
>
> C. Two
>
> D. Three

It may help you to simply circle the two years that answer the question. Make sure you've read the question thoroughly and once you've made your determination, double check your work. The correct answer is C.

SECTION 4
HELPFUL HINTS

Study Tips

1. **You are what you eat.** Certain foods aid the learning process by releasing natural memory enhancers called CCKs (cholecystokinin) composed of tryptophan, choline, and phenylalanine. All of these chemicals enhance the neurotransmitters associated with memory and certain foods release memory enhancing chemicals. A light meal or snacks of one of the following foods fall into this category:

   - Milk
   - Rice
   - Eggs
   - Fish
   - Nuts and seeds
   - Oats
   - Turkey

   The better the connections, the more you comprehend!

2. **See the forest for the trees.** In other words, get the concept before you look at the details. One way to do this is to take notes as you read, paraphrasing or summarizing in your own words. Putting the concept in terms that are comfortable and familiar may increase retention.

3. **Question authority.** Ask why, why, why? Pull apart written material paragraph by paragraph and don't forget the captions under the illustrations. For example, if a heading reads *Stream Erosion* put it in the form of a question (Why do streams erode? What is stream erosion?) then find the answer within the material. If you train your mind to think in this manner you will learn more and prepare yourself for answering test questions.

4. **Play mind games.** Using your brain for reading or puzzles keeps it flexible. Even with a limited amount of time your brain can take in data (much like a computer) and store it for later use. In ten minutes you can: read two paragraphs (at least), quiz yourself with flash cards, or review notes. Even if you don't fully understand something on the first pass, your mind stores it for recall, which is why frequent reading or review increases chances of retention and comprehension.

5. **The pen is mightier than the sword.** Learn to take great notes. A by-product of our modern culture is that we have grown accustomed to getting our information in short doses. We've subconsciously trained ourselves to assimilate information into neat little packages. Messy notes fragment the flow of information. Your notes can be much clearer with proper formatting. *The Cornell Method* is one such format. This method was popularized in *How to Study in College*, Ninth Edition, by Walter Pauk. You can benefit from the method without purchasing an additional book by simply looking up the method online. Below is a sample of how *The Cornell Method* can be adapted for use with this guide.

$\leftarrow 2\frac{1}{2}" \rightarrow$ **Cue Column**	$\longleftarrow$ 6" $\longrightarrow$ **Note Taking Column**
	1. Record: During your reading, use the note-taking column to record important points.
	2. Questions: As soon as you finish a section, formulate questions based on the notes in the right-hand column. Writing questions helps to clarify meanings, reveal relationships, establish community, and strengthen memory. Also, the writing of questions sets the state for exam study later.
	3. Recite: Cover the note-taking column with a sheet of paper. Then, looking at the questions or cue-words in the question and cue column only, say aloud, in your own words, the answers to the questions, facts, or ideas indicated by the cue words.
	4. Reflect: Reflect on the material by asking yourself questions.
	5. Review: Spend at least ten minutes every week reviewing all your previous notes. Doing so helps you retain ideas and topics for the exam.
$\uparrow$ 2" $\downarrow$	**Summary** After reading, use this space to summarize the notes from each page.

*Adapted from How to Study in College, Ninth Edition, by Walter Pauk, ©2008 Wadsworth

6. **Place yourself in exile and set the mood.** Set aside a particular place and time to study that best suits your personal needs and biorhythms. If you're a night person, burn the midnight oil. If you're a morning person set yourself up with some coffee and get to it. Make your study time and place as free from distraction as possible and surround yourself with what you need, be it silence or music. Studies have shown that music can aid in concentration, absorption, and retrieval of information. Not all music, though. Classical music is said to work best

7. **Get pointed in the right direction.** Use arrows to point to important passages or pieces of information. It's easier to read than a page full of yellow highlights. Highlighting can be used sparingly, but add an arrow to the margin to call attention to it.

8. **Check your budget.** You should at least review all the content material before your test, but allocate the most amount of time to the areas that need the most refreshing. It sounds obvious, but it's easy to forget. You can use the study rubric above to balance your study budget.

> *The proctor will write the start time where it can be seen and then, later, provide the time remaining, typically fifteen minutes before the end of the test.*

Testing Tips

1. **Get smart, play dumb.** Sometimes a question is just a question. No one is out to trick you, so don't assume that the test writer is looking for something other than what was asked. Stick to the question as written and don't overanalyze.

2. **Do a double take.** Read test questions and answer choices at least twice because it's easy to miss something, to transpose a word or some letters. If you have no idea what the correct answer is, skip it and come back later if there's time. If you're still clueless, it's okay to guess. Remember, you're scored on the number of questions you answer correctly and you're not penalized for wrong answers. The worst case scenario is that you miss a point from a good guess.

3. **Turn it on its ear.** The syntax of a question can often provide a clue, so make things interesting and turn the question into a statement to see if it changes the meaning or relates better (or worse) to the answer choices.

4. **Get out your magnifying glass.** Look for hidden clues in the questions because it's difficult to write a multiple-choice question without giving away part of the answer in the options presented. In most questions you can readily eliminate one or two potential answers, increasing your chances of answering correctly to 50/50, which will help out if you've skipped a question and gone back to it (see tip #2).

5. Call it intuition. Often your first instinct is correct. If you've been studying the content you've likely absorbed something and have subconsciously retained the knowledge. On questions you're not sure about trust your instincts because a first impression is usually correct.

6. Graffiti. Sometimes it's a good idea to mark your answers directly on the test booklet and go back to fill in the optical scan sheet later. You don't get extra points for perfectly blackened ovals. If you choose to manage your test this way, be sure not to mismark your answers when you transcribe to the scan sheet.

7. Become a clock-watcher. You have a set amount of time to answer the questions. Don't get bogged down laboring over a question you're not sure about when there are ten others you could answer more readily. If you choose to follow the advice of tip #6, be sure you leave time near the end to go back and fill in the scan sheet.

Do the Drill

No matter how prepared you feel it's sometimes a good idea to apply Murphy's Law. So the following tips might seem silly, mundane, or obvious, but we're including them anyway.

1. Remember, you are what you eat, so bring a snack. Choose from the list of energizing foods that appear earlier in the introduction.

2. You're not too sexy for your test. Wear comfortable clothes. You'll be distracted if your belt is too tight or if you're too cold or too hot.

3. Lie to yourself. Even if you think you're a prompt person, pretend you're not and leave plenty of time to get to the testing center. Map it out ahead of time and do a dry run if you have to. There's no need to add road rage to your list of anxieties.

4. Bring sharp number 2 pencils. It may seem impossible to forget this need from your school days, but you might. And make sure the erasers are intact, too.

5. No ticket, no test. Bring your admission ticket as well as **two** forms of identification, including one with a picture and signature. You will not be admitted to the test without these things.

6. You can't take it with you. Leave any study aids, dictionaries, notebooks, computers, and the like at home. Certain tests **do** allow a scientific or four-function calculator, so check ahead of time to see if your test does.

7. **Prepare for the desert.** Any time spent on a bathroom break **cannot** be made up later, so use your judgment on the amount you eat or drink.

8. **Quiet, Please!** Keeping your own time is a good idea, but not with a timepiece that has a loud ticker. If you use a watch, take it off and place it nearby but not so that it distracts you. And **silence your cell phone**.

To the best of our ability, we have compiled the content you need to know in this book and in the accompanying online resources. The rest is up to you. You can use the study and testing tips or you can follow your own methods. Either way, you can be confident that there aren't any missing pieces of information and there shouldn't be any surprises in the content on the test.

If you have questions about test fees, registration, electronic testing, or other content verification issues please visit *www.ets.org*.

Good luck!

Sharon Wynne
Founder, XAMonline

DOMAIN I

ALGEBRA AND
NUMBER THEORY

PERSONALIZED STUDY PLAN

KNOWN MATERIAL/ SKIP IT

PAGE	COMPETENCY AND SKILL	
3	**1:**	**Algebra and number theory**	☐
	1.1:	Demonstrate an understanding of the structure of number systems and the ability to perform basic operations	☐
	1.2:	Compare and contrast properties of number systems under various operations	☐
	1.3:	Demonstrate an understanding of the properties of counting numbers	☐
	1.4:	Solve ratio, proportion, percent, and average problems	☐
	1.5:	Work with algebraic expressions, formulas, and equations; polynomials; algebraic fractions; operations involving complex numbers, radicals, and exponents	☐
	1.6:	Solve and graph systems of equations and inequalities	☐
	1.7:	Interpret algebraic principles geometrically	☐
	1.8:	Recognize and use algebraic representations of lines, planes, conic sections, and spheres	☐
	1.9:	Solve problems in two and three dimensions	☐

COMPETENCY 1
ALGEBRA AND NUMBER THEORY

Underlying many of the more involved fields of mathematics is an understanding of basic algebra and number theory. A foundation in these concepts allows for expansion of knowledge into trigonometry, calculus, and other areas. The following discussion covers the essential properties of standard sets of numbers (such as real and complex numbers).

Real Numbers

The following chart shows the relationships among the subsets of the real numbers.

Real Numbers

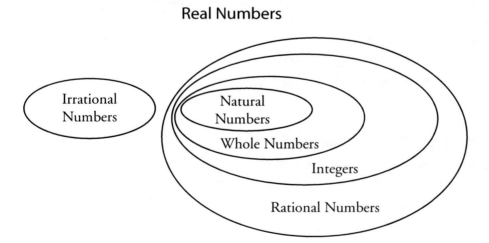

REAL NUMBERS are denoted by $\mathbb{R}$ and are numbers that can be shown by an infinite decimal representation such as 3.286275347 . . . . Real numbers include rational numbers, such as 242 and –23/129, and irrational numbers, such as $\sqrt{2}$ and π, and can be represented as points along an infinite number line. Real numbers are also known as "the unique complete Archimedean *ordered field*." Real numbers are to be distinguished from imaginary numbers.

> **REAL NUMBERS:** numbers that can be represented by an infinite decimal representation

Real numbers are classified as follows:

CLASSIFICATIONS OF REAL NUMBERS	
Natural Numbers Denoted by $\mathbb{N}$	The counting numbers. 1, 2, 3, . . .
Whole Numbers	The counting numbers along with zero. 0, 1, 2, 3, . . .
Integers, Denoted by $\mathbb{Z}$	The counting numbers, their negatives, and zero. . . . , –2, –1, 0, 1, 2, . . .
Rationals, Denoted by $\mathbb{Q}$	All of the fractions that can be formed using whole numbers. Zero cannot be the denominator. In decimal form, these numbers will be either terminating or repeating decimals. Simplify square roots to determine if the number can be written as a fraction.
Irrationals	Real numbers that cannot be written as a fraction. The decimal forms of these numbers neither terminate nor repeat. Examples include π, e and $\sqrt{2}$.

Operations on Whole Numbers

Mathematical operations include addition, subtraction, multiplication, and division. Addition can be indicated by these expressions: *sum, greater than, and, more than, increased by, added to*. Subtraction can be expressed by the phrases *difference, fewer than, minus, less than, and decreased by*. Multiplication is shown by *product, times, multiplied by*, and *twice*. Division is indicated by *quotient, divided by*, and *ratio*.

Addition and subtraction

There are two main procedures used in addition and subtraction: adding or subtracting single digits and "carrying" or "borrowing."

Example: Find the sum of 346 + 225 using place value.

PLACE VALUE		
100	10	1
3 2	4 2	6 5
5	6	11
5	7	1

Standard algorithm for addition check:

$$
\begin{array}{r}
3\ {}^{1}4\ 6 \\
+\,2\ \ \ 2\ 5 \\
\hline
5\ \ \ 7\ 1
\end{array}
$$

Example: Find the difference 234 − 46 using place value.

PLACE VALUE		
100	10	1
1	13 4	4 6

PLACE VALUE		
100	10	1
1	12 4	14 6
1	8	8

Standard algorithm for subtraction check:

$$
\begin{array}{r}
2\ 3\ 4 \\
-\ \ \ 4\ 6 \\
\hline
1\ 8\ 8
\end{array}
$$

Multiplication and division

Multiplication is one of the four basic number operations. In simple terms, multiplication is the addition of a number to itself a certain number of times. For example, 4 multiplied by 3 is the equal to $4 + 4 + 4$ or $3 + 3 + 3 + 3$. Another way of conceptualizing multiplication is to think in terms of groups. For example, if we have 4 groups of 3 students, the total number of students is 4 multiplied by 3. We call the solution to a multiplication problem the PRODUCT.

PRODUCT: a solution to a multiplication problem

Example: A student buys 4 boxes of crayons. Each box contains 16 crayons. How many total crayons does the student have?

The total number of crayons is 16×4.

$$\begin{array}{r} 16 \\ \times\ \ 4 \\ \hline 64 \end{array}$$ Total number of crayons equals 64 crayons.

Division, the inverse of multiplication, is another of the four basic number operations. When we divide one number by another, we determine how many times we can multiply the divisor (number divided by) before we exceed the number we are dividing (dividend). For example, 8 divided by 2 equals 4 because we can multiply 2 four times to reach 8 ($2 \times 4 = 8$ or $2 + 2 + 2 + 2 = 8$). Using the grouping conceptualization we used with multiplication, we can divide 8 into 4 groups of 2 or 2 groups of 4. We call the answer to a division problem the QUOTIENT.

QUOTIENT: the answer to a division problem

If the divisor does not divide evenly into the dividend, we express the leftover amount either as a remainder or as a fraction with the divisor as the denominator. For example, 9 divided by 2 equals 4 with a remainder of 1 or $4\frac{1}{2}$.

Example: Each box of apples contains 24 apples. How many boxes must a grocer purchase to supply a group of 252 people with one apple each? The grocer needs 252 apples. Because he must buy apples in groups of 24, we divide 252 by 24 to determine how many boxes he needs to buy.

$$\begin{array}{r} 10 \\ 24\overline{)252} \\ -24 \\ \hline 12 \\ -0 \\ \hline 12 \end{array}$$ → The quotient is 10 with a remainder of 12.

Thus, the grocer needs 10 full boxes plus 12 more apples. Therefore, the minimum number of boxes the grocer must purchase is 11 boxes.

Adding and Subtracting Decimals

When adding and subtracting decimals, we align the numbers by place value as we do with whole numbers. After adding or subtracting each column, we bring the decimal down, placing it in the same location as in the numbers added or subtracted.

Example: Find the sum of 152.3 and 36.342.

```
  152.300
+  36.342
  188.642
```

Note that we placed two zeroes after the final place value in 152.3 to clarify the column addition.

Example: Find the difference of 152.3 and 36.342.

```
   2 9 10            (4)11(12)
  152.300           152.300
-  36.342          -  36.342
       58           115.958
```

Note how we borrowed to subtract from the zeros in the hundredths and thousandths place of 152.300.

Operations with Signed Numbers

When adding numbers with the same sign, the result will also have the same sign. When adding numbers that have different signs, subtract the smaller number from the larger number (ignoring the sign) and then use the sign of the larger number. When subtracting a negative number, change the sign of the number to a positive sign and then add it (i.e., replace the two negative signs by a positive sign).

Examples:

$(3) + (4) = 7$

$(-8) + (-4) = -12$

$(6) - (5) = 1$

$(3) - (6) = -3$

$(-4) - (2) = -6$

$(-6) - (-10) = 4$

When we multiply two numbers with the same sign, the result is positive. If the two numbers have different signs, the result is negative. The same rule follows for division.

Examples:

$(5)(5) = 25$

$(5)(-6) = -30$

$(-19)(-2) = 38$

$16 \div 4 = 4$

$(-34) \div 2 = -17$

$(-18) \div (-2) = 9$

$27 \div (-3) = -9$

Order of Operations

The Order of Operations is to be followed when evaluating expressions with multiple operations. Remember the mnemonic PEMDAS (Please Excuse My Dear Aunt Sally) to follow these steps in order:

1. Simplify inside grouping characters such as parentheses, brackets, radicals, fraction bars, etc.

2. Multiply out expressions with exponents.

3. Do multiplication or division from left to right.

   Note: Multiplication and division are equivalent even though multiplication is mentioned before division in the mnemonic PEMDAS.

4. Do addition or subtraction from left to right.

   Note: Addition and subtraction are equivalent even though addition is mentioned before "subtraction in the mnemonic PEMDAS.

Example:

Evaluate: $\dfrac{12(9 - 7) + 4 \times 5}{3^4 + 2^3}$

$\dfrac{12(9 - 7) + 4 \times 5}{3^4 + 2^3}$

$= \dfrac{12(2) + 4 \times 5}{3^4 + 2^3}$ Simplify within parentheses.

$= \dfrac{12(2) + 4 \times 5}{81 + 8}$ Multiply out exponent expressions.

$= \dfrac{24 + 20}{81 + 8}$ Do multiplication and division.

$= \dfrac{44}{89}$ Do addition and subtraction.

Complex Numbers

The set of complex numbers is denoted by $\mathbb{C}$. The set $\mathbb{C}$ is defined as $\{a + bi : a, b \in \mathbb{R}\}$ ($\in$ means "element of"). In other words, complex numbers are an extension of real numbers made by attaching an imaginary number i, which satisfies the equality $i^2 = -1$. COMPLEX NUMBERS are of the form $\boldsymbol{a} + \boldsymbol{bi}$, where a and b are real numbers and $i = \sqrt{-1}$. Thus, a is the real part of the number and b is the imaginary part of the number. When i appears in a fraction, the fraction is usually simplified so that i is not in the denominator. The set of complex numbers includes the set of real numbers, where any real number n can be written in its equivalent complex form as $n + 0i$. In other words, it can be said that $\mathbb{R} \subseteq \mathbb{C}$ (or $\mathbb{R}$ is a subset of $\mathbb{C}$).

COMPLEX NUMBERS: numbers of the form $a + bi$, where a and b are real numbers and $i = \sqrt{-1}$

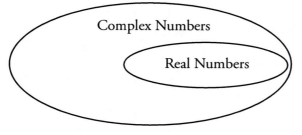

The number $3i$ has a real part 0 and imaginary part 3; the number 4 has a real part 4 and an imaginary part 0. As another way of writing complex numbers, we can express them as ordered pairs:

Complex number	Ordered pair
$3 + 2i$	$(3, 2)$
$\sqrt{3} + \sqrt{3}i$	$(\sqrt{3}, \sqrt{3})$
$7i$	$(0, 7)$
$\dfrac{6 + 2i}{7}$	$\left(\dfrac{6}{7}, \dfrac{2}{7}\right)$

The basic operations for complex numbers can be summarized as follows, where $z_1 = a_1 + b_1 i$ and $z_2 = a_2 + b_2 i$. Note that the operations are performed in the standard manner, where i is treated as a standard radical value. The result of each operation is written in the standard form for complex numbers. Also note that the COMPLEX CONJUGATE of a complex number $z = a + bi$ is denoted as $z^* = a - bi$.

COMPLEX CONJUGATE: for a complex number $z = a + bi$, this is denoted as $z^* = a - bi$

$$z_1 + z_2 = (a_1 + a_2) + (b_1 + b_2)i$$
$$z_1 - z_2 = (a_1 - a_2) + (b_1 - b_2)i$$
$$z_1 z_2 = (a_1 a_2 - b_1 b_2) + (a_1 b_2 - a_2 b_1)i$$
$$\frac{z_1}{z_2} = \frac{z_1}{z_2}\frac{z_2^*}{z_2^*} = \frac{a_1 a_2 + b_1 b_2}{a_2^2 + b_2^2} + \frac{a_2 b_1 + a_1 b_2}{a_2^2 + b_2^2}i$$

Compare and contrast properties *(e.g., closure, commutativity, associativity, distributivity)* **of number systems under various operations**

Fields and Rings

Any set that includes at least two nonzero elements that satisfies the field axioms for addition and multiplication is a FIELD. The real numbers, $\mathbb{R}$, as well as the complex numbers, $\mathbb{C}$, are each a field, with the real numbers being a subset of the complex numbers. The field axioms are summarized below.

> **FIELD:** any set that includes at least two nonzero elements that satisfies the field axioms for addition and multiplication

FIELD AXIOMS	
ADDITION	
Commutativity	$a + b = b + a$
Associativity	$a + (b + c) = (a + b) + c$
Identity	$a + 0 = a$
Inverse	$a + (-a) = 0$
MULTIPLICATION	
Commutativity	$ab = ba$
Associativity	$a(bc) = (ab)c$
Identity	$a \times 1 = a$
Inverse	$a \times \frac{1}{a} = 1 \qquad (a \neq 0)$
ADDITION AND MULTIPLICATION	
Distributivity	$a(b + c) = (b + c)a = ab + ac$

Note that both the real numbers and the complex numbers satisfy the axioms summarized above.

> **RING:** an integral domain with two binary operations (addition and multiplication) where, for every nonzero element a and b in the domain, the product *ab* is nonzero

A RING is an integral domain with two binary operations (addition and multiplication) where, for every nonzero element a and b in the domain, the product ab is nonzero. A field is a ring in which multiplication is commutative, or $a \times b = b \times a$, and all nonzero elements have a multiplicative inverse. The set $\mathbb{Z}$ (integers) is a ring that is not a field in that it does not have the multiplicative inverse; therefore, integers are not a field. A polynomial ring is also not a field, as it also has no multiplicative inverse. Furthermore, matrix rings do not constitute fields because matrix multiplication is not generally commutative.

> ***Note:*** *Multiplication is implied when there is no symbol between two variables. Thus, a $\times$ b can be written ab. Multiplication can also be indicated by a raised dot (·).*

Real numbers are an ordered field and can be ordered

As such, an ordered field F must contain a subset P (such as the positive numbers) such that if a and b are elements of P, then both $a + b$ and ab are also elements of P. (In other words, the set P is closed under addition and multiplication.) Furthermore, it must be the case that for any element c contained in F, exactly one of the following conditions is true: c is an element of P, $-c$ is an element of P, or $c = 0$.

The rational numbers also constitute an ordered field

The set P can be defined as the positive rational numbers. For each a and b that are elements of the set $\mathbb{Q}$ (the rational numbers), $a + b$ is also an element of P, as is ab. (The sum $a + b$ and the product ab are both rational if a and b are rational.) Since P is closed under addition and multiplication, $\mathbb{Q}$ constitutes an ordered field.

Complex numbers, unlike real numbers, cannot be ordered

Consider the number $i = \sqrt{-1}$ contained in the set $\mathbb{C}$ of complex numbers. Assume that $\mathbb{C}$ has a subset P (positive numbers) that is closed under both addition and multiplication. Assume that $i > 0$. A difficulty arises in that $i^2 = -1 < 0$, so i cannot be included in the set P. Likewise, assume $i < 0$. The problem once again arises that $i^4 = 1 > 0$, so i cannot be included in P. It is clearly the case that $i \neq 0$, so there is no place for i in an ordered field. Thus, the complex numbers cannot be ordered.

Example: Prove that for every integer y, if y is an even number, then y^2 is even.

The definition of *even* implies that for each integer y there is at least one integer x such that $y = 2x$.

$$y = 2x$$
$$y^2 = 4x^2$$

Since $4x^2$ is always evenly divisible by two ($2x^2$ is an integer), y^2 is even for all values of y.

Example: If a, b, and c are positive real numbers, prove that $c(a + b) = (b + a)c$.

Use the properties of the set of real numbers.

$$
\begin{aligned}
c(a + b) &= c(b + a) && \text{Additive commutativity} \\
&= cb + ca && \text{Distributivity} \\
&= bc + ac && \text{Multiplicative commutativity} \\
&= (b + a)c && \text{Distributivity}
\end{aligned}
$$

Example: Given real numbers a, b, c, and d, where ad = -bc, prove that (a + bi)(c + di) is real.

Expand the product of the complex numbers.

$$(a + bi)(c + di) = ac + bci + adi + bdi^2$$

Use the definition of i^2.

$$(a + bi)(c + di) = ac - bd + bci + adi$$

Apply the fact that ad = -bc.

$$(a + bi)(c + di) = ac - bd + bci - bci = ac - bd$$

Since a, b, c and d are all real, $ac - bd$ must also be real.

Closure

Another useful property that can describe arbitrary sets of numbers (including fields and rings) is CLOSURE. A set is closed under an operation if the operation performed on any given elements of the set always yields a result that is likewise an element of the set. For instance, the set of real numbers is closed under multiplication, because for any two real numbers a and b, the product ab is also a real number.

> **CLOSURE:** a set is closed under an operation if the operation performed on any given elements of the set always yields a result that is likewise an element of the set

Example: Determine if the set of integers is closed under division.

For the set of integers to be closed under division, it must be the case that $\frac{a}{b}$ is an integer for any integers a and b. Consider $a = 2$ and $b = 3$.

$$\frac{a}{b} = \frac{2}{3}$$

This result is not an integer. Therefore, the set of integers is not closed under division.

SKILL 1.3 **Demonstrate an understanding of the properties of counting numbers** *(e.g., prime, composite, prime factorization, even, odd, factors, multiples)*

Natural (Counting) Numbers

The set of NATURAL NUMBERS, $\mathbb{N}$, includes 1, 2, 3, 4, ... (For some definitions, $\mathbb{N}$ includes zero.) The natural numbers are sometimes called the counting numbers (especially if the definition of $\mathbb{N}$ excludes zero). The set $\mathbb{N}$ constitutes neither a ring nor a field, because there is no additive inverse (since there are no negative numbers).

> **NATURAL NUMBERS:** the numbers 1, 2, 3, 4, . . . ; they are sometimes called the counting numbers

The set $\mathbb{N}$ obeys the properties of associativity, commutativity, distributivity and identity for multiplication and addition (assuming, for the case of addition, that zero is included in some sense in the natural numbers). The set of natural numbers does *not* obey additive or multiplicative inverses, however, as there are no noninteger fractions or negative numbers.

Natural numbers can be either *even* or *odd*. Even numbers are evenly divisible by two; odd numbers are not evenly divisible by two (alternatively, they leave a remainder of one when divided by two). Any natural number n that is divisible by at least one number that is not equal to 1 or n is called a COMPOSITE NUMBER. A natural number *n* that is only divisible by 1 or n is called a PRIME NUMBER.

> **COMPOSITE NUMBER:** any natural number *n* that is divisible by at least one number that is not equal to 1 or *n*

> **PRIME NUMBER:** a natural number *n* that is only divisible by 1 or *n*

Divisibility tests

1. A number is *divisible by 2* if that number is an even number (i.e., the last digit is 0, 2, 4, 6 or 8).

   Consider a number *abcd* defined by the digits *a*, *b*, *c* and *d* (for instance, 1,234). Rewrite the number as follows.
   $$10abc + d = abcd$$

   Note that $10abc$ is divisible by 2. Thus, the number *abcd* is only divisible by 2 if *d* is divisible by two; in other words, *abcd* is divisible by two only if it is an even number. For example, the last digit of 1,354 is 4, so it is divisible by 2. On the other hand, the last digit of 240,685 is 5, so it is not divisible by 2.

2. A number is *divisible by 3* if the sum of its digits is evenly divisible by 3.

   Consider a number *abcd* defined by the digits *a*, *b*, *c* and *d*. The number can be written as
   $$abcd = 1000a + 100b + 10c + d$$

   The number can also be rewritten as
   $$abcd = (999 + 1)a + (99 + 1)b + (9 + 1)c + d$$
   $$abcd = 999a + 99b + 9c + (a + b + c + d)$$

   Note that the first three terms in the above expression are all divisible by 3. Thus, the number is evenly divisible by 3 only if $a + b + c + d$ is divisible by 3. The same logic applies regardless of the size of the number. This proves the rules for divisibility by 3.

   The sum of the digits of 964 is $9 + 6 + 4 = 19$. Since 19 is not divisible by 3, neither is 964. The digits of 86,514 is $8 + 6 + 5 + 1 + 4 = 24$. Since 24 is divisible by 3, 86,514 is also divisible by 3.

3. A number is *divisible by 4* if the number in its last two digits is evenly divisible by 4.

Let a number *abcd* be defined by the digits *a*, *b*, *c* and *d*.

$$ab(100) + cd = abcd$$

Since 100 is divisible by 4, 100*ab* is also divisible by 4. Thus, *abcd* is divisible by 4 only if *cd* is divisible by 4.

$$25ab + \frac{cd}{4} = \frac{abcd}{4}$$

The number 113,336 ends with the number 36 for the last two digits. Since 36 is divisible by 4, 113,336 is also divisible by 4. The number 135,627 ends with the number 27 for the last two digits. Since 27 is not evenly divisible by 4, 135,627 is also not divisible by 4.

4. A number is *divisible by 5* if the number ends in either a 5 or a 0.

Use the same number abcd.

$$100ab + cd = abcd$$

The first term is evenly divisible by 5, but the second term is only evenly divisible by 5 if it is 0, 5, 10, 15, . . . , 95. In other words, *abcd* is divisible by 5 only if it ends in a 0 or a 5. For instance, 225 ends with a 5, so it is divisible by 5. The number 470 is also divisible by 5 because its last digit is a 0. The number 2,358 is not divisible by 5 because its last digit is an 8.

5. A number is *divisible by 6* if the number is divisible by both 2 and 3. Thus any even number that is divisible by 3 is also divisible by 6. For instance, 4,950 is an even number and its digits add up to 18 (4 + 9 + 5 + 0 = 18). Since it is even and the sum of its digits is divisible by 3, the number 4,950 is divisible by 3 and by 6 as well. On the other hand, 326 is an even number, but its digits add up to 11. Since 11 is not divisible by 3, 326 is not divisible by 3 or by 6.

6. A number is *divisible by 8* if the number in its last three digits is evenly divisible by 8.

The logic for the proof of this case follows that of numbers divisible by 2 and 4. The number 113,336 ends with the 3-digit number 336 in the last three columns. Since 336 is divisible by 8, then 113,336 is also divisible by 8. The number 465,627 ends with the number 627 in the last three columns. Since 627 is not evenly divisible by 8, then 465,627 is also not divisible by 8.

7. A number is *divisible by 9* if the sum of its digits is evenly divisible by 9.

The logic for the proof of this case follows that for the case of numbers that are divisible by 3 and 6. The sum of the digits of 874, for example, is 8 +

$7 + 4 = 19$. Since 19 is not divisible by 9, neither is 874. The sum of the digits of 116,514 is $1 + 1 + 6 + 5 + 1 + 4 = 18$. Since 18 is divisible by 9, 116,514 is also divisible by 9.

The Fundamental Theorem of Arithmetic

Every integer greater than 1 can be written uniquely in the form

$$p_1^{e_1} p_2^{e_2} \cdots p_k^{e_k}.$$

The p_i are distinct prime numbers and the e_i are positive integers.

Greatest common factor

GCF is the abbreviation for the GREATEST COMMON FACTOR. The GCF is the largest number that is a factor of all the numbers given in a problem. The GCF can be no larger than the smallest number given in the problem. If no other number is a common factor, then the GCF will be the number 1. To find the GCF, list all possible factors of the smallest number given (include the number itself). Starting with the largest factor (which is the number itself), determine if it is also a factor of all the other given numbers. If so, that is the GCF. If that factor does not work, try the same method on the next smaller factor. Continue until a common factor is found. This is the GCF. Note: There can be other common factors besides the GCF.

> **GREATEST COMMON FACTOR:** the largest number that is a factor of all the numbers given in a problem

> *The GCF can be no larger than the smallest number given in the problem.*

Example: Find the GCF of 12, 20, and 36.

The smallest number in the problem is 12. The factors of 12 are 1, 2, 3, 4, 6 and 12. 12 is the largest factor, but it does not divide evenly into 20. Neither does 6, but 4 will divide into both 20 and 36 evenly. Therefore, 4 is the GCF.

Example: Find the GCF of 14 and 15.

Factors of 14 are 1, 2, 7 and 14. 14 is the largest factor, but it does not divide evenly into 15. Neither does 7 or 2. Therefore, the only factor common to both 14 and 15 is the number 1, which is the GCF.

The Euclidean Algorithm is a formal method for determining the greatest common divisor (GCD, another name for GCF) of two positive integers. The algorithm can be formulated in a recursive manner that simply involves repetition of a few steps until a terminating point is reached. The algorithm can be summarized as follows, where a and b are the two integers for which determination of the GCD is to be undertaken. (Assign a and b such that $a > b$.)

1. If $b = 0$, a is the GCD

2. Calculate $c = a \bmod b$

3. If $c = 0$, b is the GCD

4. Go back to step 2, replacing a with b and b with c

Note that the mod operator in this case is simply a remainder operator. Thus, a mod b is the remainder of division of a by b.

Example: Find the GCD of 299 and 351.
To find the GCD, first let $a = 351$ and $b = 299$. Begin the algorithm as follows.
Step 1: $b \neq 0$
Step 2: $c = 351$ mod $299 = 52$
Step 3: $c \neq 0$

Perform the next iteration, starting with step 2.
Step 2: $c = 299$ mod $52 = 39$
Step 3: $c \neq 0$

Continue to iterate recursively until a solution is found.
Step 2: $c = 52$ mod $39 = 13$
Step 3: $c \neq 0$

Step 2: $c = 39$ mod $13 = 0$
Step 3: $c = 0$: GCD $= 13$

Thus, the GCD of 299 and 351 is thus 13.

Least common multiple

LCM is the abbreviation for LEAST COMMON MULTIPLE. The least common multiple of a group of numbers is the smallest number that all of the given numbers will divide into. The least common multiple will always be the largest of the given set of numbers, or a multiple of the largest number.

> **LEAST COMMON MULTIPLE:** of a group of numbers is the smallest number that all of the given numbers will divide into

The least common multiple will always be the largest of the given set of numbers, or a multiple of the largest number.

Example: Find the LCM of 20, 30 and 40.
The largest number given is 40, but 30 will not divide evenly into 40. The next multiple of 40 is 80 (2×40), but 30 will not divide evenly into 80 either. The next multiple of 40 is 120. 120 is divisible by both 20 and 30, so 120 is the LCM (least common multiple).

Example: Find the LCM of 96, 16 and 24.
The largest number is 96. 96 is divisible by both 16 and 24, so 96 is the LCM.

Proofs using the fundamental theorem of arithmetic

The Fundamental Theorem of Arithmetic can be used to show that every fraction is equivalent to a unique fraction in which the numerator and denominator are relatively prime.

Given a fraction $\frac{a}{b}$, the integers a and b can both be written uniquely as a product of prime factors.

$$\frac{a}{b} = \frac{p_1^{x_1} p_2^{x_2} p_3^{x_3} \cdots P_n^{x_n}}{q_1^{y_1} q_2^{y_2} q_3^{y_3} \cdots q_m^{y_m}}$$

When all the common factors are cancelled, the resulting numerator a_1 (the product of remaining factors $P_n^{x_n}$) and the resulting denominator b_1 (the product of remaining factors $q_m^{y_m}$) have no common divisor other than 1; i.e., they are *relatively prime*.

Since, according to the Fundamental Theorem of Arithmetic, the initial prime decomposition of the integers a and b is *unique*, the new reduced fraction $\frac{a_1}{b_1}$ is also unique. Hence, any fraction is equivalent to a unique fraction in which the numerator and denominator are relatively prime.

The proof that the square root of any integer, not a perfect square number, is irrational may also be demonstrated using prime decomposition.

Let n be an integer. Assuming that the square root of n is rational, we can write

$$\sqrt{n} = \frac{a}{b}$$

Since every fraction is equivalent to a unique fraction in which the numerator $\frac{a}{b}$ and denominator are relatively prime (shown earlier), we can reduce the fraction to the fraction $\frac{a_1}{b_1}$ and write

$$\sqrt{n} = \frac{a_1}{b_1}; \quad n = \frac{a_1^2}{b_1^2}$$

where a_1 and b_1 are relatively prime.

Since a_1 and b_1 are relatively prime, a_1^2 and b_1^2 must also be relatively prime. Also, since n is an integer, $\frac{a_1^2}{b_1^2}$ must be an integer. The only way the above two conditions can be satisfied is if the denominator $b_1^2 = 1$. Thus, $n = a_1^2$.

As a result, the square root of an integer can be rational only if the integer is a perfect square. Stated in an alternative manner, the square root of an integer, not a perfect square, is irrational.

> Every fraction is equivalent to a unique fraction in which the numerator and denominator are relatively prime.

SKILL 1.4 **Solve ratio, proportion, percent, and average** *(including arithmetic mean and weighted average)* **problems**

Ratios

> **RATIO:** a comparison of two numbers for the purpose of relating relative magnitudes

A RATIO is a comparison of two numbers for the purpose of relating relative magnitudes. For instance, if a class had 11 boys and 14 girls, the ratio of boys to girls could be written one of three ways:

11:14 or 11 to 14 or $\frac{11}{14}$

The ratio of girls to boys is:

14:11 or 14 to 11 or $\frac{14}{11}$

> **Note:** *Read ratio questions carefully. For example, given a group of 6 adults and 5 children, the ratio of children to the entire group would be 5:11.*

Ratios can be reduced when possible. A ratio of 12 cats to 18 dogs, for example, would reduce to 2:3, 2 to 3 or $\frac{2}{3}$.

Proportions

> **PROPORTION:** an equation in which a fraction is set equal to another fraction

A PROPORTION is an equation in which a fraction is set equal to another fraction. To solve the proportion, multiply each numerator times the other fraction's denominator. Set these two products equal to each other and solve the resulting equation. This is called cross multiplying the proportion.

Example: Find x given the proportion $\frac{4}{15} = \frac{x}{60}$.
To solve for *x*, cross multiply.

$(4)(60) = (15)(x)$
$240 = 15x$
$16 = x$

Example: Find x given the proportion $\frac{x+3}{3x+4} = \frac{2}{5}$.
To solve for *x*, cross multiply.

$5(x + 3) = 2(3x + 4)$
$5x + 15 = 6x + 8$
$7 = x$

> *The key to solving a problem involving proportions, is constructing the proportion correctly.*

The mathematics of solving for variables in proportions is not difficult; the key to solving a problem involving proportions, then, is constructing the proportion correctly. As noted above, this requires carefully reading the problem, followed by careful identification of the related values and construction of the appropriate ratios.

Percents

A PERCENT is a decimal value multiplied by 100. Another representation is the following: given some value c, the percent representation is p, where

$$c = \frac{p}{100}$$

or

$$p = 100c$$

When using percents in a problem, it is important to either use only percents or only decimals. Mixing these two types of values can lead to incorrect answers.

Averages

Problems involving averages can be solved using the tools discussed in Competency 7.

SKILL 1.5 Work with algebraic expressions, formulas, and equations; add, subtract, multiply, and divide polynomials; add, subtract, multiply, and divide algebraic fractions; perform standard algebraic operations involving complex numbers, radicals, and exponents, including fractional and negative exponents

For a detailed discussion of algebraic functions, see Competency 5.

SKILL 1.6 Solve and graph systems of equations and inequalities, including those involving absolute value

Solving Systems of Linear Equations

For a detailed discussion of solutions of systems of linear equations by way of matrix algebra, see Skill 9.2 In simple cases in which the use of matrices is unnecessary, systems of equations can be solved through *substitution*, *elimination*, or *graphing*.

Substitution method

The method of substitution simply requires solving one equation for a particular variable, then substituting this expression into another equation to eliminate that variable. This process, when repeated a sufficient number of times, yields the solution for a particular variable. This solution can then be substituted into other equations to find the solution for the other variables.

Example: Solve the following system of equations:
$$2x - 3y = -13$$
$$5x + y = 27$$

This system of equations can be solved by substitution. Solve the first equation for x.
$$2x = 3y - 13$$
$$x = \frac{3}{2}y - \frac{13}{2}$$

Substitute this result into the second equation and solve for y.
$$5\left[\frac{3}{2}y - \frac{13}{2}\right] + y = 27$$
$$\frac{15}{2}y - \frac{65}{2} + y = 27$$
$$\frac{17}{2}y = \frac{54}{2} + \frac{65}{2} = \frac{119}{2}$$
$$y = \frac{119}{17} = 7$$

Use this result to find x. Either equation can be used.
$$2x - 3(7) = -13$$
$$2x = -13 + 21 = 8$$
$$x = 4$$

The solution is then $x = 4$ and $y = 7$.

Elimination method

The method of elimination involves multiplying one of the equations in the system by a constant number and combining two equations in such a way that one of the variables is eliminated.

Example: Farmer Greenjeans bought 4 cows and 6 sheep for $1700. Mr. Ziffel bought 3 cows and 12 sheep for $2400. If all the cows were the same price and all the sheep were the same price, find the price charged for a cow and for a sheep.

Let x = price of a cow
Let y = price of a sheep

Farmer Greenjeans' equation would be: $4x + 6y = 1700$
Mr. Ziffel's equation would be: $3x + 12y = 2400$

To solve by elimination:

Multiply the first equation by -2: $-2(4x + 6y = 1700)$
Keep the other equation the same: $(3x + 12y = 2400)$
$$-8x - 12y = -3400$$

$\underline{3x + 12y = 2400}$ Add the equations

$-5x \qquad = -1000$

$x = 200 \leftarrow$ The price of a cow was $200.

Solving for y, $y = 150 \leftarrow$ The price of a sheep was $150.

Graphing method

Graphing a system of equations requires plotting each equation separately on an appropriate set of axes. In the simplest case, the equations can be plotted in a two-dimensional graph. Assuming the equations are all linear in two dimensions, it is sufficient to solve for y in each case and then plot the functions with respect to the variable x. The intersection of the lines is the solution to the system of equations.

Example: Solve the following system of equations graphically:

$6x - 7y = 3$

$-4x + 3y = -7$

First, solve each equation for y.

$7y = 6x - 3 \qquad 3y = 4x - 7$

$y = \frac{6}{7}x - \frac{3}{7} \qquad y = \frac{4}{3}x - \frac{7}{3}$

Next, plot each function and look for the intersection (solution).

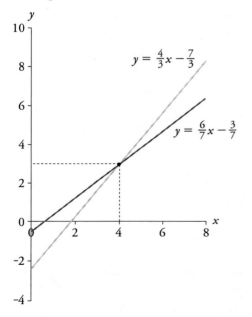

The solution can be seen by inspection: (4, 3). By inserting these values into each equation, it can be shown that this solution satisfies the system of equations.

Solving Systems of Linear Inequalities

Solving systems of linear inequalities is best performed graphically. To graph a linear inequality expressed in terms of x and y, solve the inequality for y. This renders the inequality in SLOPE-INTERCEPT FORM (for example: $y < mx + b$). The point $(0, b)$ is the y-intercept, and m is the slope of the line. If the inequality is expressed only in terms of x, solve for x. When solving an inequality, remember that dividing or multiplying by a negative number will reverse the direction of the inequality sign.

If an inequality yields any of the following results in terms of y, where a is some real number, the solution set of the inequality is bounded by a *horizontal line*:

$$y < a \qquad\qquad y \leq a \qquad\qquad y > a \qquad\qquad y \geq a$$

If the inequality yields any of the following results in terms of x, then the solution set of the inequality is bounded by a *vertical line*:

$$x < a \qquad\qquad x \leq a \qquad\qquad x > a \qquad\qquad x \geq a$$

When graphing the solution of a linear inequality, the boundary line is drawn in a dotted manner if the inequality sign is $<$ or $>$. This indicates that points on the line do not satisfy the inequality. If the inequality sign is either $\geq$ or $\leq$, then the boundary line is drawn as a solid line to indicate that the points on the line satisfy the inequality.

The line drawn as directed above is only the boundary of the solution set for an inequality. The solutions actually include the half plane bounded by the line. Since, for any line, half of the values in the full plane (for either x or y) are greater than those defined by the line and half are less, the solution of the inequality must be graphed as a half plane. (In other words, a line divides the plane in half.) Which half plane satisfies the inequality can be found by testing a point on either side of the line. The solution set can be indicated on a graph by shading the appropriate half plane.

For inequalities expressed as a function of x, shade above the line when the inequality sign is $\geq$ or $>$ Shade below the line when the inequality sign is $<$ or $\leq$. For inequalities expressed as a function of y, shade to the right for $>$ or $\geq$. Shade to the left for $<$ or $\leq$.

The solution to a system of linear inequalities consists of the portion of the graph where the shaded half planes for all the inequalities in the system overlap. For instance, if the graph of one inequality was shaded with red, and the graph of another inequality was shaded with blue, then the overlapping area would be shaded purple. The points in the purple area would be the solution set of this system.

SLOPE-INTERCEPT FORM: the form of this equation is $y = mx + b$

When solving an inequality, dividing or multiplying by a negative number will reverse the direction of the inequality sign.

When graphing the solution of a linear inequality, the boundary line is drawn in a dotted manner if the inequality sign is $<$ or $>$.

If the inequality sign is either $\leq$ or $\geq$, then the boundary line is drawn as a solid line.

Any line divides the xy-plane into two halves. The solution of an inequality must be graphed as a half-plane.

The solution to a system of linear inequalities consists of the portion of the graph where the shaded half planes for all the inequalities in the system overlap.

Example: Solve by graphing:

$$x + y \leq 6$$
$$x - 2y \leq 6$$

Solving the inequalities for y, they become the following:

$y \leq 6 - x$ (*y*-intercept of 6 and slope of -1)

$y \geq \frac{1}{2}x - 3$ (*y*-intercept of -3 and slope of $\frac{1}{2}$)

A graph with the appropriate shading is shown below:

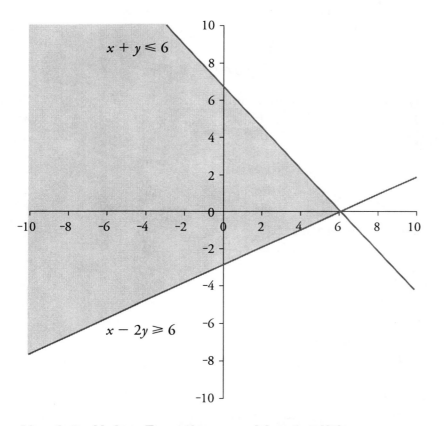

Absolute Value Equations and Inequalities

In cases where absolute values are included in the system of equations or inequalities, the process of solving can become much more complex. For each equation or inequality with an absolute value, the expression must be split into two conditional expressions. Consider, for instance, for $3|x| + y = -2$. This absolute value equation can be written as follows:

$3x + y = -2$ for $x \geq 0$; $-3x + y = -2$ for $x < 0$

The same process can likewise be applied to inequalities. Since absolute value expressions result in two different expressions (for each instance of an absolute value), the complexity of the solution process increases. A system of equations or inequalities with one absolute value expression must be solved in two different forms, each with a condition on the range of solutions (such as the condition on x in the example above). Thus, a system of equations or inequalities with absolute values may have one solution, multiple solutions, or no solution at all. In any case, it is important to check each solution to avoid any extraneous solutions.

Example: Solve the following system of equations:

$$3|x| - y = 2$$
$$-2x + 3y = 8$$

First, rewrite the system of equations as two different systems, each with a condition on the admissible values of x.

$$\begin{matrix} 3x - y = 2 \\ -2x + 3y = 8 \end{matrix}, x \geq 0 \qquad \begin{matrix} -3x - y = 2 \\ -2x + 3y = 8 \end{matrix}, x < 0$$

Solve each system individually using substitution, in this case.

$$y = 3x - 2$$
$$-2x + 3(3x - 2) = 8$$
$$-2x + 9x - 6 = 8$$
$$7x = 14$$
$$x = 2$$

$$y = -3x - 2$$
$$-2x + 3(-3x - 2) = 8$$
$$-2x - 9x - 6 = 8$$
$$-11x = 14$$
$$x = \frac{14}{11}$$

Use this x value to find y in each case.

$$y = 3(2) - 2 = 4 \qquad y = -3(\tfrac{14}{11}) - 2 = \tfrac{20}{11}$$

Check each solution:

$$3|2| - (4) = 6 - 4 = 2$$
$$-2(2) + 3(4) \ 5 \ -4 + 12 \ 5 \ 8 \text{ and}$$
$$3|\tfrac{14}{11}| - (\tfrac{20}{11}) = \tfrac{42}{11} - \tfrac{20}{11} = 2$$
$$-2(\tfrac{14}{11}) + 3(\tfrac{20}{11}) = \tfrac{28}{11} + \tfrac{60}{11} = 8$$

Also note that the first solution obeys the condition $x \geq 0$, and the second solution obeys the condition $x < 0$. Thus, each solution is valid.

The general form of an absolute value function for a linear equation is $y = m|x - h| + k$. The graph is in the shape of a $\vee$ with the point (h, k) being the location of the maximum (or minimum) point on the graph. The sign of m indicates whether the point (h, k) is a maximum or minimum. If m is positive, the graph has a minimum; if m is negative, the graph has a maximum. The magnitude of m also determines the slope of the ray on either side of the maximum or minimum point. Consider the following examples.

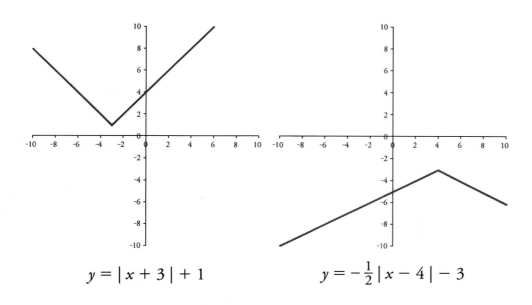

$$y = |x + 3| + 1 \qquad\qquad y = -\frac{1}{2}|x - 4| - 3$$

To sketch a graph of an absolute value function:

1. First, either convert the function into the form $y = m|x - h| + k$ or simply use the function in its current form.

2. Plot points as necessary to determine the location of the rays. (The x-value of the slope discontinuity is the value of x for which the expression in the absolute value brackets is zero.)

3. Finally, connect the points with a straight edge.

Example: Plot the system of equations below:

$$3|x| - y = 2$$
$$-2x + 3y = 8$$

These are the same equations used in the previous example. In this case, the equations can be plotted and the solution found graphically. The first equation must be plotted as follows:

$$y = 3x - 2 \text{ for } x \geq 0$$
$$y = -3x - 2 \text{ for } x < 0$$

The second equation can simply be plotted as a standard line:

$$y = \frac{2}{3}x + \frac{8}{3}$$

The graph of these functions is shown below.

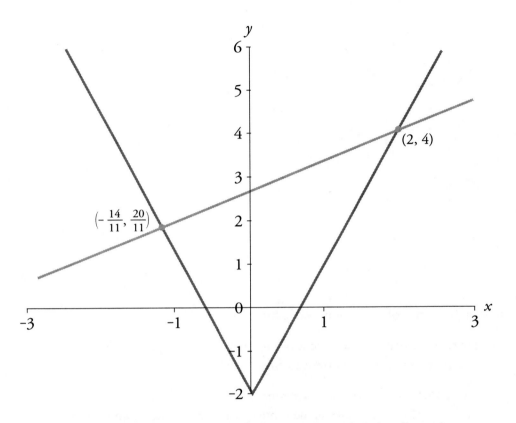

The solutions obtained algebraically above are apparent graphically in the above plot.

Example: Plot the system of inequalities given below:

$$x + 2y \leq 3$$
$$-|x| + y > 2$$

For each equation, find the equation of the line (or absolute value function) that bounds the solution areas.

$$2y \leq -x + 3 \qquad\qquad y > |x| + 2$$
$$y \leq \frac{1}{2}x + \frac{3}{2}$$

Plot both functions as follows, using a solid line for the linear equation (since the line is included in the solution set) and a dashed line for the absolute value equation (since the line is not included in the solution set). Then shade the solution regions appropriately.

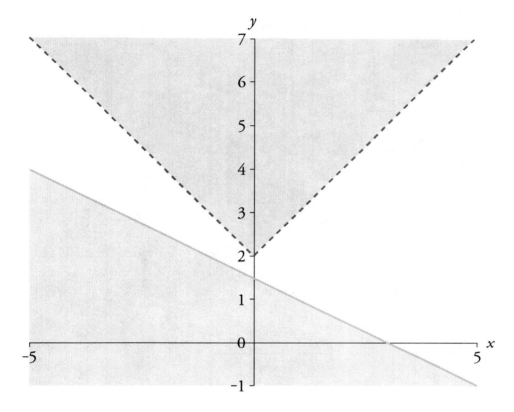

Note that there is no overlap of the solution regions for these two functions. As a result, the solution set is simply the null set (that is, there are no solutions to this system of inequalities).

If the graphs of the solution regions do not overlap, the solution to the system of inequalities is the null set.

SKILL 1.7 Interpret algebraic principles geometrically

Geometry can be a useful tool in explaining or further understanding algebraic concepts. For instance, the principle of commutativity in multiplication can be illustrated with a rectangle. The area of a rectangle is the product of the length and the width.

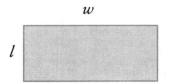

Note, however, that if we redefine the length and the width (that is, reverse the definitions), the area of the rectangle remains the same. Thus, the following two cases are equivalent.

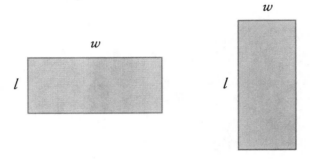

As a result, $l \times w = w \times l =$ Area.

Likewise, other geometric interpretations can be derived for various numeric and algebraic concepts. Addition, for example, can be represented as the linking of line segments of given length relative to a number line.

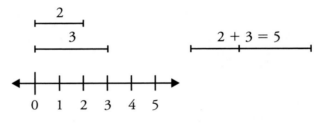

Interpreting algebraic concepts geometrically involves first assigning a geometric meaning to a particular value or concept. For instance, numbers may represent lengths. Note in the following section, for instance, how the algebraic formulas for conic sections are related to their respective geometric figures. Graphs are a helpful tool in this regard, since they can provide a visual representation of an algebraic formula or concept.

SKILL 1.8 Recognize and use algebraic representations of lines, planes, conic sections, and spheres

Algebraic representation of a geometric figure involves expressing the relationships between the coordinates of different points on the figure as an equation. It is helpful to be able to recognize and use basic algebraic representations of common functions and figures, including lines, planes, conic sections, and spheres. Lines are the simplest of these figures, and are given by the standard expression below.

$$y = mx + b$$

Here, m is the *slope* and b is the *y-intercept* of the line. Slightly more interesting is the general expression for a plane. Planes are defined in three dimensions and can be written as follows.

$$z = ax + by + c$$

Note that a plane may also have an x-intercept, a y-intercept, a z-intercept, or all three, depending on the specific expression. In general, an intercept is found by setting all nonrelevant variables to zero and then solving. For instance, to find the z-intercept, set x and y equal to zero and solve. The slope of the plane must be defined in a particular direction: for instance, the slope along the x-axis is a, and the slope along the y-axis is b.

Conic Sections

CONIC SECTIONS are aptly named as the various cross sections of a cone. Even a line and a point may in some sense be considered conic sections, although these are usually not included explicitly as such (they are sometimes called degenerate conics, because they include the vertex of the cone). Geometrically, a conic section is the intersection of an infinite cone with a plane.

CONIC SECTION: the intersection of an infinite cone with a plane

Ellipses

An ELLIPSE is a conic section that is formed as shown below. The standard algebraic expression for an ellipse is also included, along with some important parameters associated with the ellipse.

ELLIPSE: a conic section represented by the equation
$\frac{(x - h)^2}{a^2} + \frac{(y - k)^2}{b^2} = 1$

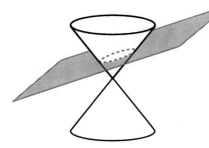

Equation: $\frac{(x - h)^2}{a^2} + \frac{(y - k)^2}{b^2} = 1$
Center: (h, k)
Foci: $(h \pm c, k)$, where $c = \sqrt{|a^2 - b^2|}$
Major axis: Maximum (a, b)
Minor axis: Minimum (a, b)

Example graph:

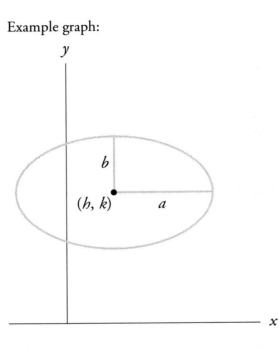

The FOCI of an ellipse are located along the major axis such that the sum of the distances from each foci to any given point on the ellipse is always constant, as shown below.

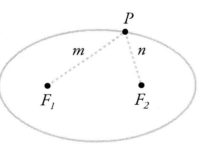

In the above diagram, $m + n$ is a constant, regardless of the position of point P on the ellipse.

Circles

Note that a CIRCLE, which is another conic section, is simply an ellipse for which the major and minor axes are of equal lengths (that is, $a = b$). The foci then coincide with the center of the ellipse, forming a circle. The equation can then be written in terms of radius r:

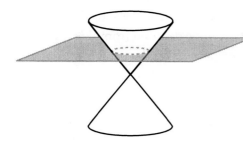

Equation: $(x - h)^2 + (y - k)^2 = r^2$

Parabolas

A parabola is a conic section that involves the cross section shown below. A PARABOLA is defined by a set of points that are equidistant from a fixed line (the directrix) and a noncollinear fixed point (the focus). The cross section and important parameters are shown below:

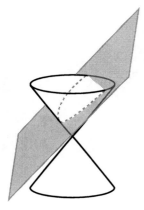

Equation: $(x - h)^2 = 4p(y - k)$
Vertex: (h, k)
Directrix: $y = k - p$
Focus: $(h, k + p)$

> **PARABOLA:** a conic section that is defined by a set of points that are equidistant from a fixed line (the directrix) and a noncollinear fixed point (the focus); the equation of a parabola is $(x - h)^2 = 4p(y - k)$

Example graph:

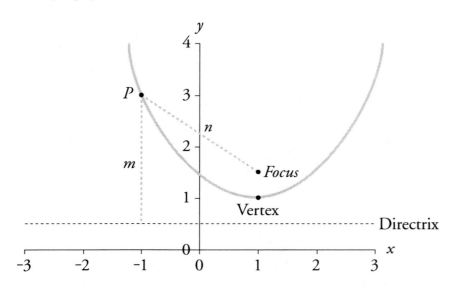

Note that the equation form above is for a parabola that is concave up. The form for concave down (or for horizontal concavity) can be deduced from this expression. Also note that m + n is a constant for any point P on the parabola.

Hyperbolas

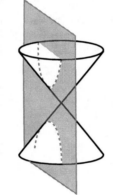

HYPERBOLA: a conic section represented by the equation
$$\frac{(x - h)^2}{a^2} - \frac{(y - k)^2}{b^2} = 1$$

A HYPERBOLA is a conic section as shown below. The hyperbola has two foci and two separate curves, and is similar in some ways to an ellipse. The defining characteristic of a hyperbola is that, for any point P on the hyperbola, the difference between the distances from P to each focus is a constant. The important characteristics of a hyperbola are shown below:

Equation: $\frac{(x - h)^2}{a^2} - \frac{(y - k)^2}{b^2} = 1$

Center: (h, k)

Foci: $(h \pm c, k)$, where $c = \sqrt{|a^2 + b^2|}$

Major axis: Maximum (a, b)

Minor axis: Minimum (a, b)

Asymptotes: $y = k + \frac{b}{a}(x - h)$, $y = k - \frac{b}{a}(x - h)$

Example graph:

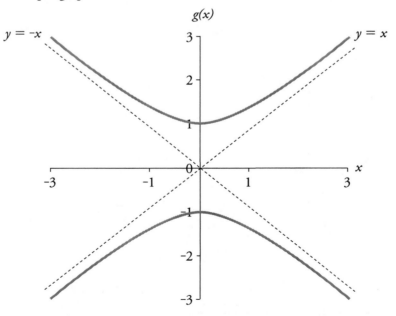

Note that $m - n$ is a constant for any point P on the hyperbola. The asymptotes are also illustrated above. The hyperbola can be oriented in an up-down manner as shown by multiplying the left side of the equation by -1. The corresponding expressions for the foci and asymptotes must also be changed accordingly.

Example: Find the equation of an ellipse with foci located at (0, 2) and (0, 0) and a minor axis of 1.

First, note that this ellipse is oriented along the y-axis. The expression for the ellipse is then the following, where $b > a$ and $a = 1$.

$$\frac{(x - h)^2}{a^2} + \frac{(y - k)^2}{b^2} = 1$$

The center of the ellipse is located halfway between the foci; by inspection, the center (h, k) is then $(0, 1)$. (Generally, the midpoint formula can be used to find the center when the foci are known.) The length of the major axis can be found using the formula

$$c = \sqrt{|a^2 - b^2|}$$

where c can be deduced from the fact that the foci are located at $(h \pm c, k)$.

$$c = 1 = \sqrt{|a^2 - b^2|}$$
$$c^2 = 1 = |a^2 - b^2| = b^2 - a^2$$
$$b^2 - (1)^2 = 1$$
$$b^2 = 2$$
$$b = \sqrt{2}$$

Finally, construct the equation for the ellipse in terms of x and y.

$$x^2 + \frac{(y - 1)^2}{2} = 1$$

The plot of this ellipse is shown below.

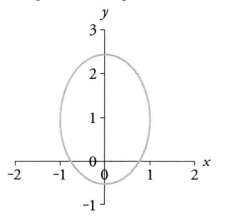

Spheres

A SPHERE, whose cross section is a circle, can also be expressed algebraically. The expression for a sphere is simply an extension of the two-dimensional representation of a circle.

$$r^2 = (x - h)^2 + (y - k)^2 + (z - j)^2$$

SPHERE: a three-dimensional circle represented by the equation: $r^2 = (x - h)^2 + (y - k)^2 + (z - j)^2$

Here, the center of the sphere is located at (h, k, j), and the radius is r. The above expression can also be viewed as the set of points (*x, y, z*) equidistant (by length *r*) from a point (*h, k, j*). Note that the distance formula uses the same format, where the square root is taken for both sides.

$$r = \sqrt{(x - h)^2 + (y - k)^2 + (z - j)^2}$$

SKILL **Solve problems in two and three dimensions** *(e.g., find the distance*
1.9 *between two points, find the coordinates of the midpoint of a line segment)*

Problems involving geometric figures or situations in which real-world activity is being considered may involve either two or three dimensions. The tools for dealing with these problems in three dimensions are largely the same as those for dealing with problems in two dimensions. The best illustrations are the examples from this Competency (for instance, the relationship of circles to spheres) and from Competency 3 (for instance, the discussion of three-dimensional figures).

DOMAIN II
MEASUREMENT, GEOMETRY, AND TRIGONOMETRY

PERSONALIZED STUDY PLAN

X KNOWN MATERIAL/ SKIP IT

PAGE	COMPETENCY AND SKILL	KNOWN MATERIAL/ SKIP IT
37	**2:** **Measurement**	☐
	2.1: Make decisions about units and scales; use unit analysis	☐
	2.2: Analyze precision, accuracy, and approximate error in measurement situations	☐
	2.3: Apply informal concepts of successive approximation, upper and lower bounds, and limit in measurement situations	☐
49	**3:** **Geometry**	☐
	3.1: Solve problems using relationships of parts of geometric figures and among geometric figures in two and three dimensions	☐
	3.2: Describe relationships among sets of special quadrilaterals	☐
	3.3: Solve problems using the properties of triangles, quadrilaterals, polygons, circles, and parallel and perpendicular lines	☐
	3.4: Solve problems using the properties of circles	☐
	3.5: Understand and apply the Pythagorean Theorem and its converse	☐
	3.6: Compute and reason about perimeter, area/surface area, or volume of two- and three-dimensional figures	☐
	3.7: Solve problems involving reflections, rotations, and translations of geometric figures in the plane	☐
94	**4:** **Trigonometry**	☐
	4.1: Define and use the six basic trigonometric relations	☐
	4.2: Apply the Law of Sines and the Law of Cosines	☐
	4.3: Apply the formulas for the trigonometric functions of $x/2$, $2x$, x, $x + y$, and $x - y$; prove trigonometric identities	☐
	4.4: Solve trigonometric equations and inequalities	☐
	4.5: Convert between rectangular and polar coordinate systems	☐

COMPETENCY 2
MEASUREMENT

> **SKILL Make decisions about units and scales that are appropriate for**
> **2.1 problem situations involving measurement; use unit analysis**

In ancient times, baskets, jars and bowls were used to measure capacity. An inch originated as the length of three barley grains placed end to end. The word "carat," used for measuring precious gems, was derived from carob seeds. Even now, nonstandard units are sometimes used when standard instruments might not be available. For example, students might measure the length of a room by their arm spans. Seeds or stones might be used for measuring weight.

Systems of Units

The Customary (Imperial) System
CUSTOMARY OR IMPERIAL UNITS are the familiar everyday units used in the United States.

Customary System units
Inch, foot, yard and mile are commonly used units of length.

1 yard	=	3 feet	=	36 inches
1 mile	=	1,760 yards		

Rod, furlong, and acre (a unit of area) are less familiar units defined in terms of yards:

1 rod	=	5 ½ yards		
1 furlong	=	220 yards		
1 acre	=	4,840 sq. yards	=	160 sq. rods

> *"When you can measure what you are speaking about and express it in numbers, you know something about it; but when you cannot measure it, when you cannot express it in numbers, your knowledge is of a meager and unsatisfactory kind."*
> —*Lord Kelvin*

> **CUSTOMARY OR IMPERIAL UNITS:** are the familiar everyday units used in the United States

The basic unit of weight is pound (lb).

1 pound	=	16 ounces (oz)		
1 ounce	=	16 drams		
Short ton (U.S.)	=	2,000 lb		
Long ton (British)	=	2,240 lb		

The basic unit of liquid measure or liquid capacity is the gallon.

1 gallon	=	4 quarts	=	8 pints	=	16 cups	=	128 ounces

The basic unit of dry measure or dry capacity is the bushel.

1 bushel	=	4 pecks	=	32 dry quarts	=	64 dry pints	=	2,150.42 cubic inches
1 barrel	=	105 dry quarts						

The metric (SI) system

The metric or SI system is commonly used in many countries around the world for making everyday measurements. It is also the standard system used for scientific measurements. The metric system is convenient to use because units at different scales are related by multiples of ten.

The basic metric unit for *length* is the meter (m). The basic metric unit for *weight* or *mass* is the gram (g). The basic metric unit for *volume* is the liter (L).

The following table shows the most commonly used units.

COMMON METRIC UNITS		
1 cm	=	10 mm
1 m	=	1000 mm
1 m	=	100 cm
1 km	=	1000 m
1 L	=	1000 mL
1 kL	=	1000 L
1 g	=	1000 mg
1 kg	=	1000 g

Appropriate units and equivalents

Different units within the same system of measurement are selected based on the scale at which the measurement is being made. For example, the height of a person is measured in feet whereas the distances between cities are measured in miles. To estimate measurements of familiar objects, it is necessary to first determine the units to be used.

Examples of appropriate units:

LENGTH	
The coastline of Florida	miles or kilometers
The width of a ribbon	inches or millimeters
The thickness of a book	inches or centimeters
The length of a football field	yards or meters
The depth of water in a pool	feet or meters

WEIGHT OR MASS	
A bag of sugar	pounds or grams
A school bus	tons or kilograms
A dime	ounces or grams

CAPACITY	
Bucket of paint for bedroom	gallons or liters
Glass of milk	cups or liters
Bottle of soda	quarts or liters
Medicine for child	ounces or milliliters

To estimate measurements, it is helpful to have a familiar reference with a known measurement. For instance, you can use the knowledge that a dollar bill is about 6 inches long or that a nickel weighs about 5 grams to make estimates of length and weight without actually measuring with a ruler or a balance.

APPROXIMATE MEASUREMENTS OF COMMON ITEMS		
ITEM APPROXIMATELY EQUAL TO	METRIC	IMPERIAL
carton of milk	1 liter	1 quart
yardstick	1 meter	1 yard
distance between highway markers	1 kilometer	1 mile
man's foot	30 centimeters	1 foot
math textbook	1 kilogram	2 pounds
average-sized man	75 kilograms	170 pounds
large paper clip	1 gram	
thickness of a dime	2 millimeters	0.1 inch
1 football field	6400 sq. yd.	
boiling point of water	100°C	212°F
freezing point of water	0°C	32°F
1 cup of liquid	240 ml	8 fl. oz.
1 teaspoon	5 ml	

Estimate the measurement of the following items:

The length of an adult cow = _____ meters

The thickness of a compact disc = _____ millimeters

Your height = _____ meters

length of your nose = _____ centimeters

weight of your math textbook = _____ kilograms

weight of an automobile = _____ kilograms

weight of an aspirin = _____ grams

Conversions: unit analysis

There are many methods for converting measurements to other units within a system or between systems. One method is multiplication of the given measurement by a conversion factor. This conversion factor is the following ratio, which is always equal to unity.

$$\frac{\text{new units}}{\text{old units}} \quad \text{OR} \quad \frac{\text{what you want}}{\text{what you have}}$$

The fundamental feature of *unit analysis* or *dimensional analysis* is that conversion factors may be multiplied together and units cancelled in the same way as numerators and denominators of numerical fractions. The following examples help clarify this point.

Example: Convert 3 miles to yards.

Multiply the initial measurement by the conversion factor, cancel the mile units and solve:

$$\frac{3 \text{ miles}}{1} \times \frac{1{,}760 \text{ yards}}{1 \text{ mile}} = 5280 \text{ yards}$$

Example: It takes Cynthia 45 minutes to get ready each morning. How many hours does she spend getting ready each week?

Multiply the initial measurement by the conversion factors from minutes to hours and from days to weeks, cancel the minute and day units and solve:

$$\frac{45 \text{ min.}}{\text{day}} \times \frac{1 \text{ hour}}{60 \text{ min.}} \times \frac{7 \text{ days}}{\text{week}} = \frac{5.25 \text{ hours}}{\text{week}}$$

Conversion factors for different types of units are listed below.

Conversion factors

MEASUREMENTS OF LENGTH (ENGLISH SYSTEM)		
12 inches (in)	=	1 foot (ft)
3 feet (ft)	=	1 yard (yd)
1760 yards (yd)	=	1 mile (mi)

MEASUREMENTS OF LENGTH (METRIC SYSTEM)		
Kilometer (km)	=	1000 meters (m)
Hectometer (hm)	=	100 meters (m)
Decameter (dam)	=	10 meters (m)
Meter (m)	=	1 meter (m)
Decimeter (dm)	=	1/10 meter (m)

MEASUREMENTS OF LENGTH (METRIC SYSTEM)		
Centimeter (cm)	=	1/100 meter (m)
Millimeter (mm)	=	1/1000 meter (m)

CONVERSION OF WEIGHT FROM METRIC TO ENGLISH		
28.35 grams (g)	=	1 ounce (oz)
16 ounces (oz)	=	1 pound (lb)
2000 pounds (lb)	=	1 ton (t) (short ton)
1 metric ton (t)	=	1.1 ton (t)

MEASUREMENTS OF WEIGHT (METRIC SYSTEM)		
kilogram (kg)	=	1000 grams (g)
gram (g)	=	1 gram (g)
milligram (mg)	=	1/1000 gram (g)

MEASUREMENT OF VOLUME (ENGLISH SYSTEM)		
8 fluid ounces (oz)	=	1 cup (c)
2 cups (c)	=	1 pint (pt)
2 pints (pt)	=	1 quart (qt)
4 quarts (qt)	=	1 gallon (gal)

MEASUREMENT OF VOLUME (METRIC SYSTEM)		
Kiloliter (kl)	=	1000 liters (l)
Liter (l)	=	1 liter (l)
Milliliter (ml)	=	1/1000 liter (ml)

CONVERSION OF VOLUME FROM ENGLISH TO METRIC		
1 teaspoon (tsp)	≈	5 milliliters
1 fluid ounce	≈	29.57 milliliters
1 cup	≈	0.24 liters
1 pint	≈	0.47 liters
1 quart	≈	0.95 liters
1 gallon	≈	3.8 liters

Note: (′) represents feet and (″) represents inches.

Example: Convert 8,750 meters to kilometers.

$$\frac{8{,}750 \text{ meters}}{1} \times \frac{1 \text{ kilometer}}{1000 \text{ meters}} = \underline{\hspace{2cm}} \text{km}$$
$$= 8.75 \text{ kilometers}$$

Example: 4 mi. = _____ yd.

1760 yd. = 1 mi.

$$4 \text{ mi.} \times 1760\frac{\text{yd.}}{\text{mi.}} = 7040 \text{ yd.}$$

Square units can be derived with knowledge of basic units of length by squaring the equivalent measurements.

1 square foot (sq. ft. or ft²) = 144 sq. in.

1 sq. yd. = 9 sq. ft.

1 sq. yd. = 1296 sq. in.

Example: 14 sq. yd. = _____ sq. ft.

1 sq. yd. = 9 sq. ft.

14 sq. yd. $\times$ 9 $\frac{\text{sq. ft.}}{\text{sq. yd.}}$ = 126 sq. ft.

Example: A car skidded 170 yards on an icy road before coming to a stop. How long is the skid distance in kilometers?

Since 1 yard $\approx$ 0.9 meters, multiply 170 yards by 0.9 meters/1 yard.

170 yd. $\times$ $\frac{0.9 \text{ m}}{1 \text{ yd.}}$ = 153 m

Since 1000 meters = 1 kilometer, multiply 153 meters by 1 kilometer/1000 meters.

153 m $\times$ $\frac{1 \text{ km}}{1000 \text{ m}}$ = 0.153 km

Example: The distance around a race course is exactly 1 mile, 17 feet, and $9\frac{1}{4}$ inches. Approximate this distance to the nearest tenth of a foot.

Convert the distance to feet.

1 mile = 1 = 1760 yards = 1760 $\times$ 3 feet = 5280 feet.

$9\frac{1}{4}$ in. = $\frac{37}{4}$ in. $\times$ $\frac{1 \text{ ft.}}{12 \text{ in.}}$ = $\frac{37}{48}$ ft. = 0.77083 ft.

So 1 mile, 17 ft. and $9\frac{1}{4}$ in. = 5280 ft. + 17 ft. + 0.77083 ft.

= 5297.$\underline{7}$7083 ft.

Now, we need to round to the nearest tenth digit. The underlined 7 is in the tenths place. The digit in the hundredths place, also a 7, is greater than 5. Therefore, the 7 in the tenths place needs to be rounded up to 8 to get a final answer of 5297.8 feet.

Example: If the temperature is 90° F, what is it expressed in Celsius units?

To convert between Celsius (C) and Fahrenheit (F), use the following formula.

$\frac{C}{5} = \frac{F - 32}{9}$

If F = 90, then C = 5$\frac{(90 - 32)}{9}$ = $\frac{5 \times 58}{9}$ = 32.2.

Example: A map shows a scale of 1 inch = 2 miles. Convert this scale to a numerical ratio so that any unit system (such as metric) can be used to measure distances.

The scale is a ratio—1 inch: 2 miles. If either value is converted so that the two values have the same units, then this scale can be converted to a purely numerical ratio. To avoid fractions, convert miles to inches.

$$2 \text{ mi} = 2 \text{ mi} \times \frac{5{,}280 \text{ ft}}{1 \text{ mi}} \times \frac{12 \text{ in.}}{1 \text{ ft.}} = 126{,}720 \text{ in}$$

The ratio is then 1:126,720.

SKILL 2.2 Analyze precision, accuracy, and approximate error in measurement situations

Most numbers in mathematics are "exact" or "counted." Measurements are "approximate" and usually involve interpolation—for instance, figuring out which mark on the ruler is the closest. Any measurement obtained with a measuring device is approximate. Variations in measurement are defined in terms of precision and accuracy.

PRECISION measures the degree of variation in a particular measurement without reference to a true or real value. If a measurement is precise, it can be made repeatedly with little variation in the result. The precision of a measuring device is the smallest fractional or decimal division on the instrument. The smaller the unit or fraction of a unit on the measuring device, the more precisely it can measure.

The GREATEST POSSIBLE ERROR of measurement is always equal to one-half the smallest fraction of a unit on the measuring device. For example, if the smallest unit was mm, then the greatest possible error would be $\pm \frac{1}{2}$ mm.

ACCURACY is a measure of how close the result of measurement comes to the "true" value. In the game of darts, the true value is the bull's eye. If three darts are tossed and each lands on the bull's eye, the dart thrower is both precise (all land near the same spot) and accurate (the darts all land on the "true" value).

The greatest allowable measure of error is called the TOLERANCE. The least acceptable value is called the LOWER LIMIT, and the greatest acceptable value is called the UPPER LIMIT. The difference between the upper and lower limits is called the TOLERANCE INTERVAL. For example, a specification for an automobile part might be 14.625 ± 0.005 mm. This means that the smallest acceptable length of the part is 14.620 mm and the largest length acceptable is 14.630 mm. The tolerance interval is 0.010 mm. One can see how it would be important for automobile

PRECISION: measures the degree of variation in a particular measurement without reference to a true or real value

GREATEST POSSIBLE ERROR: equal to one-half the smallest fraction of a unit on the measuring device

ACCURACY: a measure of how close the result of measurement comes to the "true" value

TOLERANCE: the greatest allowable measure of error

LOWER LIMIT: the smallest acceptable value of measurement given a particular tolerance

parts to be within a set of limits in terms of physical dimensions. If the part is too long or too short, it will not fit properly and vibrations may occur, thereby weakening the part and eventually causing damage to other parts.

Error in measurement may also be expressed by a percentage of error. For example, a measurement of 12 feet may be said to be off by 2%. This means that the actual measurement could be between

$12 - (2\%$ of $12)$ and $12 + (2\%$ of $12)$

$12 - (.02)12$ and $12 + (.02)12$

11.76 ft. and 12.24 feet

To determine the percent error between a measurement of a value and the actual value, use the following formula.

$$\text{Percent Error} = \frac{|\text{Measured} - \text{Actual}|}{\text{Actual}} \times 100$$

Rounding

Error in measurement may also be indicated by the terms "rounded" or "to the nearest." When rounding to a given place value, it is necessary to look at the number in the next smaller place. If this number is 5 or more, the number in the place to which we are rounding is increased by 1 and all numbers to the right are changed to zero. If the number is less than 5, the number in the place to which we are rounding stays the same and all numbers to the right are changed to zero. For example, the length of a side of a square to the nearest inch may be 10 inches. This means that the actual length of the side could be between 9.5 inches and 10.4 inches (since all of these values round to 10).

SKILL 2.3 **Apply informal concepts of successive approximation, upper and lower bounds, and limit in measurement situations**

Successive Approximation

The concept of SUCCESSIVE APPROXIMATION is used in many areas of mathematics as a computational tool. Even though it is implemented in many different ways, the general idea is to calculate a value by starting with a rough approximation and then to refine that approximation through successive iterations. Ideally, with each iteration, the result gets progressively closer to the correct result. In a typical scenario of this type, each approximation of a calculation provides the upper and lower bounds within which the answer must lie. With each new approximation, the range between bounds narrows so that, in the limit (i.e., after a very large or infinite number of iterations), the method points to the exact answer.

To illustrate this principle in the context of measurement, approximate a circle by a polygon with a large number of sides. Start with a square and then increase the number of sides of the polygon in successive iterations to see how well the area and the circumference of the circle are approximated.

In the diagram below, a circle of radius r is inscribed in a square of side A and a smaller square of side a is inscribed within the circle. The two squares provide the bounds within which the area and circumference of the circle must lie:

$$4a < \text{circumference} < 4A$$
$$a^2 < \text{area} < A^2$$

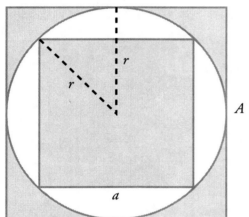

Studying the geometry of the figure we can see that:

$$A = 2r$$
$$r^2 = \left(\tfrac{a}{2}\right)^2 + \left(\tfrac{a}{2}\right)^2 \rightarrow r^2 = 2\left(\tfrac{a}{2}\right)^2 \rightarrow a = \sqrt{2}\,r$$

Thus, the upper and lower bounds for the area and circumference of the circle can be rewritten as

$$4\sqrt{2}\,r < \text{circumference} < 8r; \rightarrow 5.6r < \text{circumference} < 8r$$
$$2r^2 < \text{area} < 4r^2$$

It is clear that even a very simple polygon such as a square provides reasonable bounds for the actual circumference ($2\pi r = 6.28r$) and area ($\pi r^2 = 3.14r^2$) of a circle.

Next consider a circle inscribed within a hexagon of radius A and having a smaller hexagon of radius a inscribed within it.

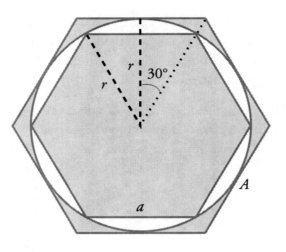

From the geometry of the figure (interior angle of 120°), we see that

$$a = r$$

$$\tan 30° = \frac{\frac{A}{2}}{r}; \rightarrow A = 2r \tan 30°; \rightarrow A = 1.15r$$

Since the area of a regular hexagon of side a is given by $\frac{3\sqrt{3}}{2}a^2$, the area and circumference of the circle bounded by the two hexagons may be expressed as follows:

$$6r < \text{circumference} < 6.9r$$

$$2.6r^2 < \text{area} < 3.44r^2$$

Try one more iteration with a circle bounded by two octagons.

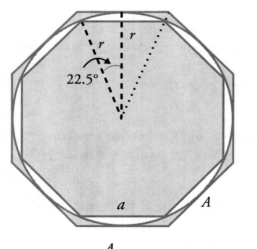

$$\tan 22.5° = \frac{\frac{A}{2}}{r}; \rightarrow A = 2r \tan 22.5°; \rightarrow A = 0.83r$$

$$\sin 22.5° = \frac{\frac{a}{2}}{r}; \rightarrow a = 2r \sin 22.5°; \rightarrow a = 0.77r$$

The area of a regular octagon of side a is given by

$$\frac{2}{\tan 22.5°}a^2 = 4.83a^2$$

Hence, the bounds on the circumference and area of the circle are given by:

$6.16r <$ circumference $< 6.64r$

$2.86r^2 <$ area $< 3.33r^2$

Summarizing the results:

POLYGON	CIRCUMFERENCE	AREA
Square	$5.6r <$ circumference $< 8r$	$2r^2 <$ area $< 4r^2$
Hexagon	$6r <$ circumference $< 6.9r$	$2.6r^2 <$ area $< 3.44r^2$
Octagon	$6.16r <$ circumference $< 6.64r$	$2.86r^2 <$ area $< 3.33r^2$
Circle	$6.28r$	$3.14r^2$

The table above shows how each iteration improves with respect to the previous one and provides a narrower range of more accurate bounds for the circumference and area of the circle.

COMPETENCY 3
GEOMETRY

SKILL **Solve problems using relationships of parts of geometric figures**
3.1 *(e.g., medians of triangles, inscribed angles in circles)* **and among geometric figures** *(e.g., congruence and similarity)* **in two and three dimensions**

EUCLIDEAN GEOMETRY is the study of the properties of two-dimensional (planar) and three-dimensional (solid) figures. It is based on the undefined concepts of point, line, and plane and a set of self-evident statements or AXIOMS. Starting from these building blocks, deductive reasoning is used to prove a set of propositions or theorems about the properties of different geometric figures. The axioms and theorems and the process of formal proof provide a consistent logical framework that can be used to derive further results. The following review of geometric concepts provides a basic overview of proof relating to geometry, as well as the characteristics of various types of polygons, circles, compound shapes and three-dimensional figures.

EUCLIDEAN GEOMETRY: the study of the properties of two-dimensional (planar) and three-dimensional (solid) figures

AXIOMS: a self-evident mathematical statement

Formal Proofs

DEDUCTIVE REASONING: the process of arriving at a conclusion based on other statements that are known to be true, such as theorems, axioms, or postulates

DEDUCTIVE REASONING is the process of arriving at a conclusion based on other statements that are known to be true, such as theorems, axioms, or postulates. Valid mathematical arguments are deductive in nature.

A DIRECT PROOF demonstrates the truth of a proposition by beginning with the given information and showing that it leads to the proposition through logical steps. An INDIRECT PROOF of a proposition can be carried out by demonstrating that the opposite of the proposition is untenable.

DIRECT PROOF: demonstrates the truth of a proposition by beginning with the given information and showing that it leads to the proposition through logical steps

A proof of a geometrical proposition is typically presented in a format that has two columns side-by-side. In a two-column proof, the left column consists of the given information or statements that can be proved by deductive reasoning. The right column consists of the reasons used to justify each statement on the left. The right side should identify given information or state the theorems, postulates, definitions, or algebraic properties used to show that the corresponding steps are valid.

INDIRECT PROOF: demonstrates that the opposite of the proposition is untenable

The following algebraic postulates are frequently used as justifications for statements in two-column geometric proofs:

In a two-column proof, the left column consists of the given information or statements that can be proved by deductive reasoning. The right column consists of the reasons used to justify each statement on the left.

ALGEBRAIC POSTULATES	
Addition Property	If $a = b$ and $c = d$, then $a + c = b + d$
Subtraction Property	If $a = b$ and $c = d$, then $a - c = b - d$
Multiplication Property	If $a = b$, then $ac = bc$
Division Property	If $a = b$ and $c \neq 0$, then $a/c = b/c$
Reflexive Property	$a = a$
Symmetric Property	If $a = b$, then $b = a$
Transitive Property	If $a = b$ and $b = c$, then $a = c$
Distributive Property	$a(b + c) = ab + ac$
Substitution Property	If $a = b$, then b may be substituted for a in any other expression (a may also be substituted for b)

Definitions of Geometric Figures

A POINT is a dimensionless location and has no length, width, or height.

A LINE connects a series of points and continues "straight" infinitely in two directions. Lines extend in one dimension. A line is defined by any two points that fall on the line; therefore, a line may have multiple names.

A LINE SEGMENT is a portion of a line. A line segment is the shortest distance between two endpoints and is named using those endpoints. Line segments therefore have exactly two names (e.g., $\overline{AB}$ or $\overline{BA}$). Because line segments have two endpoints, they have a defined length or distance.

A RAY is a portion of a line that has only one endpoint and continues infinitely in one direction. Rays are named using the endpoint as the first point and any other point on the ray as the second.

Note that the symbol for a line includes two arrows (indicating infinite extent in both directions), the symbol for a ray includes only one arrow (indicating that it has one endpoint), and the symbol for a line segment has no arrows (indicating two endpoints).

Example: Using the diagram below, calculate the length of $\overline{AB}$ given that $\overline{AC}$ is 6 cm and $\overline{BC}$ is twice as long as $\overline{AB}$

$\overline{AB} + \overline{BC} = \overline{AC}$
Let $x = \overline{AB}$
$x + 2x = 6$ cm
$3x = 6$ cm
$x = 2$ cm

A PLANE is a flat surface defined by three points. Planes extend indefinitely in two dimensions. A common example of a plane is the x-y plane used in the Cartesian coordinate system.

In geometry, the point, line, and plane are key concepts and can be discussed in relation to each other.

Collinear points
are all on the same line.

Noncollinear points
are not on the same line.

POINT: a dimensionless location and has no length, width, or height

LINE: connects a series of points and continues "straight" infinitely in two directions

LINE SEGMENT: a portion of a line; a line segment has two endpoints

RAY: a portion of a line that has only one endpoint and continues infinitely in one direction

PLANE: a flat surface defined by three points; planes extend indefinitely in two dimensions

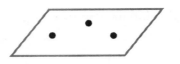

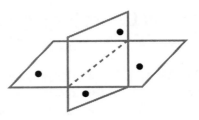

Coplanar points
are on the same plane.

Noncoplanar points
are not on the same plane.

Congruence

CONGRUENT figures have the same size and shape; i.e., if one of the figures is superimposed on the other, the boundaries coincide exactly. Congruent line segments have the same length; congruent angles have equal measures. The symbol $\cong$ is used to indicate that two figures, line segments, or angles are congruent.

The reflexive, symmetric and transitive properties described for algebraic equality relationships may also be applied to congruence. For instance, if $\angle A \cong \angle B$ and $\angle A \cong \angle D$, then $\angle B \cong \angle D$ (transitive property).

The polygons (pentagons) *ABCDE* and *VWXYZ* shown below are congruent since they are exactly the same size and shape.

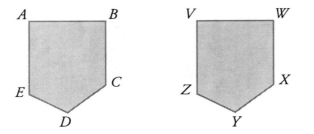

$$ABCDE \cong VWXYZ$$

Corresponding parts are congruent angles and congruent sides. For the polygons shown above:

corresponding angles	corresponding sides
$\angle A \leftrightarrow \angle V$	$AB \leftrightarrow VW$
$\angle B \leftrightarrow \angle W$	$BC \leftrightarrow WX$
$\angle C \leftrightarrow \angle X$	$CD \leftrightarrow XY$
$\angle D \leftrightarrow \angle Y$	$DE \leftrightarrow YZ$
$\angle E \leftrightarrow \angle Z$	$AE \leftrightarrow VZ$

Two triangles are congruent if each of the three angles and three sides of one triangle match up in a one-to-one fashion with congruent angles and sides of the second triangle. To see how the sides and angles match up, it is sometimes necessary to imagine rotating or reflecting one of the triangles so the two figures are oriented in the same position.

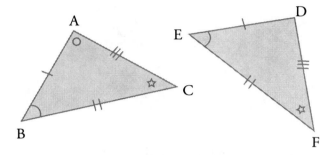

In the example above, the two triangles ABC and DEF are congruent if these 6 conditions are met:

1. $\angle A \cong \angle D$ 4. $\overline{AB} \cong \overline{DE}$
2. $\angle B \cong \angle E$ 5. $\overline{BC} \cong \overline{EF}$
3. $\angle C \cong \angle F$ 6. $\overline{AC} \cong \overline{DF}$

The congruent angles and segments "correspond" to each other.

It is not always necessary to demonstrate all of the above six conditions to prove that two triangles are congruent. There are several "shortcut" methods described below.

The SAS POSTULATE (side-angle-side) states that if two sides and the included angle of one triangle are congruent to two sides and the included angle of another triangle, then the two triangles are congruent.

> **SAS POSTULATE:** also called side-angle-side; states that if two sides and the included angle of one triangle are congruent to two sides and the included angle of another triangle, then the two triangles are congruent

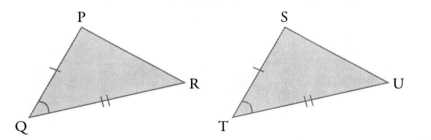

To see why this is true, imagine moving the triangle PQR (shown above) in such a way that the point P coincides with the point S, and line segment PQ coincides with line segment ST. Point Q will then coincide with T, since PQ $\cong$ ST. Also, segment QR will coincide with TU, because $\angle Q \cong \angle T$. Point R will coincide with U, because QR $\cong$ TU. Since P and S coincide and R and U coincide, line PR will coincide with SU because two lines cannot enclose a space. Thus the two triangles match perfectly point for point and are congruent.

Example: Are the following triangles congruent?

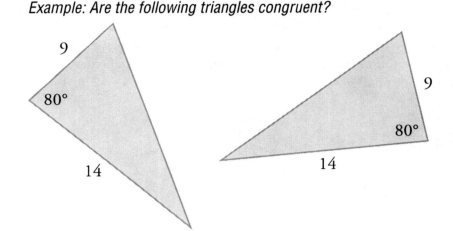

Each of the two triangles has a side that is 14 units and another that is 9 units. The angle included in the sides is 80° in both triangles. Therefore, the triangles are congruent by SAS.

The SSS POSTULATE (side-side-side) states that if three sides of one triangle are congruent to three sides of another triangle, then the two triangles are congruent.

> **SSS POSTULATE:** also called side-side-side; states that if three sides of one triangle are congruent to three sides of another triangle, then the two triangles are congruent

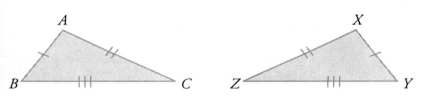

Since $AB \cong XY$, $BC \cong YZ$ and $AC \cong XZ$, then $\triangle ABC \cong \triangle XYZ$.

Example: Given isosceles triangle ABC with D being the midpoint of base AC, prove that the two triangles ABD and ACD are congruent.

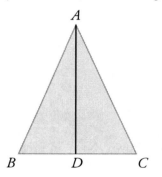

Proof:

1. Isosceles triangle ABC,
   D midpoint of base AC   Given

2. $AB \cong AC$ An isosceles triangle has two congruent sides

3. $BD \cong DC$ Midpoint divides a line into two equal parts

4. $AD \cong AD$ Reflexive property

5. $\triangle ABD \cong \triangle ACD$ SSS

The ASA POSTULATE (angle-side-angle) states that if two angles and the included side of one triangle are congruent to two angles and the included side of another triangle, the triangles are congruent.

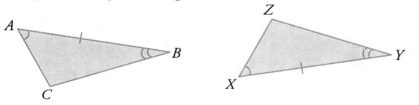

$\angle A \cong \angle X$, $\angle B \cong \angle Y$, $AB \cong XY$ then $\triangle ABC \cong \triangle XYZ$ by ASA

> **ASA POSTULATE:** also called angle-side-angle; states that if two angles and the included side of one triangle are congruent to two angles and the included side of another triangle, the triangles are congruent

Example: Given two right triangles with one leg (AB and KL) of each measuring 6 cm and the adjacent angle 37°, prove the triangles are congruent.

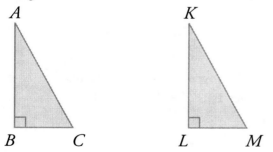

Proof:

1. Right $\triangle ABC$ and $\triangle KLM$
   AB = KL = 6 cm
   $\angle A = \angle K = 37°$ Given

2. $AB \cong KL$; $\angle A \cong \angle K$ Figures with the same measure are congruent

3. $\angle B \cong \angle L$ All right angles are congruent

4. $\triangle ABC \cong \triangle KLM$ ASA

Example: What method could be used to prove that triangles ABC and AED are congruent?

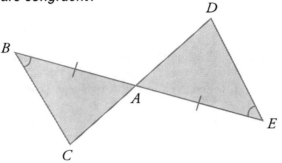

The sides AB and AE are given as congruent, as are $\angle ABC$ and $\angle AED$. $\angle BAC$ and $\angle DAE$ are vertical angles and are therefore congruent. Thus triangles $\triangle ABC$ and $\triangle AED$ are congruent by the ASA postulate.

> **HL THEOREM:** states that if the hypotenuse and leg of one right triangle are congruent to the hypotenuse and leg of another right triangle, then the two triangles are congruent

The HL THEOREM (hypotenuse-leg) is a congruence shortcut that can only be used with right triangles. According to this theorem, if the hypotenuse and leg of one right triangle are congruent to the hypotenuse and leg of the other right triangle, then the two triangles are congruent.

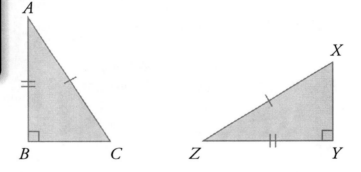

If $\angle B$ and $\angle Y$ are right angles and $AC \cong XZ$ (hypotenuse of each triangle), $AB \cong YZ$ (corresponding leg of each triangle), then $\triangle ABC \cong \triangle ZYX$ by HL.

Proof:

1. $\angle B \cong \angle Y$
   $AB \cong YZ$
   $AC \cong XZ$ Given

2. $BC = \sqrt{AC^2 - AB^2}$ Pythagorean theorem

3. $XY = \sqrt{XZ^2 - YZ^2}$ Pythagorean theorem

4. $XY = \sqrt{AC^2 - AB^2} = BC$ Substitution ($XZ \cong AC$, $YZ \cong AB$)

5. $\triangle ABC \cong \triangle ZYX$ SAS ($AB \cong YZ$, $\angle B \cong \angle Y$, $BC \cong XY$)

Similarity

Two figures that have the same shape are SIMILAR. To be the same shape, corresponding angles must be equal. Therefore, polygons are similar if and only if there is a one-to-one correspondence between their vertices such that the corresponding angles are congruent. For similar figures, the lengths of corresponding sides are proportional. The symbol ~ is used to indicate that two figures are similar.

> **SIMILAR:** figures that have the same shape but not necessarily the same size are similar

The polygons *ABCDE* and *VWXYZ* shown below are similar.

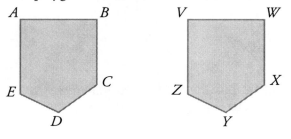

$$ABCDE \sim VWXYZ$$

> *For similar figures, the lengths of corresponding sides are proportional.*

Corresponding angles: $\angle A = \angle V, \angle B = \angle W, \angle C = \angle X, \angle D = \angle Y, \angle E = \angle Z$

Corresponding sides: $\dfrac{AB}{VW} = \dfrac{BC}{WX} = \dfrac{CD}{XY} = \dfrac{DE}{YZ} = \dfrac{AE}{VZ}$

Example: Given two similar quadrilaterals, find the lengths of sides x, y, and z.

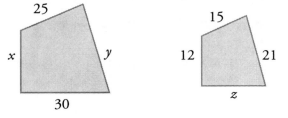

Since corresponding sides are proportional, 15/25 = 3/5, so the scale factor is 3/5.

$$\frac{12}{x} = \frac{3}{5} \qquad\qquad \frac{21}{y} = \frac{3}{5} \qquad\qquad \frac{z}{30} = \frac{3}{5}$$
$$3x = 60 \qquad\qquad 3y = 105 \qquad\qquad 5z = 90$$
$$x = 20 \qquad\qquad y = 35 \qquad\qquad z = 18$$

Just as for congruence, there are shortcut methods that can be used to prove similarity.

According to the AA SIMILARITY POSTULATE, if two angles of one triangle are congruent to two angles of another triangle, then the triangles are similar. It is obvious that if two of the corresponding angles are congruent, the third set of corresponding angles must be congruent as well. Hence, showing AA is sufficient to prove that two triangles are similar.

> **AA SIMILARITY POSTULATE:** states that if two angles of one triangle are congruent to two angles of another triangle, then the triangles are similar

SAS SIMILARITY THEOREM: states that if an angle of one triangle is congruent to an angle of another triangle, and the sides adjacent to those angles are in proportion, then the triangles are similar

The SAS SIMILARITY THEOREM states that if an angle of one triangle is congruent to an angle of another triangle, and the sides adjacent to those angles are in proportion, then the triangles are similar.

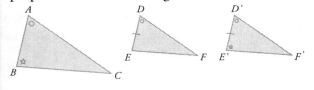

If $\angle A = \angle D$ and $\frac{AB}{DE} = \frac{AC}{DF}$, $\Delta ABC \sim \Delta DEF$.

Example: A graphic artist is designing a logo containing two triangles. The artist wants the triangles to be similar. Determine whether the artist has created similar triangles.

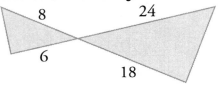

The sides are proportional ($\frac{8}{24} = \frac{6}{18} = \frac{1}{3}$) and vertical angles are congruent. The two triangles are therefore similar by the SAS similarity theorem.

SSS SIMILARITY THEOREM: states that if the sides of two triangles are in proportion, then the triangles are similar

According to the SSS SIMILARITY THEOREM, if the sides of two triangles are in proportion, then the triangles are similar.

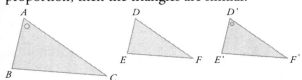

If $\frac{AB}{DE} = \frac{AC}{DF} = \frac{BC}{EF}$, $\Delta ABC \sim \Delta DEF$

Example: Tommy draws and cuts out 2 triangles for a school project. One of them has sides of 3, 6, and 9 inches. The other triangle has sides of 2, 4, and 6. Is there a relationship between the two triangles?

Determine the proportions of the corresponding sides.

$$\frac{2}{3} \qquad \frac{4}{6} = \frac{2}{3} \qquad \frac{6}{9} = \frac{2}{3}$$

The smaller triangle is $\frac{2}{3}$ the size of the large triangle, therefore they are similar triangles by the SSS similarity theorem.

SKILL 3.2 **Describe relationships among sets of special quadrilaterals, such as the square, rectangle, parallelogram, rhombus, and trapezoid**

Properties of Polygons

A POLYGON is a simple closed figure composed of line segments. Here we will consider only CONVEX POLYGONS, i.e., polygons for which the measure of each internal angle is less than 180°. Of the two polygons shown below, the one on the left is a convex polygon.

A REGULAR POLYGON is one for which all sides are the same length and all interior angles are the same measure.

The sum of the measures of the interior angles of a polygon can be determined using the following formula, where n represents the number of angles in the polygon.

Sum of $\angle s = 180(n - 2)$

The measure of each angle of a regular polygon can be found by dividing the sum of the measures by the number of angles.

Measure of $\angle = \frac{180(n - 2)}{n}$

Example: Find the measure of each angle of a regular octagon. Since an octagon has eight sides, each angle equals:

$$\frac{180(8 - 2)}{8} = \frac{180(6)}{8} = 135°$$

The sum of the measures of the *exterior angles* of a polygon, taken one angle at each vertex, equals 360°.

The measure of each exterior angle of a regular polygon can be determined using the following formula, where *n* represents the number of angles in the polygon.

POLYGON: a simple closed figure composed of line segments

CONVEX POLYGON: a polygon in which the measure of each internal angle is less than 180 degrees

REGULAR POLYGON: a polygon for which all sides are the same length and all interior angles are the same measure

Measure of exterior $\angle$ of regular polygon

$$\angle = 180 - \frac{180(n - 2)}{n} = \frac{360}{n}$$

Example: Find the measure of the interior and exterior angles of a regular pentagon.

Since a pentagon has five sides, each exterior angle measures:

$$\frac{360}{5} = 72°$$

Since each exterior angle is supplementary to its interior angle, the interior angle measures $180 - 72$ or $108°$.

Properties of Quadrilaterals

A QUADRILATERAL is a polygon with four sides. The sum of the measures of the angles of a convex quadrilateral is 360°.

A TRAPEZOID is a quadrilateral with exactly one pair of parallel sides.

The two parallel sides of a trapezoid are called the bases, and the two nonparallel sides are called the legs. If the two legs are the same length, then the trapezoid is called an ISOSCELES TRAPEZOID.

The segment connecting the two midpoints of the legs is called the median. The median has the following two properties:

1. The median is parallel to the two bases

2. The length of the median is equal to one-half the sum of the length of the two bases

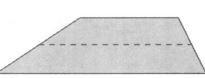

In an isosceles trapezoid, the nonparallel sides are congruent.

An isosceles trapezoid has the following properties:

1. The diagonals of an isosceles trapezoid are congruent

2. The base angles of an isosceles trapezoid are congruent

QUADRILATERAL: a polygon with four sides

TRAPEZOID: a quadrilateral with exactly one pair of parallel sides

ISOSCELES TRAPEZOID: a trapezoid with two legs of equal length

Example: An isosceles trapezoid has a diagonal of 10 and a base angle measuring 30°. Find the measure of the other three angles.

Based on the properties of trapezoids, the measure of the other base angle is 30° and the measure of the other diagonal is 10. The other two angles have a measure of:

$$360 = 30(2) + 2x$$
$$x = 150°$$

The other two angles measure 150° each.

A PARALLELOGRAM is a quadrilateral with two pairs of parallel sides. A parallelogram has the following properties:

1. The diagonals bisect each other

2. Each diagonal divides the parallelogram into two congruent triangles

3. Both pairs of opposite sides are congruent

4. Both pairs of opposite angles are congruent

5. Two adjacent angles are supplementary

Example: Find the measures of the other three angles of a parallelogram if one angle measures 38°.

Since opposite angles are equal, there are two angles measuring 38°. Since adjacent angles are supplementary, $180 - 38 = 142$. Hence the other two angles measure 142° each.

Example: The measures of two adjacent angles of a parallelogram are 3x + 40 and x + 70. Find the measure of each angle.

$$2(3x + 40) + 2(x + 70) = 360$$
$$6x + 80 + 2x + 140 = 360$$
$$8x + 220 = 360$$
$$8x = 140$$
$$x = 17.5$$
$$3x + 40 = 92.5$$
$$x + 70 = 87.5$$

Thus the angles measure 92.5°, 92.5°, 87.5°, and 87.5°.

RECTANGLE: a parallelogram with a right angle

A RECTANGLE is a parallelogram with a right angle. Since a rectangle is a special type of parallelogram, it exhibits all the properties of a parallelogram. All the angles of a rectangle are right angles because of congruent opposite angles. Additionally, the diagonals of a rectangle are congruent.

RHOMBUS: a parallelogram with all sides equal in length

A RHOMBUS is a parallelogram with all sides equal in length. A rhombus has all the properties of a parallelogram. Additionally, its diagonals are perpendicular to each other, and they bisect its angles.

SQUARE: a rectangle with all sides equal in length

A SQUARE is a rectangle with all sides equal in length. A square has all the properties of a rectangle and of a rhombus.

TRUE OR FALSE?	
All squares are rhombuses	True
All parallelograms are rectangles	False—*Some* parallelograms are rectangles
All rectangles are parallelograms	True
Some rhombuses are squares	True
Some rectangles are trapezoids	False—Trapezoids have only <u>one</u> pair of parallel sides
All quadrilaterals are parallelograms	False—*Some* quadrilaterals are parallelograms
Some squares are rectangles	False—*All* squares are rectangles
Some parallelograms are rhombuses	True

Example: In rhombus ABCD, side AB = 3x − 7 and side CD = x + 15. Find the length of each side.

Since all the sides are the same length,

$3x - 7 = x + 15$

$2x = 22$

$x = 11$

Since $3(11) - 7 = 26$ and $11 + 15 = 26$, each side measures 26 units.

> ### SKILL 3.3 Solve problems using the properties of triangles, quadrilaterals, polygons, circles, and parallel and perpendicular lines

For information on solving problems using the properties of polygons and quadrilaterals, see Skill 3.2. For information on solving problems using the properties of circles, see Skill 3.4.

Parallel and Perpendicular Lines and Planes

PARALLEL LINES in two dimensions can be sufficiently defined as lines that do not intersect. In three dimensions, however, this definition is insufficient. Parallel lines in three dimensions are defined as lines for which every pair of nearest points on the lines has a fixed distance.

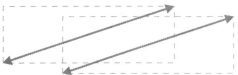

> **PARALLEL LINES:** in two dimensions, lines that do not intersect; in three dimensions, lines for which every pair of nearest points on the lines has a fixed distance

Lines in three dimensions that do not intersect and are not parallel are called SKEW LINES. Parallel lines are coplanar; skew lines are not.

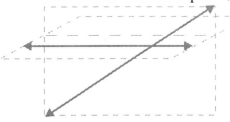

> **SKEW LINES:** lines in three dimensions that do not intersect and are not parallel

Two planes intersect on a single line. If two planes do not intersect, then they are parallel. Parallel and nonparallel planes are shown in the diagrams below.

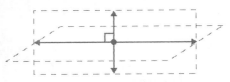

Parallelism between two planes may also be defined in the same way as parallel lines: the distance between any pair of nearest points (one point on each plane) is constant.

Perpendicularity of lines and planes in three dimensions is largely similar to that of two dimensions. Two lines are PERPENDICULAR LINES, in two or three dimensions, if they intersect at a point and form 90° angles between them. Consequently, perpendicular lines are always coplanar.

PERPENDICULAR LINES: when two lines are perpendicular, in two or three dimensions, they intersect at a point and form 90° angles between them

Notice that, for any line and coincident point on that line, there are an infinite number of perpendicular lines to the line through that point. In two dimensions, there is only one.

Two planes are perpendicular if they intersect and the angles formed between them are 90°. For any given plane and line on that plane, there is only one perpendicular plane.

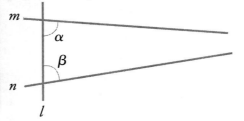

Properties of Parallel Lines

PARALLEL POSTULATE: in Euclidean planar geometry this postulate states that if a line l is crossed by two other lines m and n (where the crossings are not at the same point on l), then m and n intersect on the side of l on which the sum of the interior angles α and β is less than 180°

The PARALLEL POSTULATE in Euclidean planar geometry states that if a line l is crossed by two other lines m and n (where the crossings are not at the same point on l), then m and n intersect on the side of l on which the sum of the interior angles α and β is less than 180°. This scenario is illustrated below.

Based on this definition, a number of implications and equivalent formulations can be derived. First, note that the lines m and n intersect on the right-hand side of l above only if $\alpha + \beta < 180°$. This implies that if α and β are both 90° and, therefore, $\alpha + \beta = 180°$, then the lines do not intersect on either side. This is illustrated below.

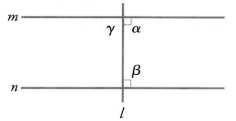

The supplementary angles formed by the intersection of l and m (and the intersection of l and n) must sum to 180°:

$$\alpha + \gamma = 180° \qquad \beta + \delta = 180°$$

Since these sums are both equal to 180°, the lines m and n do not intersect on either side of l. That is to say, these lines are parallel.

Let the nonintersecting lines m and n used in the above discussion remain parallel, but adjust l such that the interior angles are no longer right angles.

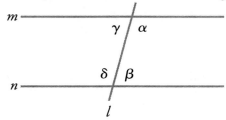

The Parallel Postulate still applies, and it is therefore still the case that $\alpha + \beta = 180°$ and $\gamma + \delta = 180°$. Combined with the fact that $\alpha + \gamma = 180°$ and $\beta + \delta = 180°$, the ALTERNATE INTERIOR ANGLE THEOREM can be justified. This theorem states that if two parallel lines are cut by a transversal, the alternate interior angles are congruent.

By manipulating the four relations based on the above diagram, the relationships between alternate interior angles (γ and β form one set of alternate interior angles, and α and δ form the other) can be established.

$$\alpha = 180° - \beta$$
$$\alpha + \gamma = 180° = 180° - \beta + \gamma$$
$$-\beta + \gamma = 0$$
$$\gamma = \beta$$

> **ALTERNATE INTERIOR ANGLE THEOREM:** states that if two parallel lines are cut by a transversal, the alternate interior angles are congruent

By the same reasoning,

$\gamma = 180° - \delta$

$\alpha + \gamma = 180° = \alpha + 180° - \delta$

$\alpha = \delta$

One of the consequences of the Parallel Postulate, in addition the Alternate Interior Angle Theorem, is that *corresponding angles* are equal. If two parallel lines are cut by a transversal line, then the corresponding angles are equal. The diagram below illustrates one set of corresponding angles (α and β) for the parallel lines *m* and *n* cut by *l*.

> *If two parallel lines are cut by a transversal line, then the corresponding angles are equal.*

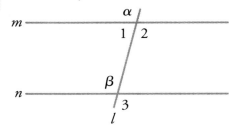

That α and β are equal can be proven as follows.

Proof:

$\angle\beta = \angle 2$	Alternate Interior Angle Theorem
$\angle 1 + = \angle 2 = 180°$	Supplementary angles
$\angle 2 = 180° - \angle 1$	
$\angle 1 + \angle\alpha = 180°$	Supplementary angles
$\angle\alpha = 180° - \angle 1$	
$\angle 2 = 180° - \angle 1 = \angle\alpha$	
$\angle 2 = \angle\alpha$	
$\angle\beta = \angle 2 = \angle\alpha$	
$\angle\beta = \angle\alpha$	

Thus, it has been proven that corresponding angles are equal.

Note, also, that the above proof also demonstrates that vertical angles are equal ($\angle 2 = \angle\alpha$). Thus, opposite angles formed by the intersection of two lines (called vertical angles) are equal. Furthermore, *alternate exterior angles* (angles α and 3 in the diagram above) are also equal.

Proof:

$\angle\beta = \angle 3$	Vertical angles
$\angle\alpha = \angle 2$	Vertical angles
$\angle\beta = \angle 2$	Alternate Interior Angle Theorem
$\angle\alpha = \angle 2 = \angle\beta = \angle 3$	
$\angle\alpha = \angle 3$	

Properties of Triangles

The three angles within a triangle are known as the INTERIOR ANGLES. The sum of the measures of the interior angles of a triangle is 180°. This property can be justified as follows. Consider a triangle with angles α, β and γ. Draw two parallel lines such that one parallel line coincides with any side of the triangle, and the other parallel line intersects the vertex opposite that side.

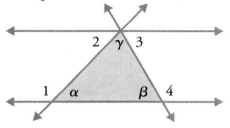

Proof:

$\angle\alpha = \angle 2$ Alternate interior angles

$\angle\beta = \angle 3$ Alternate interior angles

$\angle 2 + \angle 3 + \angle\gamma = 180°$ Supplementary angles

$\angle\alpha + \angle\beta + \angle\gamma = 180°$ Substitution

Thus, the sum of all the interior angles of a triangle is always 180°.

Example: Can a triangle have two right angles?

No. A right angle measures 90°; therefore, the sum of two right angles would be 180°, and there could not be a third angle.

Example: Can a right triangle have two obtuse angles?

No. Since an obtuse angle measures more than 90°, the sum of two obtuse angles would be greater than 180°.

Example: Can a right triangle be obtuse?

No. Once again, the sum of the angles would be more than 180°.

Two adjacent angles form a LINEAR PAIR when they have a common side and their remaining sides form a straight angle. Angles in a linear pair are supplementary. An EXTERIOR ANGLE of a triangle forms a linear pair with an angle of the triangle.

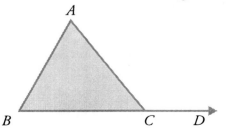

∠ACD is an exterior angle of triangle ABC, forming a linear pair with ∠ACB.

> **LINEAR PAIR:** when two adjacent angles have a common side and their remaining sides form a straight angle

> **EXTERIOR ANGLE:** an angle that forms a linear pair with an angle of the triangle

According to the EXTERIOR ANGLE THEOREM, the measure of an exterior angle of a triangle is equal to the sum of the measures of the two nonadjacent interior angles. We can easily demonstrate this by taking the above triangle ABC as an example. In this triangle, $\angle ABC + \angle BAC + \angle ACB = 180°$ (the sum of interior angles of a triangle). Also, $\angle ACD + \angle ACB = 180°$ (exterior angle and adjacent interior angle are supplementary). Therefore, $\angle ACD = \angle ABC + \angle BAC$.

Example: In triangle ABC, the measure of $\angle A$ is twice the measure of $\angle B$. $\angle C$ is 30° more than their sum. Find the measure of the exterior angle formed at $\angle C$.

Let x = the measure of $\angle B$

$2x$ = the measure of $\angle A$

$x + 2x + 30$ = the measure of $\angle C$

$$x + 2x + x + 2x + 30 = 180$$
$$6x + 30 = 180$$
$$6x = 150$$
$$x = 25$$
$$2x = 50$$

It is not necessary to find the measure of the third angle, since the exterior angle equals the sum of the opposite interior angles. Thus, the exterior angle at $\angle C$ measures 75°.

Concurrence theorems

If three or more segments intersect in a single point, the point is called a POINT OF CONCURRENCY. The concurrence theorems, given below, make statements about the concurrence of the following sets of special segments associated with triangles:

1. ANGLE BISECTORS: An angle bisector is a line segment that bisects one of the angles of a triangle. *The three angle bisectors of a triangle intersect in a single point equidistant from all three sides of the triangle.* (Recall that the distance from a point to a side is measured along the perpendicular from the point to the side.) This point is known as the *incenter* and is the center of the *incircle* inscribed within the triangle tangent to each of the three sides.

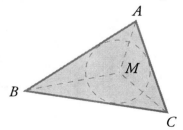

2. **MEDIANS**: A median of a triangle is a segment that connects a vertex to the midpoint of the side opposite from that vertex. *The three medians of a triangle are concurrent and intersect each other in a ratio of 2:1 at the centroid of the triangle.*

The medians of the triangle ABC shown below intersect in the centroid G such that $\frac{AG}{GF} = \frac{BG}{GE} = \frac{CG}{GD} = \frac{2}{1}$.

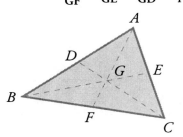

> **MEDIAN:** a segment that connects a vertex to the midpoint of the side opposite from that vertex

> *The three medians of a triangle are concurrent and intersect each other in a ratio of 2:1 at the centroid of the triangle.*

3. **ALTITUDES**: An altitude of a triangle is a segment that extends from one vertex and is perpendicular to the side opposite that vertex. In some cases, the side opposite the vertex will need to be extended in order for the altitude to form a perpendicular to the opposite side. The length of the altitude is used when referring to the height of the triangle. *The altitudes of a triangle are concurrent* and meet at the orthocenter of the triangle.

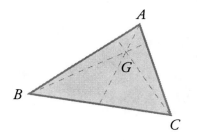

> **ALTITUDE:** a segment that extends from one vertex and is perpendicular to the side opposite that vertex

4. **PERPENDICULAR BISECTORS**: A perpendicular bisector of a triangle bisects one of the sides and is perpendicular to it. *The three perpendicular bisectors of a triangle meet in a point equidistant from the vertices of the triangle.* This point is known as the circumcenter and is the center of the circumcircle that circumscribes the triangles.

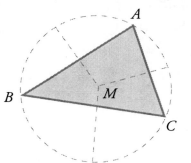

> **PERPENDICULAR BISECTOR:** a line that bisects one of the sides of a triangle and is perpendicular to it

> *The three perpendicular bisectors of a triangle meet in a point equidistant from the vertices of the triangle.*

The points of concurrency can lie inside the triangle, outside the triangle, or on one of the sides of the triangle. The following table summarizes this information.

POSSIBLE LOCATION(S) OF THE POINTS OF CONCURRENCY			
	INSIDE THE TRIANGLE	OUTSIDE THE TRIANGLE	ON THE TRIANGLE
Angle Bisectors	X		
Medians	X		
Altitudes	X	X	X
Perpendicular Bisectors	X	X	X

Example: BE and CD are altitudes of equilateral triangle ABC and intersect at the point G. What is the ratio of the area of triangle BDG to the area of triangle ABC?

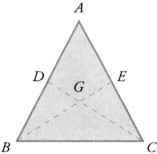

The area of triangle $ABC = \frac{1}{2}AB \times CD$. The area of triangle $BDG = \frac{1}{2}BD \times DG$. Since ABC is an equilateral triangle, the altitudes of the triangles are also medians. Therefore, $BD = \frac{1}{2}AB$ and $GD = \frac{1}{3}CD$. Thus, the area of triangle $BDG = \frac{1}{2}(\frac{1}{2}AB) \times (\frac{1}{3}CD) = \frac{1}{12}AB \times CD$. Hence the area of triangle BDG is one-sixth the area of triangle ABC.

The TRIANGLE INEQUALITY THEOREM states that the sum of the lengths of any two sides of a triangle is greater than the length of the remaining side. In the triangle below,

$a + b > c$
$a + c > b$
$b + c > a$

> **TRIANGLE INEQUALITY THEOREM:** states that the sum of the lengths of any two sides of a triangle is greater than the length of the remaining side

If a triangle has an unknown side, the Triangle Inequality Theorem can be applied to determine a reasonable range of possible values for the unknown side.

Example: Determine the range of possible values for the unknown side, p.

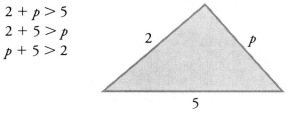

$2 + p > 5$
$2 + 5 > p$
$p + 5 > 2$

The expressions could be arranged to show: $p > 5 - 2$ or $p > 3$

$$7 > p$$
$$p > -3.$$

Thus, p is a value between 3 and 7.

An angle-side relationship exists between angles of a triangle and the sides opposite them. The side of the triangle that is opposite the largest angle is the longest side. The side opposite the smallest angle is the shortest side. This rule can be used to determine a reasonable range of measurement for an unknown angle.

The side of the triangle that is opposite the largest angle is the longest side. The side opposite the smallest angle is the shortest side.

SKILL 3.4 Solve problems using the properties of circles, including those involving inscribed angles, central angles, chords, radii, tangents, secants, arcs, and sectors

Properties of Circles

The distance around a circle is called the CIRCUMFERENCE. The ratio of the circumference to the diameter is represented by the Greek letter pi, where $\pi \approx 3.14$. The circumference of a circle is given by the formula $C = 2\pi r$ or $C = \pi d$, where r is the radius of the circle and d is the diameter. The area of a circle is given by the formula $A = \pi r^2$.

CIRCUMFERENCE: the distance around a circle

We can extend the area formula of a regular polygon to obtain the area of a circle by considering the fact that a circle is essentially a regular polygon with an infinite number of sides. The radius of a circle is equivalent to the apothem of a regular polygon. Thus, applying the area formula for a regular polygon to a circle, we get

$$\tfrac{1}{2} \times perimeter \times apothem = \tfrac{1}{2} \times 2\pi r \times r = \pi r^2$$

If two circles have radii that are in a ratio of $a : b$, then the following ratios also apply to the circles:

1. The diameters are in the ratio $a : b$

2. The circumferences are in the ratio $a : b$

3. The areas are in the ratio $a^2 : b^2$, or the ratio of the areas is the square of the ratio of the radii.

CENTRAL ANGLE: the angle formed by two radii that intersect in the center of a circle

If you draw two radii in a circle, the angle they form with the center as the vertex is a CENTRAL ANGLE. The piece of the circle "inside" the angle is an arc. Just like a central angle, an arc can have any degree measure from 0 to 360. The measure of an arc is equal to the measure of the central angle that forms the arc. Since a diameter forms a semicircle and the measure of a straight angle like a diameter is 180°, the measure of a semicircle is also 180°.

MINOR ARC: an arc with measure less than 180°

Given two points on a circle, the two points form two different arcs. Except in the case of semicircles, one of the two arcs will always be greater than 180°, and the other will be less than 180°. The arc less than 180° is a MINOR ARC and the arc greater than 180° is a MAJOR ARC.

MAJOR ARC: an arc with measure greater than 180°.

Examples:

1.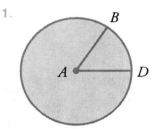

$m \angle BAD = 45°$

What is the measure of the major arc BD?

minor arc $BD = m \angle BAD = 45°$

$360 - 45 = $ major arc BD

Thus, major arc $BD = 315°$.

A major and minor arc always add up to 360°.

2.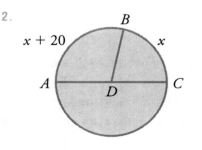

$\overline{AC}$ is a diameter of circle D.

What is the measure of $\angle BDC$?

$m \angle ADB + m \angle BDC = 180°$

$x + 20 + x = 180$

$2x + 20 = 180$

$2x = 160$

$x = 80$

A diameter forms a semicircle that has a measure of 180°.

minor arc $BC = 80°$	A central angle has the same
$m\angle BDC = 80°$	measure as the arc it forms.

Although an arc has a measure associated to the degree measure of a central angle, it also has a length that is a fraction of the circumference of the circle. For each central angle and its associated arc, there is a sector of the circle that resembles a pie piece. The area of such a sector is a fraction of the area of the circle. The fractions used for the area of a sector and length of its associated arc are both equal to the ratio of the central angle to 360°.

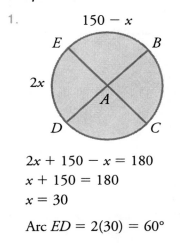

$$\frac{\angle PQR}{360°} = \frac{\text{length of arc } RP}{\text{circumference of circle}} = \frac{\text{area of sector } PQR}{\text{area of circle}}$$

Examples:

1.

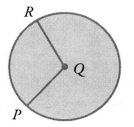

Circle A has a radius of 4 cm. What is the length of arc *ED*?

$2x + 150 - x = 180$

$x + 150 = 180$

$x = 30$

Arc *BE* and arc *ED* make a semicircle.

Arc $ED = 2(30) = 60°$

The ratio 60° to 360° is equal to the ratio of arc length *ED* to the circumference of circle A.

$$\frac{60}{360} = \frac{\text{arc length } ED}{2\pi 4}$$

$$\frac{1}{6} = \frac{\text{arc length}}{8\pi}$$

$$\text{arc length} = \frac{8\pi}{6} = \frac{4\pi}{3}$$

Cross multiply and solve for the arc length.

2.

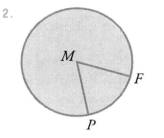

The radius of circle M is 3 cm. The length of arc *PF* is 2π cm. What is the area of sector *MPF*?

Circumference of circle M = $2\pi(3) = 6\pi$

Find the circumference and area of the circle.

Area of circle M = $\pi \times 3^2 = 9\pi$

$\dfrac{\text{area of MPF}}{9\pi} = \dfrac{2\pi}{6\pi}$

The ratio of the sector area to the circle area is the same as the arc length to the circumference.

$\dfrac{\text{area of } MPF}{9\pi} = \dfrac{1}{3}$

area of $MPF = \dfrac{9\pi}{3}$

area of $MPF = 3\pi$

Solve for the area of the sector.

TANGENT LINE: a line to a circle that intersects or touches the circle in exactly one point

A TANGENT LINE to a circle intersects or touches the circle in exactly one point. If a radius is drawn to that point, the radius will be perpendicular to the tangent.

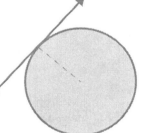

SECANT LINE: a line that intersects a circle in two points

A SECANT LINE intersects a circle in two points and includes a CHORD, which is a line segment with endpoints on the circle. If a radius or diameter is perpendicular to a chord, the radius will cut the chord into two equal parts, and vice versa.

CHORD: a line segment with endpoints on a circle

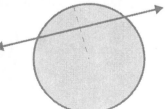

If two chords in the same circle have the same length, the two chords will have arcs that are the same length, and the two chords will be equidistant from the center of the circle. Distance from the center to a chord is measured by finding the length of a segment from the center perpendicular to the chord.

Examples:

1.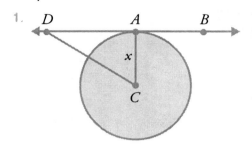

$\overleftrightarrow{DB}$ is tangent to circle C at *A*.
$m\angle ADC = 40°$ Find *x*.

$\overline{AC} \perp \overleftrightarrow{DB}$

A radius is $\perp$ to a tangent at the point of tangency.

$m\angle DAC = 90°$

Two segments that are $\perp$ form a 90° angle.

$40 + 90 + x = 180$

The sum of the angles of a triangle is 180°.

$x = 50°$

Solve for *x*.

2.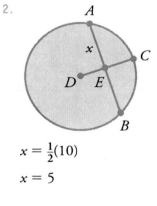

$\overline{CD}$ is a radius and $\overline{CD} \perp$ chord $\overline{AB}$.

$\overline{AB} = 10$. Find *x*.

$x = \frac{1}{2}(10)$

$x = 5$

If a radius is $\perp$ to a chord, the radius bisects the chord.

An INSCRIBED ANGLE is an angle whose vertex is on the circumference of a circle. Such an angle could be formed by two chords, a diameter and a chord, two secants, or a secant and a tangent. An inscribed angle has one arc of the circle in its interior. The measure of the inscribed angle is one-half the measure of its intercepted arc. If two inscribed angles intercept the same arc, the two angles are congruent (i.e. their measures are equal). If an inscribed angle intercepts an entire semicircle, the angle is a right angle.

When two chords intersect inside a circle, two sets of vertical angles are formed in the interior of the circle. Each set of vertical angles intercepts two arcs that are across from each other. The measure of an angle formed by two chords in a circle is equal to one-half the sum of the arc intercepted by the angle and the arc intercepted by its vertical angle.

INSCRIBED ANGLE: an angle whose vertex is on the circumference of a circle

If an angle has its vertex outside of the circle and each side of the angle intersects the circle, then the angle contains two different arcs. The measure of the angle is equal to one-half the difference of the two arcs.

Examples:

1.

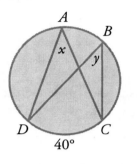

$40°$

Find x and y.

$m\angle DAC = \frac{1}{2}(40) = 20°$

$\angle DAC$ and $\angle DBC$ are both inscribed angles, so each one has a measure equal to one-half the measure of arc DC.

$m\angle DBC = \frac{1}{2}(40) = 20°$

$x = 20°$ and $y = 20°$

2.

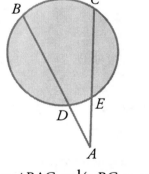

Find the measure of arc BC if the measure of arc DE is 30° and angle $BAC = 20°$.

$m\angle BAC = \frac{1}{2}(mBC - mDE)$

$\rightarrow 2 \times m\angle BAC = mBC - mDE$

$\rightarrow mBC = 2 \times m\angle BAC + mDE = 2 \times 20° + 30° = 70°$

If *two chords intersect inside a circle*, each chord is divided into two smaller segments. The product of the lengths of the two segments formed from one chord equals the product of the lengths of the two segments formed from the other chord.

If *two tangent segments intersect outside of a circle*, the two segments have the same length.

If *two secant segments intersect outside a circle*, a portion of each segment will lie inside the circle and a portion (called the exterior segment) will lie outside the circle. The product of the length of one secant segment and the length of its exterior segment equals the product of the length of the other secant segment and the length of its exterior segment.

If *a tangent segment and a secant segment intersect outside a circle*, the square of the length of the tangent segment equals the product of the length of the secant segment and its exterior segment.

Examples:

1.

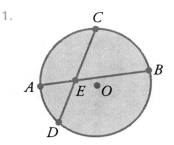

$\overline{AB}$ and $\overline{CD}$ are chords.

$CE = 10$, $ED = x$, $AE = 5$, $EB = 4$

$(AE)(EB) = (CE)(ED)$

Since the chords intersect in the circle, the products of the segment pieces are equal.

$5(4) = 10x$
$20 = 10x$
$x = 2$

Solve for x.

2.

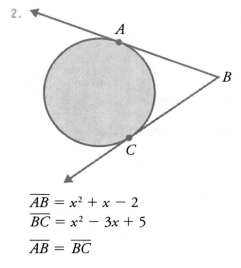

$\overline{AB}$ and $\overline{CB}$ are tangents.

$\overline{AB} = x^2 + x - 2$

$\overline{CB} = 5 - 3x + x^2$

Find the length of $\overline{AB}$ and $\overline{BC}$

$\overline{AB} = x^2 + x - 2$
$\overline{BC} = x^2 - 3x + 5$

Given

$\overline{AB} = \overline{BC}$

Intersecting tangents are equal.

$x^2 + x - 2 = x^2 - 3x + 5$

Set the expressions equal to each other and solve.

$$4x = 7$$
$$x = 1.75$$
$$(1.75)^2 + 1.75 - 2 = \overline{AB}$$
$$\overline{AB} = \overline{BC} = 2.81$$

Substitute and solve.

RIGHT TRIANGLE: a triangle with one right angle

Pythagorean Theorem

A RIGHT TRIANGLE is a triangle with one right angle. The side opposite the right angle is called the hypotenuse. The other two sides are the legs.

The Pythagorean Theorem states that, for any right triangle, the square of the length of the hypotenuse is equal to the sum of the squares of the lengths of the legs. Symbolically, this is stated as:

$$c^2 = a^2 + b^2$$

The Pythagorean Theorem states that, for any right triangle, the square of the length of the hypotenuse is equal to the sum of the squares of the lengths of the legs.

Example: Given the right triangle below, find the missing side.

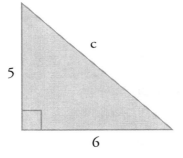

$c^2 = a^2 + b^2$	1. Write formula.
$c^2 = 5^2 + 6^2$	2. Substitute known values.
$c^2 = 61$	3. Take square root.
$c^2 = \sqrt{61}$ or 7.81	4. Solve.

The Converse of the Pythagorean Theorem states that if the square of one side of a triangle is equal to the sum of the squares of the other two sides, then the triangle is a right triangle.

The Converse of the Pythagorean Theorem states that if the square of one side of a triangle is equal to the sum of the squares of the other two sides, then the triangle is a right triangle.

Example: Given ΔXYZ, with sides measuring 12, 16, and 20 cm, is this a right triangle?

$$c^2 = a^2 + b^2$$
$$20^2 \; \underline{?} \; 12^2 + 16^2$$
$$400 \; \underline{?} \; 144 + 256$$
$$400 = 400$$

Yes, the triangle is a right triangle.

This theorem can be expanded to determine if triangles are obtuse or acute.

If the square of the longest side of a triangle is greater than the sum of the squares of the other two sides, then the triangle is an obtuse triangle. If the square of the longest side of a triangle is less than the sum of the squares of the other two sides, then the triangle is an acute triangle.

Example: Given ΔLMN with sides measuring 7, 12, and 14 inches, is the triangle right, acute, or obtuse?

$$14^2 \; \underline{?} \; 7^2 + 12^2$$
$$196 \; \underline{?} \; 49 + 144$$
$$196 > 193$$

Therefore, the triangle is obtuse.

When an altitude is drawn to the hypotenuse of a right triangle, then the two triangles formed are similar to the original triangle and to each other.

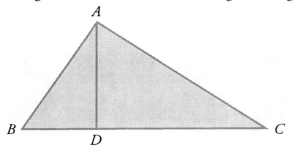

Given right triangle ABC with right angle at A, altitude AD drawn to hypotenuse BD at D, ΔABC ~ ΔDBA ~ ΔDAC.

If *a*, *b*, and *c* are positive numbers such that $\frac{a}{b} = \frac{b}{c}$, then b is called the GEOMETRIC MEAN of *a* and *c*.

The geometric mean is significant when the altitude is drawn to the hypotenuse of a right triangle.

> **When an altitude is drawn to the hypotenuse of a right triangle, then the two triangles formed are similar to the original triangle and to each other.**

> **GEOMETRIC MEAN:** if *a*, *b*, and *c* are positive numbers such that $\frac{a}{b} = \frac{b}{c}$, then b is called the geometric mean of *a* and *c*

The length of the altitude is the geometric mean between each segment of the hypotenuse. Also, each leg is the geometric mean between the hypotenuse and the segment of the hypotenuse that is adjacent to the leg.

Example:

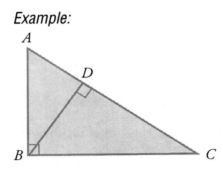

$\triangle$ABC is a right triangle and $\angle$ABC is a right angle. AB = 6 and AC = 12. Find AD, CD, BD, and BC.

$$\frac{12}{6} = \frac{6}{AD} \qquad\qquad \frac{3}{BD} = \frac{BD}{9} \qquad\qquad \frac{12}{BC} = \frac{BC}{9}$$

$$12(AD) = 36 \qquad (BD)^2 = 27 \qquad (BC)^2 = 108$$

$$AD = 3$$

$$BD = \sqrt{27} = \sqrt{9 \times 3} = 3\sqrt{3}$$

$$BC = 6\sqrt{3}$$

$$CD = 12 - 3 = 9$$

SKILL 3.6 **Compute and reason about perimeter, area/surface area, or volume of two- and three-dimensional figures or of regions or solids that are combinations of these figures**

Perimeter and Area

PERIMETER: the sum of the lengths of the sides of a polygon

AREA: the number of square units covered by the figure or the space that the figure occupies

The PERIMETER of any polygon is the sum of the lengths of the sides. The AREA of a polygon is the number of square units covered by the figure or the space that the figure occupies. In the area formulae below, b refers to the base and h to the height or altitude of a figure. For a trapezoid, a and b are the two parallel bases.

For a rectangle, L is the length and W is the width.

AREA AND PERIMETER FORMULAS		
FIGURE	**AREA FORMULA**	**PERIMETER FORMULA**
Rectangle	LW	$2(L + W)$
Triangle	$\frac{1}{2}bh$	sum of lengths of sides
Parallelogram	bh	sum of lengths of sides
Trapezoid	$\frac{1}{2}h(a + b)$	sum of lengths of sides

Even though different figures have different area formulae, the formulae are connected, and one can go easily from one to another. For instance, it is easy to see from the diagram below that the area of the triangle ABD is half that of rectangle EABD, and the area of triangle ADC is half that of rectangle AFDC. Thus, the area of triangle ABC is half that of rectangle EFBC and is equal to

$$\frac{1}{2}BC \times EB = \frac{1}{2}BC \times AD$$

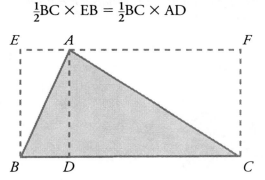

The area of a parallelogram may similarly be shown to be equal to that of an equivalent rectangle. Since triangles ACE and BDF are congruent in the diagram below (AE and BF are altitudes), parallelogram ABCD is equal in area to rectangle AEFB, which has the same base (CD=EF) and height.

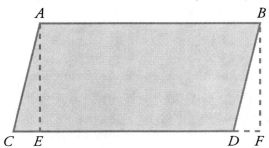

The area of a trapezoid is the sum of the areas of two triangles, each of which has one of the parallel sides as a base. In the diagram below,

area of trapezoid ABCD = area of ABC + area of ACD

$$= \tfrac{1}{2}BC \times AE + \tfrac{1}{2}AD \times CF$$

$$= \tfrac{1}{2}AE(BC + AD) \text{ (Since AE = CF)}$$

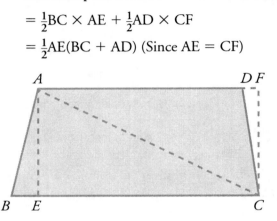

Example: A farmer has a piece of land shaped as shown below. He wishes to fence this land at an estimated cost of $25 per linear foot. What is the total cost of fencing this property to the nearest foot?

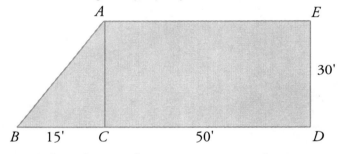

From the right triangle ABC, AC = 30 and BC = 15.

Since $(AB)^2 = (AC)^2 + (BC)^2$, $(AB)^2 = (30)^2 + (15)^2$. So, $\sqrt{(AB)^2} = AB = \sqrt{1125} = 33.5410$ feet. To the nearest foot, AB = 34 feet. The perimeter of the piece of land is

$$AB + BC + CD + DE + EA = 34 + 15 + 50 + 30 + 50 = 179 \text{ feet}$$

The cost of fencing is $25 \times 179 = \$4,475.00$.

The area of any regular polygon having n sides may be expressed as a sum of the areas of n congruent triangles. If each side of the polygon is of length a, and the apothem (distance from center of polygon to one side) is h,

area of the polygon $= n \times \tfrac{1}{2} \times a \times h$ (n times the area of one triangle)

Since $n \times a$ is the perimeter of the polygon, we can also write area of the polygon $= \frac{1}{2} \times$ perimeter $\times$ apothem

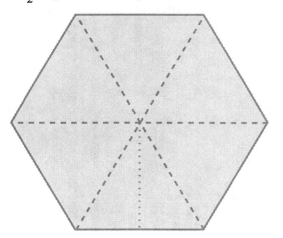

Three-Dimensional Figures

Three-dimensional figures require slightly more complicated mathematical manipulations to derive or apply such properties as surface area and volume. In some instances, two-dimensional concepts can be applied directly. In other instances, a more rigorous approach is needed.

To represent three-dimensional objects in a coordinate system, three coordinates are required. Thus, a point in three dimensions must be represented as (x, y, z) instead of simply (x, y), as is used in the two-dimensional representation.

The volume and surface area of three-dimensional figures can be derived most clearly (in some cases) using integral calculus. (See Competency 6.0 for more information on integrals relating to the area and volume of geometric figures.) For instance, the volume of a sphere of radius r can be derived by revolving a semicircular area around the axis defined by its diameter.

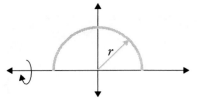

The result of this revolution is a solid sphere of radius r. To perform the integral, use the function f(x) for the semicircle of radius r.

$$f(x) = \sqrt{r^2 - x^2}$$
$$V = \pi \int_{-r}^{r} [\sqrt{r^2 - x^2}]^2 dx$$
$$V = \pi \int_{-r}^{r} (r^2 - x^2) dx$$
$$V = \pi [r^2 x - \frac{x^3}{3}]_{-r}^{r} = \pi [(r^3 + r^3) - (\frac{r^3}{3} + \frac{r^3}{3})]$$
$$V = \pi [2r^3 - \frac{2r^3}{3}] = \frac{4}{3}\pi r^3$$

The surface area can also be found by a similar integral that calculates the surface of revolution around the diameter, but there is a simpler method. Note that the differential change in volume of a sphere (dV) for a differential change in the radius (dr) is an infinitesimally thick spherical shell.

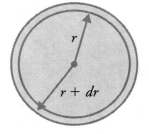

This infinitesimally thick shell is simply a surface with an area but no volume. Find the derivative of the volume to get the surface area.

$$S = \frac{dV}{dr} = \frac{d}{dr}\frac{4}{3}\pi r^3$$
$$S = 4\pi r^2$$

For right circular cylinders, the volume is simply the area of a cross section (a circle of radius r) multiplied by the height h of the cylinder. The *lateral surface area* (the surface area excluding the area on the ends of the figure) is simply the circumference of the circular cross section multiplied by the height h.

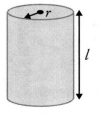

$$V = \pi r^2 h$$
$$S = 2\pi r h$$

The volumes and surface areas of these figures are summarized below.

VOLUME AND SURFACE AREA FORMULAS		
FIGURE	**VOLUME**	**TOTAL SURFACE AREA**
Right Cylinder	$\pi r^2 h$	$2\pi r h + 2\pi r^2$
Right Cone	$\frac{\pi r^2 h}{3}$	$\pi r \sqrt{r^2 + h^2} + \pi r^2$
Sphere	$\frac{4}{3}\pi r^3$	$4\pi r^2$

For figures such as pyramids and prisms, the volume and surface area must be derived by breaking the figure into portions for which these values can be calculated easily. For instance, consider the following figure.

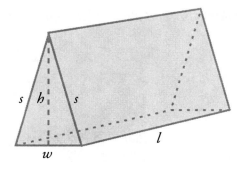

The volume of this figure can be found by calculating the area of the triangular cross section and then multiplying by l.

$$V = \tfrac{1}{2}hwl$$

The lateral surface area can be found by adding the areas of each side.

$$S = 2sl + lw$$

Similar reasoning applies to other figures composed of sides that are defined by triangles, quadrilaterals, and other planar or linear elements.

For a rectangular right prism:

- Surface area S = 2(lw + hw + lh)
  (where l = length, w = width, and h = height)

- Volume V = lwh

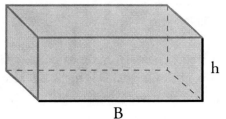

For a regular pyramid:

- Volume V = $\tfrac{1}{3}$ Bh (where B = area of the base of the pyramid and h = the height of the pyramid)

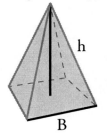

Example: Find the height of a box whose volume is 120 cubic meters if the area of the base is 30 square meters.

$V = Bh$

$120 = 30h$

$h = 4$ meters

Example: How much material is needed to make a basketball that has a diameter of 15 inches? How much air is needed to fill the basketball?

Draw and label a sketch:

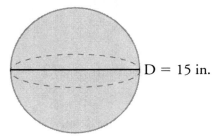

D = 15 in.

Surface Area	Volume	
SA $= 4\pi r^2$	V $= \frac{4}{3}\pi r^3$	1. Write formula.
$= 4\pi(7.5)^2$	$= \frac{4}{3}\pi(7.5)^3$	2. Substitute.
$= 706.858$ in^2	$= 1767.1459$ in^3	3. Solve

> *The ratio of any two corresponding measurements of similar solids is the scale factor.*

Similar solids share the same shape but are not necessarily the same size. The ratio of any two corresponding measurements of similar solids is the scale factor. For example, the scale factor for two triangular prisms, one with a side measuring 2 inches and the other with a corresponding side measuring 4 inches, is 2:4.

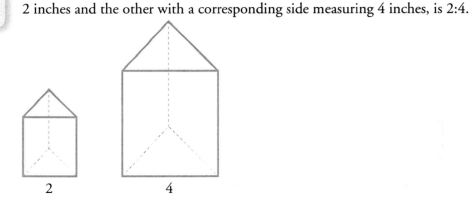

2   4

The base perimeter, the surface area, and the volume of similar solids are directly related to the scale factor. If the scale factor of two similar solids is a:b, then

- ratio of base perimeters $= a : b$

- ratio of areas $= a^2 : b^2$

- ratio of volumes $= a^3 : b^3$

Thus, for the above example,

- ratio of base perimeters $= 2 : 4$

- ratio of areas $= 2^2 : 4^2 = 4 : 16$

- ratio of volumes $= 2^3 : 4^3 = 8 : 64$

Example: What happens to the volume of a square pyramid when the lengths of the sides of the base and the height are doubled?

scale factor $= a : b = 1:2$

ratio of volume $= 1^3 : 2^3 = 1 : 8$

The volume is increased 8 times.

Example: Given the following measurements for two similar cylinders with a scale factor of 2:5 (cylinder A to cylinder B), determine the height, radius, and volume of each cylinder.

cylinder A: $r = 2$

cylinder B: $h = 10$

For cylinder A,

$$\frac{h_a}{10} = \frac{2}{5}$$

$5h_a = 20$ Solve for h_a

$h_a = 4$

Volume of cylinder A $= \pi r^2 h = \pi(2)^2 4 = 16\pi$

For cylinder B,

$$\frac{2}{r_b} = \frac{2}{5}$$

$2r_b = 10$ Solve for r_b

$r_b = 5$

Volume of cylinder B $= \pi r^2 h = \pi(5)^2 10 = 250\pi$

SKILL Solve problems involving reflections, rotations, and translations of
3.7 geometric figures in the plane

Transformational Geometry

TRANSFORMATIONAL GEOMETRY is the study of the manipulation of objects through movement, rotation, and scaling. The transformation of an object is called its image. If the original object is labeled with letters, such as *ABCD*, the image can be labeled with the same letters followed by a prime symbol: *A'B'C'D'*. Transformations can be characterized in different ways.

Types of transformations

An **ISOMETRY** is a linear transformation that maintains the dimensions of a geometric figure.

SYMMETRY is exact similarity between two parts or halves, as if one were a mirror image of the other.

A **TRANSLATION** is a transformation that "slides" an object a fixed distance in a given direction. The original object and its translation have the same shape and size, and they face in the same direction.

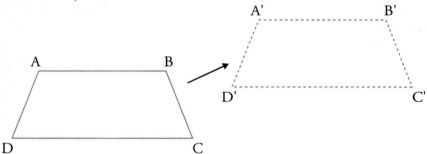

A **ROTATION** is a transformation that turns a figure about a fixed point, which is called the center of rotation. An object and its rotation are the same shape and size, but the figures may be oriented in different directions. Rotations can occur in either a clockwise or a counterclockwise direction.

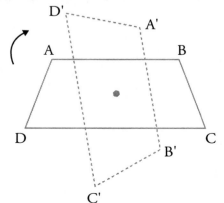

> **TRANSFORMATIONAL GEOMETRY:** the study of the manipulation of objects through movement, rotation, and scaling

> **ISOMETRY:** a linear transformation that maintains the dimensions of a geometric figure

> **SYMMETRY:** the exact similarity between two parts or halves, as if one were a mirror image of the other

> **TRANSLATION:** a transformation that "slides" an object a fixed distance in a given direction

> **ROTATION:** a transformation that turns a figure about a fixed point, which is called the center of rotation

An object and its REFLECTION have the same shape and size, but the figures face in opposite directions. The line (where a hypothetical mirror may be placed) is called the line of reflection. The distance from a point to the line of reflection is the same as the distance from the point's image to the line of reflection.

REFLECTION: when an object and another figure have the same shape and size, but they face in opposite directions

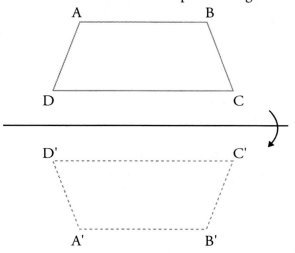

The examples of a translation, a rotation, and a reflection given above are for polygons, but the same principles apply to the simpler geometric elements of points and lines. In fact, a transformation performed on a polygon can be viewed equivalently as the same transformation performed on the set of points (vertices) and lines (sides) that compose the polygon. Thus, to perform complicated transformations on a figure, it is helpful to perform the transformations on all the points (or vertices) of the figure, then reconnect the points with lines as appropriate.

Multiple transformations can be performed on a geometrical figure. The order of these transformations may or may not be important. For instance, multiple translations can be performed in any order, as can multiple rotations (around a single fixed point) or reflections (across a single fixed line). The order of the transformations becomes important when several types of transformations are performed or when the point of rotation or the line of reflection change among transformations. For example, consider a translation of a given distance upward and a clockwise rotation by 90° around a fixed point. Changing the order of these transformations changes the result.

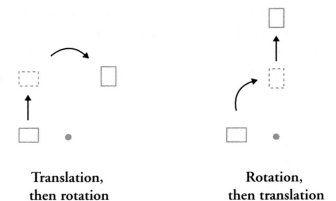

**Translation,
then rotation**

**Rotation,
then translation**

As shown, the final position of the box is different, depending on the order of the transformations. Thus, it is crucial that the proper order of transformations (whether determined by the details of the problem or some other consideration) be followed.

Example: Find the final location of a point at (1, 1) that undergoes the following transformations: rotate 90° counterclockwise about the origin; translate distance 2 in the negative y direction; reflect about the y-axis.

First, draw a graph of the *x*- and *y*-axes and plot the point at (1, 1).

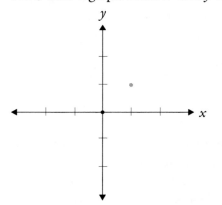

Next, perform the rotation. The center of rotation is the origin, and the rotation is in the counterclockwise direction. In this case, the even value of 90° makes the rotation simple to do by inspection. Next, perform a translation of distance 2 in the negative *y* direction (down). The results of these transformations are shown below.

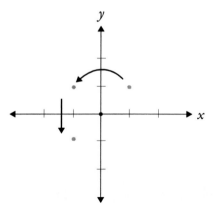

Finally, perform the reflection about the *y*-axis. The final result, shown below, is a point at (1, −1).

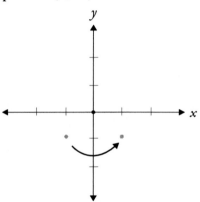

Using this approach, polygons can be transformed on a point-by-point basis.

For some problems, there is no need to work with coordinate axes. For instance, the problem may simply require transformations without respect to any absolute positioning.

Example: Rotate the following regular pentagon by 36° about its center, and then reflect it about a horizontal line.

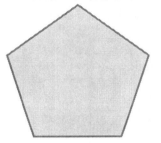

First, perform the rotation. In this case, the direction is not important because the pentagon is symmetric. As it turns out in this case, a rotation of 36° yields the same result as flipping the pentagon vertically (assuming the vertices of the pentagon are indistinguishable).

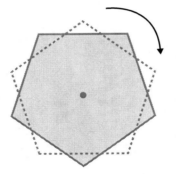

Finally, perform the reflection. Note that the result here is the same as a downward translation (assuming the vertices of the pentagon are indistinguishable).

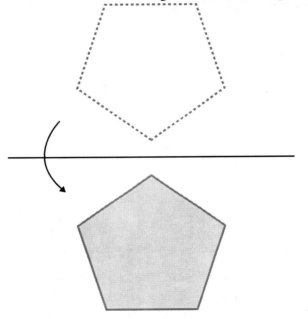

Proofs Using Coordinate Geometry

**COORDINATE
GEOMETRY:** the
application of algebraic
methods to geometry

COORDINATE GEOMETRY involves the application of algebraic methods to geometry. The locations of points in space are expressed in terms of coordinates on a Cartesian plane. The relationships between the coordinates of different points are expressed as equations.

Proofs using coordinate geometry techniques employ the following commonly used formulae and relationships:

1. Midpoint formula: The midpoint (x, y) of the line joining points (x_1, y_1) and (x_2, y_2) is given by $(x, y) = (\frac{x_1 + x_2}{2}, \frac{y_1 + y_2}{2})$

2. Distance formula: The distance between points (x_1, y_1) and (x_2, y_2) is given by $D = \sqrt{(x_2 - x_1)^2 + (y_2 - y_1)^2}$

3. **Slope formula:** The slope m of a line passing through the points (x_1, y_1) and (x_2, y_2) is given by $m = \frac{y_2 - y_1}{x_2 - x_1}$

4. **Equation of a line:** The equation of a line is given by $y = mx + b$, where m is the slope of the line and b is the y-intercept, i.e., the y-coordinate at which the line intersects the y-axis.

5. **Parallel and perpendicular lines:** Parallel lines have the same slope. The slope of a line perpendicular to a line with slope m is $\frac{-1}{m}$.

Example: Prove that quadrilateral ABCD with vertices A(−3,0), B(−1,0), C(0,3), and D(2,3) is in fact a parallelogram using coordinate geometry:

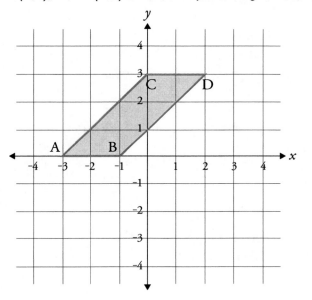

By definition, a parallelogram has diagonals that bisect each other. Using the midpoint formula, $(x, y) = (\frac{x_1 + x_2}{2}, \frac{y_1 + y_2}{2})$, find the midpoints of $\overline{AD}$ and $\overline{BC}$.

The midpoint of $\overline{BC} = (\frac{-1 + 0}{2}, \frac{0 + 3}{2}) = \frac{-1}{2}, \frac{3}{2}$

The midpoint of $\overline{AD} = (\frac{-3 + 2}{2}, \frac{0 + 3}{2}) = \frac{-1}{2}, \frac{3}{2}$

Since the midpoints of the diagonals are the same, the diagonals bisect each other. Hence the polygon is a parallelogram.

In the above example, the proof involved a specific geometric figure with given coordinates. Coordinate geometry can also be used to prove more general results.

Example: Prove that the diagonals of a rhombus are perpendicular to each other.

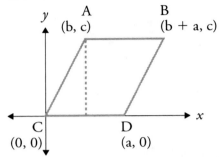

Draw a rhombus ABCD with side of length a such that the vertex C is at the origin and the side CD lies along the x-axis. The coordinates of the corners of the rhombus can then be written as shown above.

The slope m_1 of the diagonal AD is given by $m_1 = \dfrac{c}{b - a}$.

The slope m_2 of the diagonal BC is given by $m_2 = \dfrac{c}{b + a}$.

The product of the slopes is $m_1 \times m_2 = \dfrac{c}{b - a} \times \dfrac{c}{b + a} = \dfrac{c^2}{b^2 - a^2}$.

The length of side $AC = \sqrt{b^2 + c^2} = a$ (since each side of the rhombus is equal to a). Therefore,

$b^2 + c^2 = a^2$

$\rightarrow b^2 - a^2 = -c^2$

$\rightarrow \dfrac{c^2}{b^2 - a^2} = -1$

Thus the product of the slopes of the diagonals $m_1 \times m_2 = -1$. Hence the two diagonals are perpendicular to each other.

COMPETENCY 4
TRIGONOMETRY

> ### SKILL 4.1 Define and use the six basic trigonometric relations using degree or radian measure of angles; know their graphs and be able to identify their periods, amplitudes, phase displacements or shifts, and asymptotes

Trigonometry is an important tool for analyzing problems and phenomena that involve either triangles or circles. Likewise, many periodic phenomena (which are in and of themselves "circular" or cyclical) can be modeled with trigonometric functions.

This review of trigonometry starts with a review of right triangle trigonometry and its relationship with the unit circle. Next, trigonometric functions are reviewed, including their properties and applications to problems and mathematical models.

Right Triangle Trigonometry

Trigonometric functions can be related to right triangles: each trigonometric function corresponds to a ratio of certain sides of the triangle with respect to a particular angle. Thus, given the generic right triangle diagram below, the following functions can be specified.

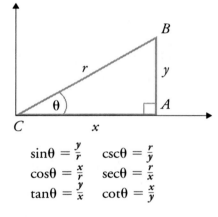

$$\sin\theta = \frac{y}{r} \qquad \csc\theta = \frac{r}{y}$$
$$\cos\theta = \frac{x}{r} \qquad \sec\theta = \frac{r}{x}$$
$$\tan\theta = \frac{y}{x} \qquad \cot\theta = \frac{x}{y}$$

Based on these definitions, the unknown characteristics of a particular right triangle can be calculated based on certain known characteristics. For instance, if the hypotenuse and one of the adjacent angles are both known, the lengths of the other two sides of the triangle can be calculated.

Angle Measures: Degrees and Radians

The argument of a trigonometric function is an angle that is typically expressed in either degrees or radians. A DEGREE constitutes an angle corresponding to a sector that is $\frac{1}{360}$th of a circle. Therefore, a circle has 360 degrees. A RADIAN, on the other hand, is the angle corresponding to a sector of a circle, where the arc length of the sector is equal to the radius of the circle. In the case of the unit circle (a circle of radius 1), the circumference is 2π. Thus, there are 2π radians in a circle. Conversion between degrees and radians is a simple matter of using the ratio between the total degrees in a circle and the total radians in a circle.

$$\text{(degrees)} = \frac{180}{\pi} \times \text{(radians)}$$
$$\text{(radians)} = \frac{\pi}{180} \times \text{(degrees)}$$

DEGREE: an angle corresponding to a sector that is $\frac{1}{360}$th of a circle

RADIAN: the angle corresponding to a sector of a circle, where the arc length of the sector is equal to the radius of the circle

Trigonometry and the Unit Circle

Trigonometry can also be understood in terms of a unit circle on the *x-y* plane. A unit circle has a radius of 1.

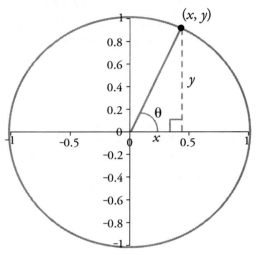

Notice that any given radius forms a right triangle with legs having lengths equal to the position of the point on the circle (*x*, *y*). Since the radius is equal to 1, the values of *x* and *y* are the following:

$x = \cos\theta$

$y = \sin\theta$

All the properties of trigonometric relationships for right triangles also apply in this case as well.

Trigonometric Functions

Trigonometric functions can be analyzed with respect to their individual behavior or with respect to solving problems that include them.

Graphs of trigonometric functions

The trigonometric functions sine, cosine, and tangent (and their reciprocals) are PERIODIC FUNCTIONS. The values of periodic functions repeat on regular intervals. The period, amplitude, and phase shift are critical properties of periodic functions that can be determined by observation of the graph or by detailed study of the functions themselves.

The PERIOD of a function is the smallest domain containing one complete cycle of the function. For example, the period of a sine or cosine function is the distance between the adjacent peaks or troughs of the graph. The AMPLITUDE of a function is half the distance between the maximum and minimum values of the function.

PERIODIC FUNCTIONS: functions whose values repeat on regular intervals

PERIOD: the smallest domain containing one complete cycle of the function

AMPLITUDE: half the distance between the maximum and minimum values of the function

The PHASE SHIFT of a function is the amount of horizontal displacement of the function from a given reference position.

Below is a generic sinusoidal graph with the period and amplitude labeled.

PHASE SHIFT: the amount of horizontal displacement of the function from a given reference position

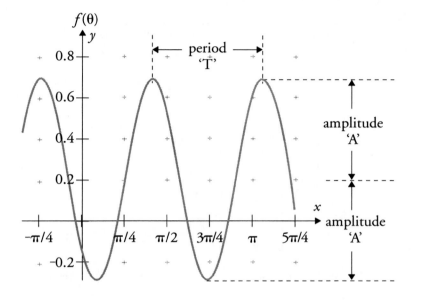

The period and amplitude for the three basic trigonometric functions are provided in the table below.

PERIOD AND AMPLITUDE OF THE BASIC TRIG FUNCTIONS		
Function	Period (radians)	Amplitude
$\sin \theta$	2π	1
$\cos \theta$	2π	1
$\tan \theta$	π	Undefined

Below are the graphs of the basic trigonometric functions, (a) $y = \sin x$; (b) $y = \cos x$; and (c) $y = \tan x$.

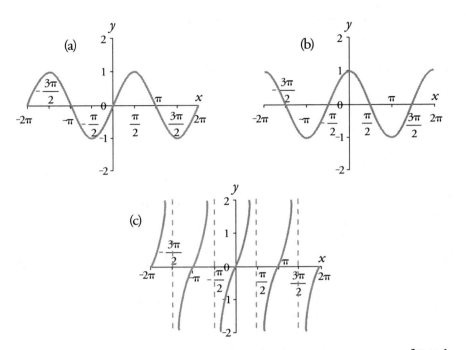

Note that the graph of the tangent function has asymptotes at $x = \frac{2n - 1}{2}\pi$, where $n = 0, \pm 1, \pm 2, \pm 3, \dots$.

The graphs of the reciprocal trigonometric functions are shown below, with (a) $y = \csc x$; (b) $y = \sec x$; and (c) $y = \cot x$.

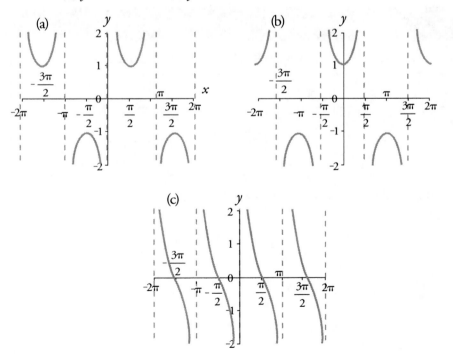

The phase and amplitude for the three reciprocal trigonometric functions are provided in the table below.

PERIOD AND AMPLITUDE OF THE RECIPROCAL TRIG FUNCTIONS		
Function	Period (radians)	Amplitude
csc θ	2π	Undefined
sec θ	2π	Undefined
cot θ	π	Undefined

Graphing a trigonometric function by hand typically requires a calculator for determining the value of the function for various angles. Nevertheless, simple functions can often be graphed by simply determining the amplitude, period, and phase shift. Once these parameters are known, the graph can be sketched approximately. The amplitude of a simple sine or cosine function is simply the multiplicative constant (or function) associated with the trigonometric function. Thus, $y = 2\cos x$, for instance, has an amplitude of 2. The phase shift is typically just a constant added to the argument of the function. For instance, $y = \sin(x + 1)$ includes a phase shift of 1. A positive phase shift constant indicates that the graph of the function is shifted to the left; a negative phase shift indicates that the graph is shifted to the right.

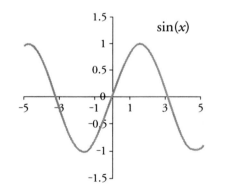

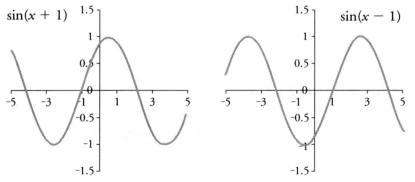

Example: Sketch the graph of the function $f(x) = 4\sin(2x + \frac{\pi}{2})$.

Notice first that the amplitude of the function is 4. Since there is no constant term added to the sine function, the function is centered on the x-axis. Find crucial points on the graph by setting f equal to zero and solving for x to find the roots.

$$f(x) = 0 = 4\sin(2x + \frac{\pi}{2})$$
$$\sin(2x + \frac{\pi}{2}) = 0$$
$$2x + \frac{\pi}{2} = n\pi$$

In the above expression, n is an integer.

$$2x = (n - \frac{1}{2})\pi$$
$$x = (n - \frac{1}{2})\frac{\pi}{2}$$

So, the roots of the function are at

$$x = \pm\frac{\pi}{4}, \pm\frac{3\pi}{4}, \pm\frac{5\pi}{4}, \ldots$$

The maxima and minima of the function are halfway between successive roots. Determine the location of a maximum by testing the function. Try $x = 0$.

$$f(0) = 4\sin(2[0] + \frac{\pi}{2}) = 4\sin(\frac{\pi}{2}) = 4$$

Thus, f is maximized at $x = 4$. The function can then be sketched.

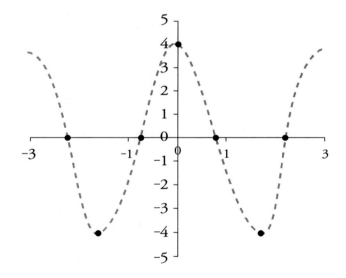

Inverse Trigonometric Functions

The inverse sine function of x is written as arcsin x or $\sin^{-1} x$ and is the angle for which the sine is x; i.e., $\sin(\arcsin x) = x$. Since the sine function is periodic, many values of arcsin x correspond to a particular x. In order to define arcsin as a function, therefore, its range needs to be restricted.

The function $y = \textbf{arcsin}\ x$ has a domain $[-1, 1]$ and range $[-\frac{\pi}{2}, \frac{\pi}{2}]$.

In some books, a restricted inverse function is denoted by a capitalized beginning letter such as in Sin^{-1} or Arctan. The arcsin function is shown below.

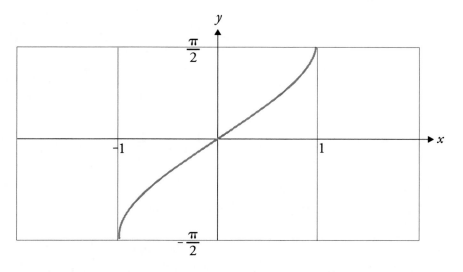

The inverse cosine and tangent functions are defined in the same way: $\cos(\text{arccos}\ x) = x$; $\tan(\text{arctan}\ x) = x$.

The function $y = \textbf{arccos}\ x$ has a domain $[-1, 1]$ and range $[0, \pi]$. The graph of this function is shown below.

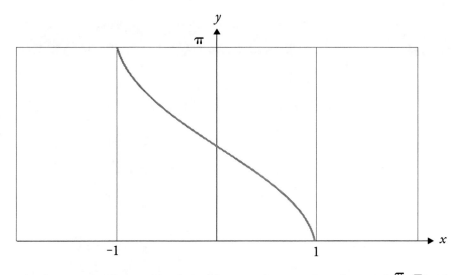

The function $y = \textbf{arctan}\ x$ has a domain $[-\infty, +\infty]$ and range $[-\frac{\pi}{2}, \frac{\pi}{2}]$. The plot of the function is shown below.

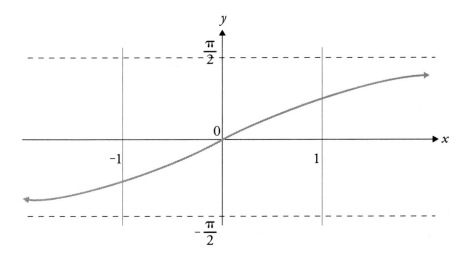

Example: Evaluate the following: (i) sin⁻¹(0) and (ii) arccos(-1)

(i) $\sin(\sin^{-1}(0)) = 0$.

The value of the inverse sine function must lie in the range $[-\frac{\pi}{2}, \frac{\pi}{2}]$. Since 0 is the only argument in the range $[-\frac{\pi}{2}, \frac{\pi}{2}]$ for which the sine function is zero, $\sin^{-1}(0) = 0$.

(ii) $\cos(\arccos(-1)) = -1$

The value of the inverse cosine function must lie in the range $[0, \pi]$. π is the only argument for which the cosine function is equal to -1 in the range $[0, \pi]$. Hence, $\arccos(-1) = \pi$.

IDENTITIES FOR THE INVERSE TRIGONOMETRIC FUNCTIONS		
$\csc^{-1}(x)$	$=$	$\sin^{-1}\left(\frac{1}{x}\right)$ for $|x| \geq 1$
$\sec^{-1}(x)$	$=$	$\cos^{-1}\left(\frac{1}{x}\right)$ for $|x| \geq 1$
$\cot^{-1}(x)$	$=$	$\tan^{-1}\left(\frac{1}{x}\right)$ for $x > 0$
	$=$	$\tan^{-1}\left(\frac{1}{x}\right) + \pi$ for $x < 0$
	$=$	$\frac{\pi}{2}$ for $x = 0$

$\sin^{-1} x$	$=$	$\cos^{-1}\left(\sqrt{1-x^2}\right)$	$\cos^{-1} x$	$=$	$\sin^{-1}\left(\sqrt{1-x^2}\right)$
$\tan^{-1} x$	$=$	$\cos^{-1}\left(\dfrac{1}{\sqrt{1+x^2}}\right)$	$\cos^{-1} x$	$=$	$\tan^{-1}\left(\dfrac{\sqrt{1-x^2}}{x}\right)$
$\tan^{-1} x$	$=$	$\sin^{-1}\left(\dfrac{x}{\sqrt{1+x^2}}\right)$	$\sin^{-1} x$	$=$	$\tan^{-1}\left(\dfrac{x}{\sqrt{1-x^2}}\right)$

Example: Simplify the expression cos(arcsin x) + sin(arccos x)

$\arcsin x = \arccos(\sqrt{1-x^2})$ identity

$\rightarrow \cos(\arcsin x) = \sqrt{1-x^2}$

$\arccos x = \arcsin(\sqrt{1-x^2})$ identity

$\rightarrow \sin(\arccos x) = \sqrt{1-x^2}$

Hence, $\cos(\arcsin x) + \sin(\arccos x) = \sqrt{1-x^2} + \sqrt{1-x^2} = 2\sqrt{1-x^2}$

Example: Using the identities given above, prove the identity

$$\sin^{-1} x + \cos^{-1} x = \frac{\pi}{2}$$

Since $\sin\left(\frac{\pi}{2}\right) = 1$, the identity may be proven by showing that

$\sin(\sin^{-1} x + \cos^{-1} x) = 1$

$\sin(\sin^{-1} x + \cos^{-1} x) = \sin(\sin^{-1} x)\cos(\cos^{-1} x)$

$\qquad\qquad + \cos(\sin^{-1} x)\sin(\cos^{-1} x)$ sine sum formula

$\qquad\qquad = x \times x + \sqrt{1-x^2}\sqrt{1-x^2}$ inverse identities

$\qquad\qquad = x^2 + 1 - x^2 = 1$

Other similar identities include the following:

$$\tan^{-1} x + \cot^{-1} x = \frac{\pi}{2}$$
$$\sec^{-1} x + \csc^{-1} x = \frac{\pi}{2}$$

SKILL 4.2 Apply the Law of Sines and the Law of Cosines

Trigonometric functions can also be applied to nonright triangles by way of the law of sines and the law of cosines. Consider the arbitrary triangle shown below with angles *A*, *B* and *C* and corresponding opposite sides *a*, *b* and *c*.

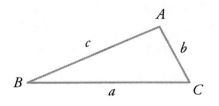

The law of sines is a proportional relationship between the lengths of the sides of the triangle and the opposite angles. The law of sines is given below:

$$\frac{a}{\sin A} = \frac{b}{\sin B} = \frac{c}{\sin C}$$

Trigonometric functions can be applied to nonright triangles by way of the Law of Sines and the Law of Cosines.

The law of cosines permits determination of the length of a side of an arbitrary triangle as long as the lengths of the other two sides, along with the angle opposite the unknown side, are known. The law of cosines is given below:

$$c^2 = a^2 + b^2 - 2ab\cos C$$

Example: An inlet is 140 feet wide. The lines of sight from each bank to an approaching ship are 79 degrees and 58 degrees. What are the distances from each bank to the ship?

First, draw an appropriate sketch of the situation with the appropriate labels for the parameters.

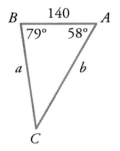

Since the sum of the angles in a triangle is 180°, angle C must be 43°. Use the law of sines to calculate the lengths of sides *a* and *b*.

For side *b*:

$$\frac{b}{\sin 79°} = \frac{140 \text{ feet}}{\sin 43°}$$

$$b = \frac{\sin 79°}{\sin 43°} 140 \text{ feet} \approx 201.5 \text{ feet}$$

And for side *a*:

$$\frac{a}{\sin 58°} = \frac{140 \text{ feet}}{\sin 43°}$$

$$a = \frac{\sin 58°}{\sin 43°} 140 \text{ feet} \approx 174.1 \text{ feet}$$

SKILL **Apply the formulas for the trigonometric functions of *x*/2, 2*x*, *x*,**
4.3 ***x* + *y*, and *x* − *y*; prove trigonometric identities**

Identities Involving Arguments of Trigonometric Functions

Sum and difference formulas

Trigonometric functions involving the sum or difference of two angles can be expressed in terms of functions of each individual angle using the following formulas.

SUM AND DIFFERENCE FORMULAS		
$\cos(\alpha + \beta)$	$=$	$\cos\alpha\cos\beta - \sin\alpha\sin\beta$
$\cos(\alpha - \beta)$	$=$	$\cos\alpha\cos\beta + \sin\alpha\sin\beta$
$\sin(\alpha + \beta)$	$=$	$\sin\alpha\cos\beta + \cos\alpha\sin\beta$
$\sin(\alpha - \beta)$	$=$	$\sin\alpha\cos\beta - \cos\alpha\sin\beta$
$\tan(\alpha + \beta)$	$=$	$\dfrac{\tan\alpha + \tan\beta}{1 - \tan\alpha\tan\beta}$
$\tan(\alpha - \beta)$	$=$	$\dfrac{\tan\alpha - \tan\beta}{1 + \tan\alpha\tan\beta}$

The cosine sum formula can be proven by considering the relationships between the angles and distances in the unit circle shown below.

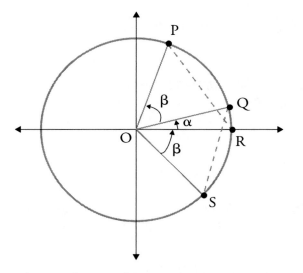

The coordinates of point P are $(\cos(\alpha + \beta), \sin(\alpha + \beta))$, the coordinates of point Q are $(\cos\alpha, \sin\alpha)$, the coordinates of point R are $(1, 0)$, and the coordinates of point S are $(\cos\beta, -\sin\beta)$.

Since $\angle POR = \angle QOS = \alpha + \beta$, $PR = QS$.

Using the distance formula to express the lengths PR and QS in terms of their coordinates, the result is the following.

$$PR = \sqrt{(\cos(\alpha+\beta)-1)^2 + (\sin(\alpha+\beta)-0)^2}$$
$$QS = \sqrt{(\cos\alpha - \cos\beta)^2 + (\sin\alpha - (-\sin\beta))^2}$$

Squaring both expressions and simplifying yields the following.

$PR = (\cos(\alpha + \beta) - 1)^2 + \sin^2(\alpha + \beta)$

$PR = \cos^2(\alpha + \beta) + 1 - 2\cos(\alpha + \beta) + \sin^2(\alpha + \beta)$

$QS = (\cos\alpha - \cos\beta)^2 + (\sin\alpha + \sin\beta)^2$

$QS = \cos^2\alpha + \cos^2\beta - 2\cos\alpha\cos\beta + \sin^2\alpha + \sin^2\beta + 2\sin\alpha\sin\beta$

Apply the Pythagorean identities $\cos^2(\alpha + \beta) + \sin^2(\alpha + \beta) = 1$, $\sin^2\alpha + \cos^2\alpha = 1$, and $\sin^2\beta + \cos^2\beta = 1$ to the above expressions.

$PR = 1 + 1 - 2\cos(\alpha + \beta) = 2 - 2\cos(\alpha + \beta)$

$QS = 2 - 2\cos\alpha\cos\beta + 2\sin\alpha\sin\beta$

Equate these two expressions and simplify.

$PR = QS$

$2 - 2\cos(\alpha + \beta) = 2 - 2\cos\alpha\cos\beta + 2\sin\alpha\sin\beta$

$-2\cos(\alpha + \beta) = -2\cos\alpha\cos\beta + 2\sin\alpha\sin\beta$

$\cos(\alpha + \beta) = \cos\alpha\cos\beta - \sin\alpha\sin\beta$

This is the cosine sum formula. The other sum and difference formulas can be proven in a similar manner.

Example: Evaluate the following using the appropriate identity.
sin (35°) cos (55°) + cos (35°) sin (55°)

Using the sine sum formula,

$\sin 35° \cos 55° + \cos 35° \sin 55°$

$= \sin(35° + 55°) = \sin(90°) = 1$

Example: Show that $\frac{\cos(x + y)}{\cos x \cos y} = 1 - \tan x \tan y$.

Apply the cosine sum formula:

$\frac{\cos(x + y)}{\cos x \cos y} = \frac{\cos x \cos y - \sin x \sin y}{\cos x \cos y}$

$= 1 - \frac{\sin x \sin y}{\cos x \cos y}$

$= 1 - \tan x \tan y$

Double- and half-angle identities

The double-angle identities and half-angle identities are summarized below.

DOUBLE-ANGLE AND HALF-ANGLE IDENTITIES				
$\cos 2\alpha$	$=$	$\cos^2\alpha - \sin^2\alpha$	$=$	$1 - 2\sin^2\alpha$
	$\sin 2\alpha$	$=$	$2\sin\alpha\cos\alpha$	

Table continued on next page

$\tan 2\alpha$	$=$	$\dfrac{2\tan\alpha}{1-\tan^2\alpha}$
$\cos\dfrac{\alpha}{2}$	$=$	$\pm\sqrt{\dfrac{1+\cos\alpha}{2}}$
$\sin\dfrac{\alpha}{2}$	$=$	$\pm\sqrt{\dfrac{1-\cos\alpha}{2}}$
$\tan\dfrac{\alpha}{2}$	$=$	$\pm\sqrt{\dfrac{1-\cos a}{1+\cos a}}$ or $\dfrac{\sin a}{1+\cos a}$ or $\dfrac{1-\cos a}{\sin a}$

The double-angle identities can be obtained using the sum formulas, as with the example of the cosine function below:

$$\cos 2\alpha = \cos(\alpha+\alpha)$$
$$= \cos\alpha\cos\alpha - \sin\alpha\sin\alpha$$
$$\cos 2\alpha = \cos^2\alpha - \sin^2\alpha$$

Example: Show that $\sin(3x) = \sin x\,(3\cos^2 x - \sin^2 x)$.

$$\sin(3x) = \sin(2x+x)$$
$$= \sin 2x\cos x + \cos 2x\sin x \qquad \text{Sine Sum Formula}$$
$$= 2\sin x\cos x\cos x$$
$$\quad + (\cos^2 x - \sin^2 x)\sin x \qquad \text{Double-Angle Identities}$$
$$= 2\sin x\cos^2 x + \sin x\cos^2 x - \sin^3 x$$
$$= 3\sin x\cos^2 x - \sin^3 x$$
$$= \sin x\,(3\cos^2 x - \sin^2 x)$$

The half-angle identities can be derived by solving the double angle identities for the sine, cosine, or tangent of a single angle. For instance,

$$\cos 2\alpha = 2\cos^2\alpha - 1$$
$$2\cos^2\alpha = 1 + \cos 2\alpha$$
$$\cos^2\alpha = \frac{1+\cos 2\alpha}{2}$$
$$\cos\alpha = \pm\sqrt{\frac{1+\cos 2\alpha}{2}}$$

Since this identity is valid for all values of α, it will continue to be valid if we replace α with $\frac{\alpha}{2}$. Therefore,

$$\cos\frac{\alpha}{2} = \pm\sqrt{\frac{1+\cos\alpha}{2}}$$

Note that the choice of the appropriate sign depends on the value of the angle $\frac{\alpha}{2}$. If $\frac{\alpha}{2}$ is in the first or fourth quadrants, then the positive sign is chosen. Otherwise, the negative sign must be chosen. The choice of the sign is in conformity with the standard characteristics of trigonometric functions.

Example: Given that $\sin 30° = \frac{1}{2}$, find the value of $\tan 15°$.

$$\cos 30° = \sqrt{1 - \sin^2 30°} = \sqrt{1 - \frac{1}{4}}$$

$$= \sqrt{\frac{3}{4}} = \frac{\sqrt{3}}{2}$$

$$\tan 15° = \frac{1 - \cos 30°}{\sin 30°} \qquad \text{Half angle identity}$$

$$= \frac{1 - \frac{\sqrt{3}}{2}}{\frac{1}{2}} = 2 - \sqrt{3} = 0.27$$

Proving Trigonometric Identities

There are two methods that may be used to prove trigonometric identities. One method is to choose one side of the equation and manipulate it until it equals the other side. The other method is to replace expressions on both sides of the equation with equivalent expressions until both sides are equal.

There are a range of trigonometric identities, including reciprocal and Pythagorean identities, as listed below.

RECIPROCAL IDENTITIES		
$\sin x = \dfrac{1}{\csc x}$	$\sin x \csc x = 1$	$\csc x = \dfrac{1}{\sin x}$
$\cos x = \dfrac{1}{\sec x}$	$\cos x \sec x = 1$	$\sec x = \dfrac{1}{\cos x}$
$\tan x = \dfrac{1}{\cot x}$	$\tan x \cot x = 1$	$\cot x = \dfrac{1}{\tan x}$
$\tan x = \dfrac{\sin x}{\cos x}$		$\cot x = \dfrac{\cos x}{\sin x}$

PYTHAGOREAN IDENTITIES		
$\sin^2 x + \cos^2 x = 1$	$1 + \tan^2 x = \sec^2 x$	$1 + \cot^2 x = \csc^2 x$

Example: Prove that $\sin^2 x + \cos^2 x = 1$.

Use the definitions of the sine and cosine functions from right triangle trigonometry.

$$\left(\frac{y}{r}\right)^2 + \left(\frac{x}{r}\right)^2 = 1$$

$$\frac{x^2 + y^2}{r^2} = 1$$

But the numerator of the above fraction, by the Pythagorean theorem, is simply r^2. Then:

$$\frac{r^2}{r^2} = 1$$

The identity has been proven.

Example: Prove that cot x + tan x = csc x sec x.

Use the reciprocal identities to convert the left side of the equation to sines and cosines. Then combine terms using a common denominator.

$$\frac{\cos x}{\sin x} + \frac{\sin x}{\cos x}$$

$$\frac{\cos^2 x}{\sin x \cos x} + \frac{\sin^2 x}{\sin x \cos x} = \frac{\sin^2 x + \cos^2 x}{\sin x \cos x} = \frac{1}{\sin x \cos x}$$

Finally, convert the expression using the reciprocal identities.

$$\frac{1}{\sin x \cos x} = \csc x \sec x$$

The identity is then proven.

Practice problems: Prove each identity.

1. $\cot\theta = \dfrac{\cos\theta}{\sin\theta}$

2. $1 + \cot^2\theta = \csc^2\theta$

SKILL 4.4 Solve trigonometric equations and inequalities

Unlike trigonometric identities, which are true for all values of the defined variable, trigonometric equations and inequalities are true for some, but not all, values of the variable. Most often, trigonometric equations are solved for values between 0 and 360 degrees or between 0 and 2π radians. For inequalities, the solution is often a set of intervals, since trigonometric functions are periodic. Solving trigonometric equations is largely the same as solving algebraic equations. Care must be taken, however, to keep in mind the periodic nature of trigonometric functions. This periodic nature often yields multiple (or an infinite number of) solutions.

Trigonometric identities, including sum and difference formulas, are often indispensable in the problem-solving process. These identities allow many complicated functions to be simplified to forms that are more easily managed algebraically.

Some algebraic operations, such as squaring both sides of an equation, will yield extraneous answers. Avoid incorrect solutions by remembering to check all solutions to be sure they satisfy the original equation.

Some algebraic operations, such as squaring both sides of an equation, will yield extraneous answers. Avoid incorrect solutions by remembering to check all solutions to be sure they satisfy the original equation.

Example: Solve the following equation for x: cos x = 1 − sin x, where 0° ≤ x ≤ 180°.

Start by squaring both sides of the equation.

$$\cos^2 x = (1 - \sin x)^2 = 1 - 2\sin x + \sin^2 x$$

Substitute using the Pythagorean identity to replace the cosine term.

$$1 - \sin^2 x = 1 - 2 \sin x + \sin^2 x$$

Simplify the results.

$$2 \sin^2 x - 2 \sin x = 0$$
$$\sin x (\sin x - 1) = 0$$

There are two possible solutions to the equation:

$$\sin x = 0 \qquad \text{and} \qquad \sin x = 1$$
$$x = 0°, 180° \qquad\qquad x = 90°$$

Thus, the apparent solutions to the problem are $x = 0°$, $90°$ and $180°$. By checking each solution, however, it is found that $x = 180°$ is not a legitimate solution and must be discarded. The actual solutions to the equation are thus $x = 0°$ and $90°$.

Example: Solve the following equation: $\cos^2 x = \sin^2 x$ for $0 \leq x \leq 2\pi$.
First, use the Pythagorean identity to convert either the cosine or sine term.

$$\cos^2 x = 1 - \cos^2 x$$

Simplify the results.

$$2 \cos^2 x = 1$$
$$\cos^2 x = \frac{1}{2}$$
$$\cos x = \pm \frac{1}{\sqrt{2}}$$

Familiarity with the properties of trigonometric functions should lead to the realization that this solution corresponds to odd integer multiples of $\frac{\pi}{4}$. Alternatively, a calculator can be used to calculate the inverse function. (A detailed review of inverse trigonometric functions is provided earlier in this discussion.)

$$x = \arccos(\pm \frac{1}{\sqrt{2}})$$

In either case, the solution is the following:

$$x = \frac{\pi}{4}, \frac{3\pi}{4}, \frac{5\pi}{4}, \frac{7\pi}{4}$$

Example: Solve for x: $\sin x \geq 0$.
Solving a trigonometric inequality involves the same general process that is used in solving any other inequality. In this case, however, the set of solutions includes an infinite number of intervals, rather than a single interval as is the case for some nonperiodic functions. First, replace the inequality symbol with an equal sign. Solve using the inverse function.

$$\sin x = 0$$
$$\arcsin [\sin x] = \arcsin [0]$$
$$x = \arcsin [0]$$

The solutions for x are the following.

$\quad x = n\pi \quad\quad n = 0, \pm1, \pm2, \pm3, \ldots$

These solutions are the points at which the sine function crosses the x-axis. Thus, some set of intervals bounded by these solutions is the set of solutions for the inequality. It is apparent that the sine function is greater than zero for x between 0 and π, and negative for x between π and 2π. This pattern then repeats. Thus, sin x is greater than zero between $2n\pi$ and $(2n + 1)\pi$ for $n = 0, \pm1, \pm2, \pm3, \ldots$

$\quad\quad \sin x \geq 0$ for $2n\pi \leq x \leq (2n + 1)\pi$ where $n=0, \pm1, \pm2, \pm3, \ldots$

Note that the endpoints of the intervals are included in the solution set. The validity of this solution can be confirmed by looking at a graph of sin x.

SKILL 4.5 Convert between rectangular and polar coordinate systems

Any ordered pair can be plotted in a plane using either Cartesian (rectangular) or polar coordinates. Complex numbers, for instance, can be plotted graphically in a Cartesian complex plane, where the x-axis represents real numbers and the y-axis represents imaginary numbers. An equivalent representation, following a graphical approach, is to use polar coordinates (a magnitude or length and an angle). These two representations are shown below for the example of $2+3i$, which can be equivalently written as (2, 3).

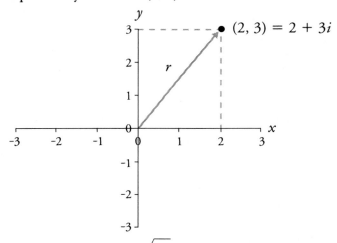

In the above case, r is $\sqrt{13}$ and θ is approximately 0.983 radians.

Thus, a complex number $a + bi$—or any ordered pair (a, b)—can be represented using a vector length r and an angle θ, measured in the counterclockwise direction from the x-axis. For a point (x, y) in rectangular coordinates, note that

$$r = \sqrt{x^2 + y^2}$$
$$\theta = \arctan \frac{y}{x}$$

To convert from polar coordinates to rectangular coordinates, apply right triangle trigonometry to the diagram above for the general case of a point (r, θ) in polar coordinates.

$$x = r \cos\theta$$
$$y = r \sin\theta$$

DOMAIN III
FUNCTIONS AND CALCULUS

PERSONALIZED STUDY PLAN

KNOWN MATERIAL/ SKIP IT

PAGE	COMPETENCY AND SKILL	
115	**5:** **Functions**	☐
	5.1: Demonstrate an understanding of functions	☐
	5.2: Find an appropriate family of functions to model particular phenomena	☐
	5.3: Determine properties of a function	☐
	5.4: Use the properties of trigonometric, exponential, logarithmic, polynomial, and rational functions to solve problems	☐
	5.5: Determine the composition of two functions	☐
	5.6: Interpret representations of functions of two variables	☐
137	**6:** **Calculus**	☐
	6.1: Demonstrate an understanding of what it means for a function to have a limit at a point	☐
	6.2: Understand the derivative of a function as a limit, as the slope of a curve, and as a rate of change	☐
	6.3: Show that a particular function is continuous	☐
	6.4: Numerically approximate derivatives and integrals	☐
	6.5: Use standard differentiation and integration techniques	☐
	6.6: Analyze the behavior of a function; solve problems involving related rates; solve applied minima-maxima problems	☐
	6.7: Demonstrate an understanding of and the ability to use the Mean Value Theorem and the Fundamental Theorem of Calculus	☐
	6.8: Demonstrate an intuitive understanding of integration	☐
	6.9: Determine the limits of sequences and simple infinite series	☐

COMPETENCY 5

FUNCTIONS

Functions are one of the essential elements of algebra, calculus, and other areas of mathematics. It is crucial to understand the basic properties of functions as well as their applications to various types of situations. The following discussion reviews the basics of functions and then goes on to discuss applications of functions to both mathematical and physical situations.

> SKILL 5.1 **Demonstrate an understanding of and the ability to work with functions in various representations** *(e.g., graphs, tables, symbolic expressions, and verbal narratives)*, **and the ability to convert flexibly among them**

Representations of Functions

Functions can be represented in a variety of ways, including as a symbolic expression (for instance, $f(x) = 3x^2 + \sin x$), a graph, a table of values, and a common-language expression (for example, "the speed of the car increases linearly from 0 to 100 miles per hour in 12 seconds"). The ability to convert among various representations of a function depends on how much information is provided. For instance, although a graph of a function can provide some clues as to its symbolic representation, it is often difficult or impossible to obtain an exact symbolic form based only on a graph. The same difficulty applies to tables.

Converting from a symbolic form to a graph or table, however, is relatively simple, especially if a computer is available. The symbolic expression need simply be evaluated for a representative set of points that can be used to produce a sufficiently detailed graph or table.

For example, the equation $y = 9x$ describes the relationship between the total amount earned, y, and the total amount of $9 sunglasses sold, x. In a relationship of this type, one of the quantities (e.g., total amount earned) is dependent on the other (e.g., number of glasses sold). These variables are known as the dependent and independent variables, respectively.

A table using this data would appear as:

Number of sunglasses sold	1	5	10	15
Total dollars earned	9	45	90	135

Each (x, y) relationship between a pair of values is called a coordinate pair and can be plotted on a graph. The coordinate pairs (1,9), (5, 45), (10, 90), and (15, 135) are plotted on the graph below.

The graph shows a linear relationship. A LINEAR RELATIONSHIP is one in which two quantities are proportional to each other. Doubling x also doubles y. On a graph, a straight line depicts a linear relationship.

> **LINEAR RELATIONSHIP:** a relationship in which two quantities are proportional to each other

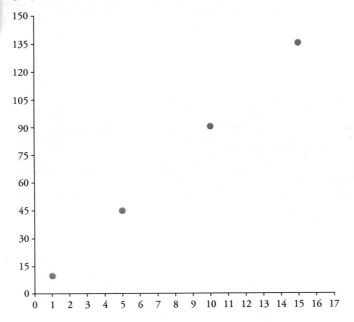

> ## SKILL 5.2 Find an appropriate family of functions to model particular phenomena *(e.g., population growth, cooling, simple harmonic motion)*

Functions that vary on a periodic basis can often be modeled using trigonometric functions.

Exponential functions often can be used to model phenomena involving growth or decay.

The process of determining an appropriate family of functions with which to model a particular phenomenon can be a challenging task. Nevertheless, there are some basic rules that can be helpful. For instance, functions that vary on a periodic basis can often be modeled using trigonometric functions. Harmonic motion (such as that of a spring or pendulum) is a particular example in which trigonometric functions can be used. If the phenomenon involves growth or decay, exponential functions are often appropriate.

It is noteworthy that some phenomena, such as the above-mentioned harmonic motion, may involve both periodicity and decay. For instance, a weight attached to a spring will oscillate, but the amplitude of the oscillations will decrease over time as air resistance and imperfections in the spring dissipate the energy of motion. In such cases, it is sometimes possible to simply model the phenomenon by using the product of two functional families (in this case, a sine function and an exponential function).

When determining the appropriate family of functions to use in the model, it is helpful to examine as much information as possible, such as a graph or table of values. It is sometimes possible to select an appropriate function by inspection. In other cases, use of a computer can be helpful to perform a trial-and-error analysis by graphing a number of different functions and comparing them to the graph of the parameter associated with the phenomenon of interest.

SKILL 5.3 **Determine properties of a function such as domain, range, intercepts, symmetries, intervals of increase or decrease, discontinuities, and asymptotes**

Properties of Functions

A RELATION is any set of ordered pairs. The DOMAIN of a relation is the set containing all the first coordinates of the ordered pairs, and the RANGE of a relation is the set containing all the second coordinates of the ordered pairs.

A FUNCTION is a relation in which each value in the domain corresponds to only one value in the range. It is notable, however, that a value in the range may correspond to any number of values in the domain. Thus, although a function is necessarily a relation, not all relations are functions, since a relation is not bound by this rule.

On a graph, use the VERTICAL LINE TEST to check whether a relation is a function. If any vertical line intersects the graph of a relation in more than one point, then the relation is not a function.

A relation is considered ONE-TO-ONE if each value in the domain corresponds to only one value in the range, and each value in the range corresponds to only one value in the domain. Thus, a one-to-one relation is also a function, but it adds an additional condition.

In the same way that the graph of a relation can be examined using the vertical line test to determine whether it is a function, the HORIZONTAL LINE TEST can be used to determine if a function is a one-to-one relation. If no horizontal lines superimposed on the plot intersect the graph of the relation in more than one place, then the relation is one-to-one (assuming it also passes the vertical line test and, therefore, is a function).

RELATION: any set of ordered pairs

DOMAIN: the set containing all the first coordinates of the ordered pairs

RANGE: the set containing all the second coordinates of the ordered pairs

FUNCTION: a relation in which each value in the domain corresponds to only one value in the range

VERTICAL LINE TEST: states that if any vertical line intersects the graph of a relation in more than one point, then the relation is not a function

A mapping is essentially the same as a function. Mappings (or maps) can be depicted using diagrams with arrows drawn from each element of the domain to the corresponding element (or elements) of the range. If two arrows originate from any single element in the domain, then the mapping is not a function. Likewise, for a function, if each arrow is drawn to a unique value in the range (that is, there are no cases where more than one arrow is drawn to a given value in the range), then the relation is one-to-one.

Example: Determine the domain and range of this mapping.

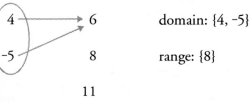

domain: {4, −5}

range: {8}

In some cases, a function (or mapping) may relate one set to another such that the range of the function consists of all the elements of a given set *S*. Thus, if the range of the function is *S*, then the function MAPS ONTO S.

Example: Determine if the function f(x) = 2x maps onto ℝ.
The range of *f* includes all the values on the real number line (note that the graph of the line 2*x* extends to both positive and negative infinity, both along the *x*- and *y*-axes). Thus, the range of *f* is ℝ, so *f* maps onto ℝ.

As mentioned above, a function is a relation in which each value in the domain corresponds to only one value in the range. Functions can be expressed discretely, as sets of ordered pairs, or they can be expressed more generally as formulas. For instance, the function $y = x$ is a function that represents an infinite set of ordered pairs (x, y), where each value in the domain (x) corresponds to the same value in the range (y).

If two parameters vary directly, then as one gets larger, the other also gets larger. If one gets smaller, then the other gets smaller as well. If x and y vary directly, there should be a constant, c, such that $y = cx$. The parameters are not necessarily limited to linear values such as x and y, but can include such expressions as x^2, ln x and sin x. For instance, the statement "y varies directly with the natural logarithm of x" leads to the equation $y = c\ln x$, where c is an unspecified multiplicative constant that determines the magnitude of variation.

If two parameters vary inversely, then, as one gets larger, the other one gets smaller instead. If x and y vary inversely, there should be a constant, c, such that $xy = c$ or $y = c/x$. As with direct variation, inverse variation can involve any number of expressions involving x or y.

Example: If $30 were paid for 5 hours work, how much would be paid for 19 hours work?

This is direct variation and $30 = 5c, so the constant c = 6 ($6/hour). So $y = 6(19)$ or $y = \$114$.

This could also be done as a proportion:
$$\frac{\$30}{5} = \frac{y}{19}$$
$$5y = 570$$
$$y = 114$$

The INTERCEPTS of a function are the points at which the function crosses the *x*- or *y*-axis. Given a function $f(x)$, the *y*-intercept is located at the point $[0, f(0)]$, and the *x*-intercept is located at the point $[f^{-1}(0), 0]$, assuming the function is one-to-one. Otherwise, the *x*-intercepts exist at points $(x_i, 0)$, where $f(x_i) = 0$ for all x_i.

INTERCEPTS: the points at which the function crosses the *x*- or *y*-axis

Symmetries in a function can also be described in terms of reflections or "mirror images." A function can be symmetric about the the *y*-axis (but not about the *x*-axis, except for the function $f(x) = 0$, since every function must pass the vertical line test). A function is symmetric about the *y*-axis if for every point (x, y) that is included on the graph of the function, the point $(-x, y)$ is also included on the graph. Consider the function $f(x) = x^2$. Note that for each point (x, x^2) on the graph, the point $(-x, x^2)$ is also on the graph. The symmetry of the function about the y-axis can also be seen in the graph below.

A function is symmetric about the y-axis if for every point (x, y) that is included on the graph of the function, the point (−x, y) is also included on the graph.

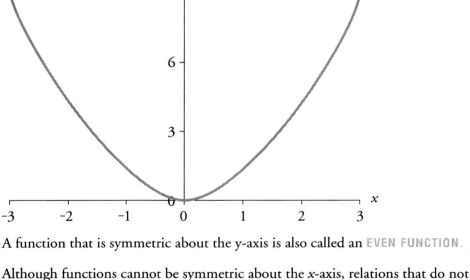

A function that is symmetric about the y-axis is also called an EVEN FUNCTION.

Although functions cannot be symmetric about the *x*-axis, relations that do not obey the vertical line test can be symmetric in this way. A relation is symmetric about the *x*-axis if for every point (x, y) in the graph of the relation, the point $(x, -y)$ is also in the graph.

EVEN FUNCTION: a function that is symmetric with respect to the *y*-axis

A relation is symmetric about the x-axis if for every point (x, y) in the graph of the relation, the point (x, y) is also in the graph.

Consider, for instance, the relation $g(x) = \pm\sqrt{x}$. For every value of x in the domain, the points $(x, \sqrt{x})$ and $(x, -\sqrt{x})$ are both in the graph, as shown below.

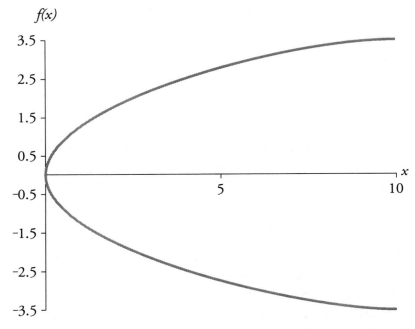

Functions may also be symmetric with respect to the origin. Such functions are called ODD (OR ANTISYMMETRIC) FUNCTIONS and are defined by the property that for any point (x, y) on the graph of the function, the point $(-x, -y)$ is also on the graph of the function. The function $f(x) = x^3$, for instance, is symmetric with respect to the origin, as shown in the graph below.

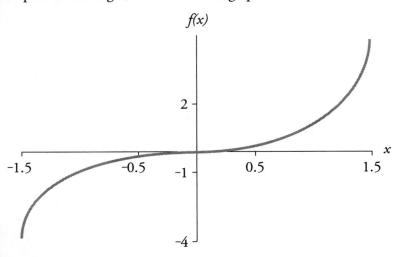

ODD (OR ANTISYMMETRIC) FUNCTIONS: a function that is symmetric with respect to the origin

A function is symmetric with respect to the origin if for any point (x, y) on the graph of the function, the point (−x, −y) is also on the graph of the function.

Functions can also be characterized in terms of *continuity*. Continuity and discontinuity in functions is discussed further in Competency 6.0.

A function may have one or more asymptotes. An ASYMPTOTE is a line for which the distance between it and a function or curve is arbitrarily small, especially as

ASYMPTOTE: a line for which the distance between it and a function or curve is arbitrarily small, especially as the function tends toward infinity in some direction

the function tends toward infinity in some direction. Asymptotes can be either vertical, horizontal or slant.

Consider, for instance, the plot of the hyperbola defined as follows.

$$g(x) = \pm\sqrt{x^2 + 1}$$

Note, for instance, that as x tends toward infinity, $g(x)$ gets arbitrarily close to x. The graph of $g(x)$ is shown below.

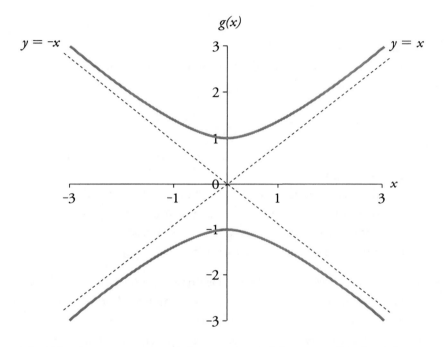

The (slant) asymptotes and their associated functions for this relation are displayed in the graph above as dashed lines.

INTERVALS OF INCREASE OR DECREASE for a function are those regions over which the function is continuously increasing or decreasing, respectively. An interval of increase for a function $f(x)$ corresponds to any subset of the domain in which the derivative of f is greater than zero. This simply means that the slope of the function is always greater than zero; thus, if $x_2 > x_1$, then $f(x_2) > f(x_1)$ for any x_1 and x_2 in the domain of the function. Likewise, an interval of decrease corresponds to any subset of the domain in which the derivative of f is less than zero. *For a review of derivatives, see Competency 6.*

> **INTERVALS OF INCREASE OR DECREASE**: those regions over which the function is continuously increasing or decreasing, respectively

Use the properties of trigonometric, exponential, logarithmic, polynomial, and rational functions to solve problems

Common Function Families

Some of the most commonly used function families include polynomial, rational, exponential, logarithmic, and trigonometric functions. These functions, separately or in various combinations, can be used to model a range of common phenomena in finances, physics, and other fields.

Polynomial Functions

POLYNOMIAL: a sum of terms, where each term is a constant multiplied by a variable raised to a positive integer power

STANDARD FORM: polynomials for which the terms are written in order of decreasing exponent value

DEGREE OF A POLY-NOMIAL FUNCTION: the value of the largest exponent to which the variable is raised

A POLYNOMIAL is a sum of terms, where each term is a constant multiplied by a variable raised to a positive integer power. The general form of a polynomial $P(x)$ is:

$$P(x) = a_n x^n + a_{n-1} x^{n-1} + \dots + a_2 x^2 + a_1 x + a_0$$

Polynomials written in STANDARD FORM have the terms written in order of decreasing exponent value, as shown above. The DEGREE OF A POLYNOMIAL FUNCTION in one variable is the value of the largest exponent to which the variable is raised. The above expression is a polynomial of degree n (assuming that $a_n \neq 0$). Any function that represents a line, for instance, is a polynomial function of degree 1. Quadratic functions are polynomials of degree 2.

There are many methods for solving problems that involve polynomial equations. For instance, in cases in which a polynomial is highly complicated or involves constants that do not permit methods such as factoring, a numerical approach may be appropriate. Newton's method is one possible approach to solving a polynomial equation numerically. At other times, solving a polynomial equation may require a graphical approach whereby the behavior of the function is examined on a visual plot. When using Newton's method, graphing the function can be helpful for estimating the locations of the roots (if any).

Polynomial equations with real coefficients cannot, in general, be solved using only real numbers. For instance, consider the quadratic function given below:

$$f(x) = x^2 + 1$$

There are no real roots for this equation, since

$$f(x) = 0 = x^2 + 1 \rightarrow x^2 = -1$$

The Fundamental Theorem of Algebra (see below), however, indicates that there must be two (possibly non-distinct) solutions to this equation. Note that if the complex numbers are permitted as solutions to this equation, then

$$x = \pm i$$

Thus, generally, solutions to any polynomial equation with real coefficients exist in the set of complex numbers.

If a phenomenon or situation can be modeled with a polynomial equation, the following theorems can be helpful in solving the equation. These theorems include the Fundamental Theorem of Algebra, the Factor Theorem, the Complex Conjugate Root Theorem, and the Rational Root Theorem.

The Fundamental Theorem of Algebra

The FUNDAMENTAL THEOREM OF ALGEBRA states that a polynomial expression of degree n must have n roots (which may be real or complex and which may not be distinct). It follows from the theorem that if the degree of a polynomial is odd, then it must have at least one real root.

Polynomial functions are in the form of $P(x)$ given below, where n is the degree of the polynomial and the constant a_n is non-zero.

$$P(x) = a_n x^n + a_{n-1} x^{n-1} + ... + a_2 x^2 + a_1 x + a_0$$

If $P(c) = 0$ for some number c, then c is said to be a *zero* (or *root*) of the function. A zero is also called a *solution* to the equation $P(x) = 0$.

The existence of n solutions can be seen by looking at a factorization of $P(x)$. For instance, consider $P(x) = x^2 - x - 6$. This second-degree polynomial can be factored into

$$P(x) = (x + 2)(x - 3)$$

Note that $P(x)$ has two roots in this case: $x = -2$ and $x = 3$. This corresponds to the degree of the polynomial, $n = 2$. In some cases, however, there may be non-distinct roots. Consider $P(x) = x^2$.

$$P(x) = (x)(x)$$

Note that the polynomial is factored in the same way as the previous example, but, in this case, the roots are identical: $x = 0$. Thus, although there are two roots for this second-degree polynomial, the roots are not distinct.

Likewise, roots of a polynomial may be complex. Consider $P(x) = x^2 + 1$. The range of this function is $P(x) \geq 1$, so there is no root in the sense that the function crosses the real x-axis. Nevertheless, if complex values of x are permitted, there are cases where $P(x)$ is zero. Factor $P(x)$ as before, but this time use complex numbers.

$$P(x) = (x + i)(x - i)$$

The solutions are x = i and x = $-i$. Thus, this second-degree polynomial still has two roots.

> **FUNDAMENTAL THEOREM OF ALGEBRA:** theorem that states that a polynomial expression of degree n must have n roots (which may be real or complex and which may not be distinct)

For a general n^{th} degree polynomial, the function $P(x)$ can be factored in a similar manner.

$$P(x) = (x - c_n)(x - c_{n-1}) \ldots (x - c_2)(x - c_1)$$

As with the second-degree polynomial examples examined above, a general nth degree polynomial can have roots c_i that are distinct or non-distinct, and real or complex. Since this is the case, if all of the roots of a polynomial are known, then a function $P(x)$ is determined based on the factoring approach shown above.

In addition, if a single root c is known, then the polynomial can be simplified (that is, it can be reduced by one degree) using division.

$$Q(x) = \frac{P(x)}{x - c}$$

Here, if $P(x)$ has degree n, then $Q(x)$ has degree $n - 1$. If some number of roots are known, the task of finding the remainder of the roots can be simplified by performing the division represented above. As each successive root is found, the degree of the polynomial can be reduced to further simplify finding the remainder of the roots.

Synthetic division

In some cases, dividing a polynomial by $(x - c)$ is simple, but generally speaking it is a complicated process. The process can be simplified using SYNTHETIC DIVISION, however.

To perform synthetic division of a polynomial $P(x)$ by $(x - c)$ to get a new polynomial $Q(x)$, first draw an upside-down division symbol as shown below, using the coefficients of $P(x)$ and the root c.

$$P(x) = a_n x^n + a_{n-1} x^{n-1} + \ldots + a_2 x^2 + a_1 x + a_0$$
$$Q(x) = \frac{P(x)}{x - c}$$

$$c \,\Big|\, a_n \;\; a_{n-1} \;\; a_{n-2} \cdots$$

The first step of synthetic division is to carry the first term, a_n.

$$c \,\Big|\, a_n \;\; a_{n-1} \;\; a_{n-2} \cdots$$
$$a_n$$

Each successive step involves multiplying c by the previously carried term and then placing the result under the next term. Then add the two results to get the next carry value.

> **SYNTHETIC DIVISION:** a shortcut method used to divide a polynomial $P(x)$ by a binomial of the form $x - c$

$$c \, \begin{array}{|ccc} a_n & a_{n-1} & a_{n-2} \cdots \\ & ca_n & \\ \hline a_n & & \end{array}$$

$$c \, \begin{array}{|ccc} a_n & a_{n-1} & a_{n-2} \cdots \\ & ca_n & \\ \hline a_n & (a_{n-1} + ca_n) & \end{array}$$

The process should be repeated until the last carry term is found. The result should be zero. (If the final carry value is non-zero, then c is not a root. This can be a useful test of whether a particular value is a root, especially for polynomials of high degrees.) The result of the division is the set of new coefficients for the quotient.

$$Q(x) = a_n x^{n-1} + (a_{n-1} + ca_n)x^{n-2} + \dots$$

Example: Divide $x^4 - 7x^2 - 6x$ by $(x + 2)$. Find the roots of the polynomial.
Use synthetic division. Notice that even the terms with coefficient zero must be included. In other words, first write the polynomial as

$$x^4 + 0x^3 - 7x^2 - 6x + 0.$$

$$-2 \, \begin{array}{|ccccc} 1 & 0 & -7 & -6 & 0 \\ & & & & \\ \hline \end{array}$$

Perform the division.

$$-2 \, \begin{array}{|ccccc} 1 & 0 & -7 & -6 & 0 \\ & & & & \\ \hline 1 & & & & \end{array}$$

$$-2 \, \begin{array}{|ccccc} 1 & 0 & -7 & -6 & 0 \\ & -2 & & & \\ \hline 1 & -2 & & & \end{array}$$

$$-2 \, \begin{array}{|ccccc} 1 & 0 & -7 & -6 & 0 \\ & -2 & 4 & & \\ \hline 1 & -2 & -3 & & \end{array}$$

$$-2 \, \begin{array}{|ccccc} 1 & 0 & -7 & -6 & 0 \\ & -2 & 4 & 6 & \\ \hline 1 & -2 & -3 & 0 & \end{array}$$

$$\begin{array}{c|ccccc} -2 & 1 & 0 & -7 & -6 & 0 \\ & & -2 & 4 & 6 & 0 \\ \hline & 1 & -2 & -3 & 0 & 0 \end{array}$$

Thus, -2 is indeed a root of the polynomial. The result is then
$$\frac{x^4 - 7x^2 - 6x}{x + 2} = x^3 - 2x^2 - 3x$$

Note that the remainder of the roots of this polynomial can be found much more easily than if the original polynomial was analyzed as is. Factor the result further.
$$x^3 - 2x^2 - 3x = x(x^2 - 2x - 3) = x(x - 3)(x + 1)$$

Thus, the roots are -2, -1, 0 and 3.

The Factor Theorem

FACTOR THEOREM:
this theorem states that a polynomial $P(x)$ has a factor $(x - a)$ if and only if $P(a) = 0$

The FACTOR THEOREM establishes the relationship between the factors and the zeros or roots of a polynomial and is useful for finding the factors of higher-degree polynomials. The theorem states that a polynomial $P(x)$ has a factor $(x - a)$ if and only if $P(a) = 0$.

Proof

The simplest proof of the Factor Theorem uses a Taylor series expansion. Since a polynomial can be differentiated an infinite number of times. Assume $x = c$ is a root of $P(x)$; write $P(x)$ as a Taylor series expansion.
$$P(x) = P(c) + P'(c)(x - c) + \frac{P''(c)(x - c)^2}{2!} + \frac{P'''(c)(x - c)^3}{3!} + ...$$

Since $x = c$ is a root, $P(c) = 0$. Then,
$$P(x) = P'(c)(x - c) + \frac{P''(c)(x - c)^2}{2!} + \frac{P'''(c)(x - c)^3}{3!} + ...$$

Note that $(x - c)$ is a factor of each term in the Taylor series. Thus, $(x - c)$ must be a factor of $P(x)$. To divide out a factor $(x - c)$ from a polynomial, synthetic division is one potential tool.

The Complex Conjugate Root Theorem

COMPLEX CONJUGATE:
if z is a complex root of $P(x)$, then the complex conjugate of z is also a root of $P(x)$. The complex conjugate of $z = a + bi$ is $\bar{z} = a - bi$

For a polynomial $P(x)$ with real coefficients, if $P(x)$ has a complex root z, then it must also have a complex root $\bar{z}$. (The bar notation indicates COMPLEX CONJUGATE. Thus, if $z = a + bi$, then $\bar{z} = a - bi$.)

Proof

This theorem can be proven easily using the tenets of complex analysis. Of main interest is that the complex conjugate of any function can be found by taking the complex conjugate of each part (that is, each additive or multiplicative term). Assume z is a complex root of $P(x)$. Then,
$$P(z) = a_n z^n + a_{n-1} z^{n-1} + ... + a_2 z^2 + a_1 z + a_0 = 0$$

Take the complex conjugate of $P(z)$. Note that the complex conjugate of zero is zero.

$$\overline{P}(z) = a_n \overline{z}^n + a_{n-1} \overline{z}^{n-1} + \ldots + a_2 \overline{z}^2 + a_1 \overline{z} + a_0 = 0$$

But this is simply $P(\overline{z})$. Thus,

$$\overline{P}(z) = P(\overline{z}) = a_n \overline{z}^n + a_{n-1} \overline{z}^{n-1} + \ldots + a_2 \overline{z}^2 + a_1 \overline{z} + a_0 = 0$$

Then $\overline{z}$ is also a root of the polynomial. If one complex root of a polynomial is known, therefore, the corresponding conjugate root is also known.

The Rational Root Theorem

The RATIONAL ROOT THEOREM, also known as the Rational Zero Theorem, allows determination of all possible rational roots (or zeroes) of a polynomial equation with integer coefficients. (A root is a value of x such that $P(x) = 0$.) Every rational root of $P(x)$ can be written as $x = \frac{p}{q}$, where p is an integer factor of the constant term a_0 and q is an integer factor of the leading coefficient a_n.

RATIONAL ROOT THEOREM: this theorem states that every rational root of the polynomial $P(x)$ can be written as $x = \frac{p}{q}$, where p is an integer factor of the constant term a_0 and q is an integer factor of the leading coefficient a_n

Proof

To prove the Rational Root Theorem, first assume that $x = \frac{p}{q}$ is a root of $P(x)$, where p and q are integers with a greatest common denominator (GCD) of 1. Then:

$$P(\tfrac{p}{q}) = a_n(\tfrac{p}{q})^n + a_{n-1}(\tfrac{p}{q})^{n-1} + \ldots + a_2(\tfrac{p}{q})^2 + a_1(\tfrac{p}{q}) + a_0 = 0$$

Multiply the entire expression by q^n.

$$a_n p^n + a_{n-1} p^{n-1} q + \ldots + a_2 p^2 q^{n-2} + a_1 p q^{n-1} + a_0 q^n = 0$$

Since each coefficient a_i is an integer, as are p and q, each term in the above expression must also be an integer. Consequently, any partial sum of the terms is an integer as well. Rewrite the sum as follows.

$$a_n p^n = -a_{n-1} p^{n-1} q - \ldots - a_2 p^2 q^{n-2} - a_1 p q^{n-1} - a_0 q^n$$

$$a_n p^n = q(-a_{n-1} p^{n-1} q^0 - \ldots - a_2 p^2 q^{n-3} - a_1 p q^{n-2} - a_0 q^{n-1})$$

$$\frac{a_n p^n}{q} = (-a_{n-1} p^{n-1} q^0 - \ldots - a_2 p^2 q^{n-3} - a_1 p q^{n-2} - a_0 q^{n-1})$$

Since p is not divisible by q (the GCD of p and q is 1), a_n must be divisible by q since the sum in the parentheses is an integer. Likewise,

$$a_0 q^n = p(-a_n p^{n-1} - a_{n-1} p^{n-2} q - \ldots - a_2 p^1 q^{n-2} - a_1 q^{n-1})$$

$$\frac{a_0 q^n}{p} = (-a_n p^{n-1} - a_{n-1} p^{n-2} q - \ldots - a_2 p^1 q^{n-2} - a_1 q^{n-1})$$

By the same reasoning, a_0 must be divisible by p. The theorem has thus been proven, since p is a factor of a_0 and q is a factor of a_n.

RATIONAL FUNCTION: this function can be written as the ratio of two polynomial expressions $p(x)$ and $q(x)$, where $q(x)$ is nonzero

Example: Find the rational roots of $P(x) = 3x^3 - 7x^2 + 3x - 2$.

By the Rational Root Theorem, the roots must be of the form

$$x = \mp \frac{1,2}{1,3}$$

The candidates are then

$$x = \pm 1, \ \pm \frac{1}{3}, \ \pm \frac{2}{3}, \ \pm 2$$

Test each possibility. The only result that works is $x = 2$.

Rational functions

A RATIONAL FUNCTION $r(x)$ can be written as the ratio of two polynomial expressions $p(x)$ and $q(x)$, where $q(x)$ is nonzero.

$$r(x) = \frac{p(x)}{q(x)}$$

Examples of rational functions (and their associated expressions) are

$$r(x) = \frac{x^2 + 2x + 4}{x - 3} \quad \text{and} \quad r(x) = \frac{x}{x^2 + 1}$$

Each of these examples is clearly the ratio of two polynomials. The following, however, is also a rational expression.

$$f(x) = \frac{1}{x + \frac{2}{x}}$$

This function can be shown to be a rational expression by converting it to standard form.

$$f(x) = \frac{1}{x + \frac{2}{x}} \cdot \frac{x}{x} = \frac{x}{x^2 + 2}$$

Since rational functions involve a denominator that is a polynomial expression (and not simply a constant), complicated division may be required to evaluate the function. Rational expressions are just like fractions and can be changed into other equivalent fractions through similar methods.

Operations on rational expressions

To reduce a rational expression with more than one term in the denominator, the expression must be factored first. Factors that are the same will cancel. Addition or subtraction of rational expressions may first require finding a common denominator. The first step to this end is to factor the denominators of both expressions to find the common factors. Then, proceed to rewrite the expressions with the common denominator by using the same methods as are used for numerical fractions.

Example: Rewrite the following fraction with a denominator of $(x + 3)$ $(x - 5)(x + 4)$:

$$\frac{x + 2}{x^2 + 7x + 12}$$

First, factor the denominator.

$$\frac{x + 2}{x^2 + 7x + 12} = \frac{x + 2}{(x + 3)(x + 4)}$$

Multiply both the numerator and denominator by $(x - 5)$.

$$\frac{x + 2}{x^2 + 7x + 12} = \frac{x + 2}{(x + 3)(x + 4)} \frac{x - 5}{x - 5} = \frac{(x + 2)(x - 5)}{(x + 3)(x - 5)(x + 4)}$$

Although it is not necessary, the numerator and denominator can be multiplied out to represent the result as a rational expression in terms of polynomials.

$$\frac{x + 2}{x^2 + 7x + 12} = \frac{x^2 - 3x - 10}{x^3 + 2x^2 - 23x - 60}$$

The use of common denominators is helpful for *addition and subtraction of rational expressions*. Multiplication and division of rational expressions follows the standard rules of these operations.

Example: Evaluate the following expression.

$$\frac{5}{x^2 - 9} - \frac{2}{x^2 + 4x + 3}$$

Let the expression above be labeled $f(x)$. First, find the common denominator, then subtract appropriately.

$$f(x) = \frac{5}{(x - 3)(x + 3)} - \frac{2}{(x + 3)(x + 1)}$$

$$f(x) = \frac{5(x + 1)}{(x - 3)(x + 3)(x + 1)} - \frac{2(x - 3)}{(x - 3)(x + 3)(x + 1)}$$

$$f(x) = \frac{5(x + 1) - 2(x - 3)}{(x - 3)(x + 3)(x + 1)} = \frac{5x + 5 - 2x + 6}{(x - 3)(x + 3)(x + 1)}$$

$$f(x) = \frac{3x + 11}{(x - 3)(x + 3)(x + 1)} = \frac{3x + 11}{x^3 + x^2 - 9x - 9}$$

The above expression is the result, both in factored form and in standard form.

Example: Evaluate the following expression.

$$(\frac{x^2 - 2x - 24}{x^2 + 6x + 8})(\frac{x^2 + 3x + 2}{x^2 - 13x + 42})$$

Label the expression as $f(x)$. First, factor each polynomial, simplifying as appropriate, then multiply.

$$f(x) = (\frac{(x - 6)(x + 4)}{(x + 2)(x + 4)})(\frac{(x + 1)(x + 2)}{(x - 6)(x - 7)})$$

$$f(x) = (\frac{(x - 6)}{(x + 2)})(\frac{(x + 1)(x + 2)}{(x - 6)(x - 7)})$$

$$f(x) = \frac{x + 1}{x - 7}$$

Solving equations involving rational expressions

To solve an equation containing rational expressions, set the expression equal to zero (which leads to the elimination of the denominator) and solve, as with simple polynomials.

$$r(x) = 0 = \frac{p(x)}{q(x)}$$

$$p(x) = 0$$

Note, however, that solutions to $p(x) = 0$ may lead to undefined values for $r(x)$ (that is, values for which $q(x) = 0$), and must be checked prior to acceptance.

This difficulty can be alleviated to some extent by factoring $p(x)$ and $q(x)$ and eliminating common factors.

Example: Find the solutions for $\dfrac{12}{2x^2 - 4x} + \dfrac{13}{5} = \dfrac{9}{x - 2}$

Factor and rearrange the equation as follows, then solve for x.

$$\frac{12}{2x(x - 2)} - \frac{9}{x - 2} = -\frac{13}{5}$$

$$\frac{12}{2x(x - 2)} - \frac{9(2x)}{2x(x - 2)} = \frac{-18x + 12}{2x(x - 2)} = -\frac{13}{5}$$

$$-18x + 12 = -\frac{13}{5}2x(x - 2) = -\frac{26}{5}x^2 + \frac{52}{5}x$$

$$\frac{26}{5}x^2 - \frac{52}{5}x - 18x + 12 = 0$$

$$0 = \frac{26}{5}x^2 - \frac{142}{5}x + 12 = 26x^2 - 142x + 60 = 13x^2 - 71x + 30$$

The solutions for x can be found by factoring the above expression.

$$13x^2 - 71x + 30 = (x - 5)(13x - 6) = 0$$

Thus, $x = 5$ or $x = \dfrac{6}{13}$. These solutions can be confirmed by substitution into the original equation.

Graphing rational functions

Rational functions can be graphed with the aid of asymptotes. Rational functions approach asymptotes for large magnitudes of the variable. Setting the denominator equal to zero and solving will give the value(s) of the vertical asymptote(s), since the function will be undefined at such points. If the value of the function approaches b as the absolute value of x increases, the equation $y = b$ is a horizontal asymptote. Horizontal asymptotes can be found using limits (for more on limits, see Competency 6.0). If either

$$\lim_{x \to \infty} f(x) = b \qquad \text{or} \qquad \lim_{x \to -\infty} f(x) = b$$

then b is a horizontal asymptote.

If there is more than one vertical asymptote, remember to choose numbers to the right and left of each asymptote to find the horizontal asymptotes. Also, use a sufficient number of points to graph the function.

Example: Graph the function $f(x) = \dfrac{3x + 1}{x - 2}$.

To find the vertical asymptote, set the denominator equal to zero.

$$x - 2 = 0$$
$$x = 2$$

The horizontal asymptote is (using L'Hopital's rule and taking derivatives of the numerator and denominator—see Competency 6.0):

$$\lim_{x \to \infty} \frac{3x + 1}{x - 2} = \lim_{x \to -\infty} \frac{3x + 1}{x - 2} = 3$$

Next, make a table of values to find the values of appropriate points for the function.

x	f(x)
−4	1.83
−2	1.25
0	−0.5
1	−4
1.5	−11
1.75	−25
2.25	31
2.5	17
3	10
5	5.33
7	4.4

Using this information, sketch the graph. The horizontal and vertical asymptotes are plotted as dashed lines.

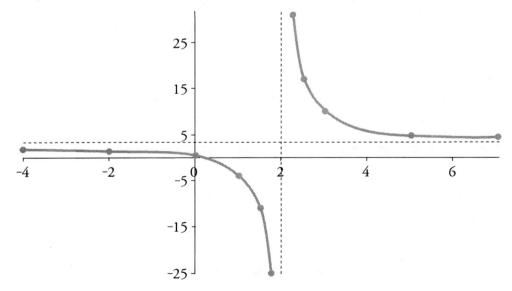

Exponential and logarithmic functions

Exponential and logarithmic functions are complementary. The general relationship for logarithmic and exponential functions is as follows.

$$y = \log_b x \quad \text{if and only if} \quad x = b^y$$

The relationship is as follows for the exponential base e and the natural logarithm (ln).

$$y = \ln x \quad \text{if and only if} \quad e^y = x$$

The following properties of logarithmic are helpful in solving equations.

PROPERTIES OF LOGARITHMS	
Multiplication Property	$\log_b mn = \log_b m + \log_b n$
Quotient Property	$\log_b \frac{m}{n} = \log_b m - \log_b n$
Powers Property	$\log_b n^r = r \log_b n$
Equality Property	$\log_b n = \log_b m$ if and only if $n = m$
Change of Base Formula	$\log_b n = \dfrac{\log_a n}{\log_a b}$ $\log_b b^x = x$ and $b^{\log_b x} = x$

Solving problems involving exponential or logarithmic functions

Solving problems involving exponentials or logarithms typically involves isolating the terms containing the exponential or logarithmic function and using the inverse operation to "extract" the argument. For instance, given the following equation,

$$\ln f(x) = c$$

the function $f(x)$ can be determined by raising e to each side of the equation.

$$e^{\ln f(x)} = f(x) = e^c$$

Alternatively, if the function is in terms of an exponent e,

$$e^{f(x)} = c$$

solve by taking the natural logarithm of both sides.

$$\ln e^{f(x)} = f(x) = \ln c$$

Although these examples are in terms of e and the natural logarithm, the same logic applies to exponentials and logarithms involving different bases as well.

Example: Find the roots of f(x) = ln(x² + 2) − 3.

Set $f(x)$ equal to zero and simplify.

$$f(x) = 0 = \ln(x^2 + 2) - 3$$
$$\ln(x^2 + 2) = 3$$

Raise e to both sides of the equation and solve for x.

$$e^{\ln(x^2 + 2)} = x^2 + 2 = e^3$$
$$x^2 = e^3 - 2$$
$$x = \pm\sqrt{e^3 - 2} \approx \pm 4.252$$

Example: Find the roots of f(x) = e^{-2x²} − 1.

Set $f(x)$ equal to zero and simplify.

$$f(x) = 0 = e^{-2x^2} - 1$$
$$e^{-2x^2} = 1$$

Solve for x by taking the natural logarithm of both sides of the equation.

$$\ln e^{-2x^2} = -2x^2 = \ln 1 = 0$$

The solution is then $x = 0$.

Trigonometric functions

Trigonometric functions and their properties are covered in depth in Competency 4.

> ### SKILL 5.5 Determine the composition of two functions; find the inverse of a one-to-one function in simple cases and know why only one-to-one functions have inverses

Composition of Functions

Composition of functions is way of combining functions such that the range of one function is the domain of another. For instance, the composition of functions f and g can be either $f \circ g$ (the composite of f with g) or $g \circ f$ (the composite of g with f). Another way of writing these compositions is $f(g(x))$ and $g(f(x))$. The domain of the composition includes all values x such that $g(x)$ is in the domain of $f(x)$.

Example: What is the composition f ∘ g for functions f(x) = ax and g(x) = bx²?

The correct answer can be found by substituting the function $g(x)$ into $f \circ g$.

$$f(g(x)) = ag(x) = abx^2$$

On the other hand, the composition $g \circ f$ would yield a different answer.

$$g(f(x)) = b(f(x))^2 = b(ax)^2 = a^2bx^2$$

Inverses of Functions

The inverse of a function $f(x)$ is typically labeled $f^{-1}(x)$ and satisfies the following two relations:

$$f(f^{-1}(x)) = x$$
$$f^{-1}(f(x)) = x$$

For a function f(x) to have an inverse, it must be one-to-one. This fact is easily seen, since both $f(x)$ and $f^{-1}(x)$ must satisfy the vertical line test (that is, both must be functions). A function takes each value in a domain and relates it to only one value in the range. Logically, then, the inverse must do the same, only backwards: relate each value in the range to a single value in the domain.

Finding inverses of functions

Finding the inverse of a function can be a difficult or impossible task, but there are some simple approaches that can be followed in many cases. The simplest method for finding the inverse of a function is to interchange the variable and the function symbols and then solve to find the inverse. The approach is summarized in the outline below, given a one-to-one function $f(x)$.

1. Replace the symbol $f(x)$ with x

2. Replace all instances of x in the function definition with $f^{-1}(x)$ (or y or some other symbol)

3. Solve for $f^{-1}(x)$

4. Check the result using $f(f^{-1}(x)) = x$ or $f^{-1}(f(x)) = x$

Example: Determine if the function f(x) = x² has an inverse. If so, find the inverse.

First, determine if $f(x)$ is one-to-one. Note that $f(1) = f(-1) = 1$, so $f(x)$ is not one-to-one, and it therefore has no inverse function.

Example: Determine if the function f(x) = x³ + 1 has an inverse. If so, find the inverse.

The function $f(x) = x^3 + 1$ has an inverse because it increases monotonically for $x > 0$ and decreases monotonically for $x < 0$. As a result, it is one-to-one, and the inverse exists. To calculate the inverse, let y be $f^{-1}(x)$. Replace $f(x)$ with x and replace x with y.

$$f(x) = x^3 + 1 \rightarrow x = y^3 + 1$$

Solve for y.

$$x - 1 = y^3$$

$$y = \sqrt[3]{x - 1}$$

$$f^{-1}(x) = \sqrt[3]{x - 1}$$

Test the result.

$$f^{-1}(f(x)) = \sqrt[3]{(x^3 + 1) - 1}$$

$$f^{-1}(f(x)) = \sqrt[3]{x^3 + 1 - 1} = \sqrt[3]{(x^3} = x$$

The result is thus correct.

SKILL **Interpret representations of functions of two variables, such as**
5.6 **three-dimensional graphs, level curves, and tables**

Functions of Two Variables

Functions of two variables can be represented in a number of ways, and, although these ways are slightly more complex than those for functions of a single variable, they follow the same fundamental principles.

Graphical representation

A function in two variables (x and y, for instance) is typically represented symbolically as $f(x, y)$. Since $f(x, y)$ represents a value (or height) corresponding to each point(x, y) on the coordinate plane, a standard two-dimensional plot is insufficient. A three-dimensional graph can be created using a perspective drawing with three axes, as shown below. The z-axis can be used to plot the value of $f(x, y)$ for each x and y.

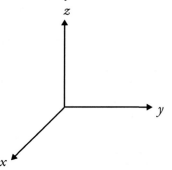

Each point can be plotted by moving the required distance parallel to each axis shown above. The points can then be used to construct a surface that represents the function, as shown in the example below.

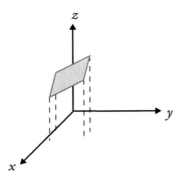

Tables of values

In addition, a function of two variables can be represented using a table of values. Consider, for instance, the function $f(x, y) = \sin xy$. The table below shows one way in which this function can be represented.

TABLE OF VALUES FOR f (x, y) = sin xy		
x	y	$\sin xy$
0	0	0
$\frac{\pi}{4}$	0	0
$\frac{\pi}{2}$	0	0
$\frac{3\pi}{4}$	0	0
π	0	0
$\frac{\pi}{4}$	$\frac{\pi}{4}$	0.578
$\frac{\pi}{2}$	$\frac{\pi}{4}$	0.944
$\frac{3\pi}{4}$	$\frac{\pi}{4}$	0.961
π	$\frac{\pi}{4}$	0.624
$\frac{\pi}{4}$	$\frac{\pi}{2}$	0.944
$\frac{\pi}{2}$	$\frac{\pi}{2}$	0.624
$\frac{3\pi}{4}$	$\frac{\pi}{2}$	−0.531
π	$\frac{\pi}{2}$	−0.975

Alternative arrangements of the values for x and y can be used in a table, but there is typically some form of organization similar to the one shown above. Furthermore, a finer distribution of values for the variables may be used.

Level curves

Another method that can be used to represent a function of two variables is level curves. A set of level curves can be defined by setting the function $f(x, y)$ equal to a set of constants, c. The expression $z = c$ defines a plane in a three-dimensional space, and the level curve is the curve defined by the intersection of the function of interest with the plane at $z = c$. The origin of the level curves is shown graphically below.

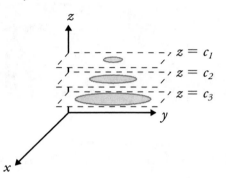

Likewise, the level curves can be plotted in a two-dimensional graph, as shown below.

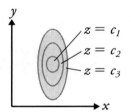

COMPETENCY 6

CALCULUS

Calculus is a mathematical skill that is crucial for solving a wide range of problems. Virtually any problem that involves rates of change or summations over continuously changing variables requires, at some point, the use of calculus. For instance, problems involving the motion of objects (particles) constitute one area in which calculus is used extensively. Various other areas of natural sciences, especially physics, require the use of calculus on a regular basis for modeling physical phenomena and for solving problems.

The development of an understanding of calculus first requires an understanding of limits. The simplest approach is then to build a foundation in differential calculus, followed by integral calculus. Integrals and derivatives are, in some sense, inverse operations.

> ### SKILL Demonstrate an understanding of what it means for a function to
> ### 6.1 have a limit at a point; calculate limits of functions or determine
> ### that the limit does not exist; solve problems using the properties
> ### of limits

Definition of Limit

LIMIT: the limit of a function is the y value that its graph approaches as the value of x approaches a certain number

Informally, the LIMIT of a function is the y value that its graph approaches as the value of x approaches a certain number. The *formal definition of a limit* is as follows.

A function $f(x)$ has a limit L as x approaches the value a, expressed as

$$\lim_{x \to a} f(x) = L$$

if and only if for a given $\varepsilon > 0$ there exists a $\delta > 0$ such that $|f(x) - L| < \varepsilon$ when $0 < |x - a| < \delta$.

This definition essentially means that for a value of x arbitrarily close to a, $f(x)$ must have a value arbitrarily close to L.

Properties of Limits

CONTINUOUS: a function $f(x)$ is continuous at $x = a$ if $\lim_{x \to a} f(x)$ exists and is equal to $f(a)$. This essentially means that the graph of the function $f(x)$ does not have a break (or discontinuity) at $x = a$

A function $f(x)$ is CONTINUOUS at $x = a$ if $\lim_{x \to a} f(x)$ exists and is equal to $f(a)$. This essentially means that the graph of the function $f(x)$ does not have a break (or discontinuity) at $x = a$.

OPERATIONS WITH LIMITS	
Sum Rule for Limits	If $\lim_{x \to a} f(x) = L$, and $\lim_{x \to a} g(x) = M$, then $\lim_{x \to a} (f(x) + g(x)) = L + M$.
	Using the sum rule for limits and the definition of continuity, we can conclude that if functions $f(x)$ and $g(x)$ are continuous at $x = a$—i.e., $L = f(a)$ and $M = g(a)$—then the function $f(x) + g(x)$ is also continuous at $x = a$.

Table continued on next page

Difference Rule for Limits	If $\lim\limits_{x \to a} f(x) = L$, and $\lim\limits_{x \to a} g(x) = M$, then $\lim\limits_{x \to a} (f(x) - g(x)) = L - M$.
	As before, using the difference rule for limits and the definition of continuity, we can conclude that if functions $f(x)$ and $g(x)$ are continuous at $x = a$ then the function $f(x) - g(x)$ is also continuous at $x = a$.
Constant Multiple Rule for Limits	If $\lim\limits_{x \to a} f(x) = L$, then, for any constant c, $\lim\limits_{x \to a} (cf(x)) = cL$.
	Again, we can conclude that if the function $f(x)$ is continuous at $x = a$, then the function $cf(x)$ is also continuous at $x = a$.
Product Rule for Limits	If $\lim\limits_{x \to a} f(x) = L$, and $\lim\limits_{x \to a} g(x) = M$, then, $\lim\limits_{x \to a} (f(x)\,g(x)) = LM$.
	Using the definition of continuity, we can conclude that if the functions $f(x)$ and $g(x)$ are continuous at $x = a$, then the function $f(x)\,g(x)$ is also continuous at $x = a$.
Quotient Rule for Limits	If $\lim\limits_{x \to a} f(x) = L$ and $\lim\limits_{x \to a} g(x) = M$, then $\lim\limits_{x \to a} \dfrac{f(x)}{g(x)} = \dfrac{L}{M}$ for $M \neq 0$.
	We can conclude that if the functions $f(x)$ and $g(x)$ are continuous at $x = a$, then the function $f(x)/g(x)$ is also continuous at $x = a$, provided $g(a)$ is not equal to zero.

Evaluating Limits

In finding a limit, there are two points to remember:

1. Factor the expression completely and cancel all common factors in fractions.

2. Substitute the number that the variable is approaching. In most cases this produces the value of the limit.

If the variable in the limit approaches ∞, factor and simplify first; then examine the result. If the result does not involve a fraction with the variable in the denominator, the limit is usually also equal to ∞. If the variable is in the denominator of the fraction, the denominator is getting larger which makes the entire fraction smaller. In other words, the limit is zero.

Example: Evaluate the following limits.

1. $\lim\limits_{x \to -3} \left(\dfrac{x^2 + 5x + 6}{x + 3} + 4x \right)$

First, factor the numerator. Then cancel the common factors.

$\lim\limits_{x \to -3} \left(\dfrac{(x + 3)(x + 2)}{x + 3} + 4x \right)$

$\lim\limits_{x \to -3} (x + 2 + 4x) = \lim\limits_{x \to -3} (5x + 2)$

$5(-3) + 2 = -15 + 2 = -13$

2. $\lim\limits_{x\to\infty} \dfrac{2x^2}{x^5}$

Cancel the common factors and take the constant outside the limit.

$2\lim\limits_{x\to\infty} \dfrac{1}{x^3}$

Evaluate the limit.

$2\dfrac{1}{\infty^3} = 0$

L'Hopital's Rule

In some cases, the evaluation of a limit yields an undefined result. In some such cases, the limit can be evaluated using an alternative method. L'HOPITAL'S RULE states that a limit can be evaluated by taking the derivative of both the numerator and denominator and then finding the limit of the resulting quotient. This rule is extremely helpful in cases where simple evaluation of a limit leads to an undefined value (positive or negative infinity). Thus, L'Hopital's rule can be expressed as follows.

> **L'HOPITAL'S RULE:** states that a limit can be evaluated by taking the derivative of both the numerator and denominator and then finding the limit of the resulting quotient

$$\lim\limits_{x\to a} \frac{f(x)}{g(x)} = \lim\limits_{x\to a} \frac{f\,'(x)}{g\,'(x)}$$

Example: Evaluate the limit of the function $f(x) = \dfrac{3x - 1}{x^2 + 2x + 3}$ as x approaches infinity.

The limit cannot be evaluated using simple substitution.

$$\lim\limits_{x\to\infty} \frac{3x - 1}{x^2 + 2x + 3} = \frac{3\infty - 1}{\infty^2 + 2\infty + 3} = \frac{\infty}{\infty}$$

Apply L'Hopital's rule by taking the derivative of the numerator and denominator individually.

$$\lim\limits_{x\to\infty} \frac{3x - 1}{x^2 + 2x + 3} = \lim\limits_{x\to\infty} = \frac{3}{2x + 2}$$

$$\lim\limits_{x\to\infty} \frac{3}{2x + 2} = \frac{3}{2\infty + 2} = 0$$

Example: Evaluate the following limit: $\lim\limits_{x\to 1} \dfrac{\ln x}{x - 1}$.

For $x = 1$, the denominator of the function becomes zero, as does the numerator. Therefore, apply L'Hopital's rule to simplify the limit.

$$\lim\limits_{x\to 1} \frac{\ln x}{x - 1} = \lim\limits_{x\to 1} \frac{\frac{1}{x}}{1}$$

$$\lim\limits_{x\to 1} \frac{\ln x}{x - 1} = \lim\limits_{x\to 1} \frac{1}{x} = \frac{1}{1} = 1$$

Derivatives

The derivative of a function has two basic interpretations:

1. Instantaneous rate of change

2. Slope of a tangent line at a given point

The following is a list summarizing some of the more common quantities referred to in rate-of-change problems.

- acceleration
- area
- decay
- distance
- frequency
- height
- population growth

- position
- pressure
- profit
- sales
- temperature
- velocity
- volume

Derivative and slope

The SLOPE of a line is simply the change in the vertical (positive *y*) direction divided by the change in the horizontal (positive *x*) direction. Since the slope of a line is constant over the entire domain of the function, any two points can be used to calculate the slope.

> **SLOPE:** the change in the vertical (positive *y*) direction divided by the change in the horizontal (positive *x*) direction

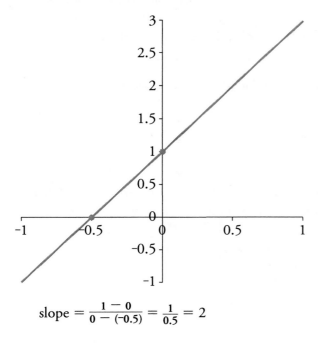

$$\text{slope} = \frac{1 - 0}{0 - (-0.5)} = \frac{1}{0.5} = 2$$

Although the specific approach used for lines cannot be used for curves, it can be used in the general sense if the distance between the points (along the x-axis) becomes zero.

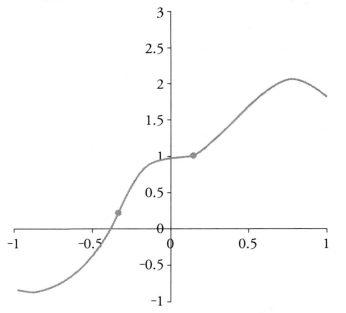

The equation for slope can be written as follows.

$$\text{slope} = \frac{f(x + \Delta x) - f(x)}{\Delta x}$$

This is also known as the difference quotient. For a curve defined by the function f, the DIFFERENCE QUOTIENT computes the slope of the secant line through the two points with x-coordinates x and $x + \Delta x$. If the two points on the line are chosen sufficiently close together so that the function does not vary significantly from the line between those points, then the difference quotient can serve as a good approximation for the slope (and, therefore, for the derivative as well). The difference quotient is used in the definition of the derivative.

Take the limit as Δx goes to zero. This is the definition of the derivative, which is written as either $f'(x)$ or as $\frac{df(x)}{dx}$.

$$f'(x) = \lim_{\Delta x \to 0} \frac{f(x + \Delta x) - f(x)}{\Delta x}$$

This fundamental definition of the derivative can be used to derive formulas for derivatives of specific types of functions. For instance, consider $f(x) = x^2$ Based on this formula, which defines the slope over an infinitesimal width Δx, the derivative can be seen as the instantaneous rate of change of the function.

$$f'(x) = \lim_{\Delta x \to 0} \frac{(x + \Delta x)^2 - x^2}{\Delta x} = \lim_{\Delta x \to 0} \frac{x^2 + 2x\Delta x + \Delta x^2 - x^2}{\Delta x}$$

$$f'(x) = \lim_{\Delta x \to 0} \frac{2x\Delta x + \Delta x^2}{\Delta x} = \lim_{\Delta x \to 0} (2x + \Delta x) = 2x$$

The same approach can be used to show generally, for instance, that $f'(x) = nx^{n-1}$ for $f(x) = x^n$.

The derivative of a function at a point can likewise be interpreted as the slope of a line tangent to the function at that same point. Pick a point (for instance, at $x = -3$) on the graph of a function and draw a tangent line at that point. Find the derivative of the function and substitute the value $x = -3$. This result will be the slope of the tangent line.

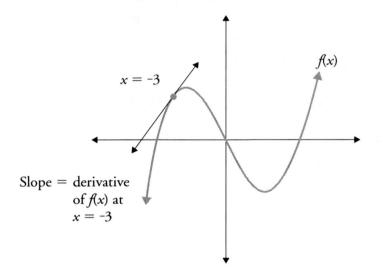

SKILL
6.3

SKILL 6.3 Show that a particular function is continuous; understand the relationship between continuity and differentiability

Continuity

Recall that the continuity of a function is easily understood graphically as the absence of missing points or breaks in the plot of the function. A more rigorous definition can be formulated, however. A function $f(x)$ is continuous at a point c if all of the following apply:

1. The function $f(x)$ is defined at $x = c$

2. The limit $\lim\limits_{x \to c} f(x)$ exists

3. The limit can be found by substitution: $\lim\limits_{x \to c} f(x) = f(c)$

A function can then be called continuous on an open interval (a, b) if the above definition applies to the function for every point c in the interval. The function is also continuous at the points $x = a$ and $x = b$ if $\lim\limits_{x \to a} f(x) = f(a)$ and $\lim\limits_{x \to b^-} f(x) = f(b)$ both exist. (The $+/-$ notation simply signifies approaching the limiting value from either the right or left, respectively.) If both of these conditions apply, then the function is continuous on the closed interval [a, b].

To check whether the limit of a function exists, make sure that

$$\lim_{x \to c^+} f(x) = \lim_{x \to c} f(x)$$

That is, the limit as x approaches c from the left must be equal to the limit as x approaches c from the right.

If it is necessary to determine whether a function is continuous over an open or closed interval, the above approach must be shown to generally apply to every point in that interval (excluding the endpoints for an open interval, but including the endpoints for a closed interval). It is often helpful to look at the graph of the function to help determine if there are any discontinuities. The graph can, at least, reveal any points that must be checked specifically.

> To demonstrate that a function is continuous at a point, check that
> 1. The function is defined at the point
> 2. The limit exists
> 3. If the limit does exist and is equal to the value of the function evaluated at the point, then the function is continuous at that point

Example: Determine whether the function ln x is continuous over the closed interval [0, 1].

One approach is to look at a plot of the function.

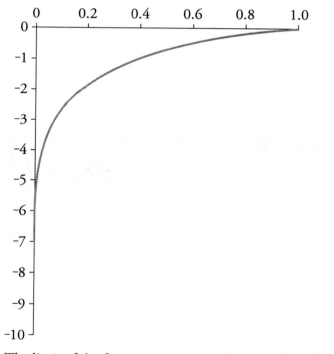

The limit of the function as x approaches zero from the right does not exist. Algebraically, this can be seen by noting that the equation $\ln x = L$ is the same as the equation $e^L = x$. For $x = 0$, the only possible value of L that satisfies this equation is $-\infty$. In other words,

$$\lim_{x \to 0} \ln x = -\infty$$

The limit does not exist, therefore, and the function is not continuous on the closed interval [0, 1]. The function is continuous on the open interval (0, 1), however. (It is also continuous on the half-open interval (0, 1].) Note that, for all $x > 0$, x is defined, and for $c > 0$,

$$\lim_{x \to c} \ln x = \ln c$$

Thus, $\ln x$ is continuous over $(0, \infty)$.

Example: Determine if the function shown in the graph is continuous at
x = 2.

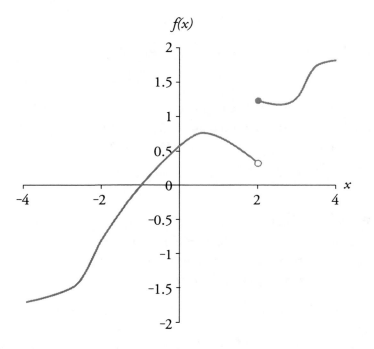

By inspection, it can be seen that the limits of the function as x approaches 2 from the right and left are not equal.

$$\lim_{x \to 2^+} f(x) \neq \lim_{x \to 2} f(x)$$

As a result, the function does not meet all of the criteria for continuity at $x = 2$ and is therefore discontinuous.

Example: Determine whether the following function is continuous at

$$x = 1 : f(x) = \begin{cases} x^2 & x \neq 1 \\ 0 & x = 1 \end{cases}$$

The plot of this piecewise function is shown below.

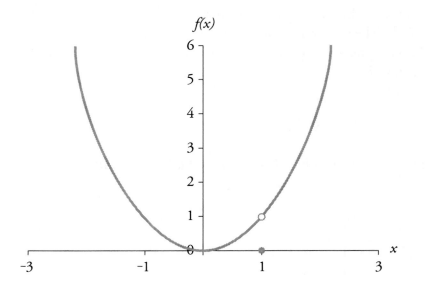

In this case, the function is defined at $x = 1$, and the limits of $f(x)$ as x approaches 1 from both the right and from the left are both equal to 1. Nevertheless, it is not the case that $\lim_{x \to 1} f(x) = f(1)$, since $\lim_{x \to 1} f(x) = 1$ and $f(1) = 0$. Thus, the function is not continuous at $x = 1$.

Differentiability of a Function

If the derivative of a function exists at x, then the function is said to be DIFFER-ENTIABLE at x. Further, if the function is differentiable at every point in an open interval (a, b), then the function is said to be differentiable on (a, b).

For a function to be differentiable at x, the limit of the difference quotient at x must exist. That is to say,

$$\lim_{\Delta x \to 0} \frac{f(x + \Delta x) - f(x)}{\Delta x}$$

must exist. A test of the existence of this limit is examination of the one-sided limits on either side of x. Consider the function at $x = c$. To determine whether the function is differentiable, determine if the following equation is valid:

$$\lim_{x \to c^+} \frac{f(x) - f(c)}{x - c} = \lim_{x \to c} \frac{f(c) - f(x)}{c - x}$$

The left side of the equation is the limit as x approaches c from the right. The right side of the equation is the limit as x approaches c from the left. Only if these two limits exist and are equal is the function differentiable at c.

Consider the following function. Although the limits of the difference quotients both exist, they are different on either side of the point at $x = -1$. As a result, the function is not differentiable at $x = -1$.

> **DIFFERENTIABLE:**
> If the derivative of a function exists at x, then the function is said to be differentiable at x

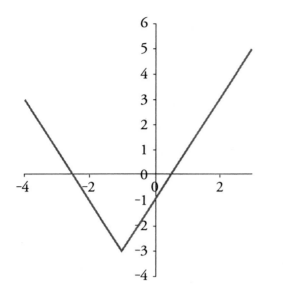

In addition to the existence and equality of both one-sided limits, a function must also be continuous at a point to be differentiable. In the above case, the function is continuous at $x = -1$, but the two one-sided limits are not equal. In the following case, the function is not continuous at $x = 1$, and, therefore, is not differentiable at this point.

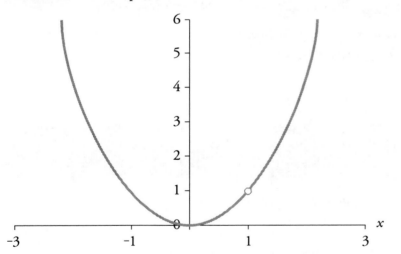

A function is continuous at a point if the function is defined at the point, the limit of the function as x approaches the corresponding value exists and the limit is equal to the function evaluated at the point. The function depicted in the above graph is not defined at $x = 1$. Nevertheless, even if the function is defined, as shown below, it can still be discontinuous.

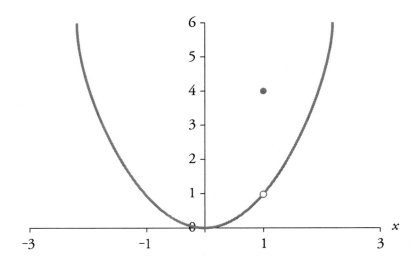

The function above would still not be differentiable at $x = 1$.

SKILL 6.4

Numerically approximate derivatives and integrals

For information on numerically approximating derivatives, see Skill 6.5; for information on numerically approximating integrals, see Skill 6.8

SKILL 6.5

Use standard differentiation and integration techniques

For information on integration techniques, see Skill 6.8

Properties of the Derivative

The following properties of the derivative allow for differentiation of a wide range of functions (although the process of differentiation may be more or less difficult, depending on the complexity of the function). For illustration, consider two arbitrary functions, $f(x)$ and $g(x)$, and an arbitrary constant, c.

DIFFERENTIATION RULES	
Rule for Multiplicative Constants	$\frac{d}{dx}(cf) = cf'$
Sum and Difference Rules	$\frac{d}{dx}(f + g) = f' + g'$ $\frac{d}{dx}(f - g) = f' - g'$
Product Rule	$\frac{d}{dx}(fg) = fg' + gf'$
Quotient Rule	$\frac{d}{dx}\left(\frac{f}{g}\right) = \frac{gf' - fg'}{g^2}$
Chain Rule	$\frac{df}{dx} = \frac{df}{du}\frac{du}{dx}$

The chain rule, as expressed above, allows for differentiation of composite functions. The variable u can be an independent variable or it can be a function (of x). Note that the differential elements du in the denominator of the first factor and in the numerator of the second factor can otherwise cancel, making the right side of the equation identical to the left side.

Derivation of Differentiation Rules

As mentioned previously, the formal definition of the derivative can be used to determine the general form of the derivative for certain families of functions. The formal definition of the derivative is expressed in terms of the limit of a difference quotient, as given below.

$$f'(x) = \lim_{\Delta x \to 0} \frac{f(x + \Delta x) - f(x)}{\Delta x}$$

Using this definition, the derivatives of algebraic functions (including, for instance, polynomial, trigonometric and logarithmic functions) can be derived. In addition, the general differentiation rules above can also be derived by applying in each case the properties of limits to the definition given above.

The use of the formal definition in deriving a general rule of differentiation for a family of functions is best illustrated by way of an example. Consider polynomial functions, as mentioned previously. Note that the sum and difference rules for differentiation, along with the multiplicative constant rule, allow polynomials to be differentiated on a term-by-term basis. Thus, it suffices to simply derive the rule for differentiating the generic term x^n, where n is a constant and x is the variable of the function. Use the formal definition of the derivative given above and substitute this algebraic term for $f(x)$ (that is, use $f(x) = x^n$).

$$f'(x) = \lim_{\Delta x \to 0} \frac{(x + \Delta x)^n - (x)^n}{\Delta x}$$

Simplify the expression and apply the binomial expansion to the result.

$$f'(x) = \lim_{\Delta x \to 0} \frac{1}{\Delta x} [(x + \Delta x)^n - x^n]$$

$$f'(x) = \lim_{\Delta x \to 0} = \frac{1}{\Delta x} [\binom{n}{0}x^n + \binom{n}{1}x^{n-1} \Delta x + \binom{n}{2}x^{n-2} (\Delta x)^2 + ... + \binom{n}{n}(\Delta x)^n - x^n]$$

In the above expression, the combinatorial form $\binom{n}{k}$ represents the number of combinations of n objects taken k at a time, or $\frac{n!}{k!(n-k)!}$.

$$f'(x) = \lim_{\Delta x \to 0} \frac{1}{\Delta x} [x^n + nx^{n-1}\Delta x + \binom{n}{2}x^{n-2} (\Delta x)^2 + ... + (\Delta x)^n - x^n]$$

$$f'(x) = \lim_{\Delta x \to 0} \frac{1}{\Delta x} [nx^{n-1}\Delta x + \binom{n}{2}x^{n-2} (\Delta x)^2 + ... + (\Delta x)^n]$$

$$f'(x) = \lim_{\Delta x \to 0} [nx^{n-1} + \binom{n}{2}x^{n-2} \Delta x + ... + (\Delta x)^{n-1}]$$

Note that, with the exception of the first term, all the terms in the brackets have a factor Δx. Thus, when the limit is applied, these terms all become zero, leaving the result of the differentiation.

$$f'(x) = nx^{n-1}$$

This is the well-known rule for differentiating polynomial terms with exponent n.

Example: Find the first derivative of the function $y = 5x^4$.

$$\frac{dy}{dx} = (5)(4)x^{4-1}$$

$$\frac{dy}{dx} = 20x^3$$

Example: Find y' where $y = \frac{1}{4x^3}$.

First, rewrite the function using a negative exponent, then apply the differentiation rule.

$$y' = \frac{1}{4}x^{-3}$$

$$y' = \frac{1}{4}(-3)x^{-3-1}$$

$$y' = -\frac{3}{4}x^{-4} = -\frac{3}{4x^4}$$

Example: Find the first derivative of $y = 3\sqrt{x^5}$.

Rewrite using $\sqrt[z]{x^n} = x^{n/z}$, then take the derivative.

$$y = 3x^{\frac{5}{2}}$$

$$\frac{dy}{dx} = (3)\left(\frac{5}{2}\right)x^{\frac{5}{2}-1}$$

$$\frac{dy}{dx} = \left(\frac{15}{2}\right)x^{\frac{3}{2}}$$

$$\frac{dy}{dx} = 7.5\sqrt{x^3} = 7.5x\sqrt{x}$$

The derivatives of other families of functions can be found in a similar manner. Below is a summary of the rules of differentiation for various transcendental (including trigonometric, logarithmic and exponential) functions.

SUMMARY OF DIFFERENTIATION RULES FOR TRANSCENDENTAL FUNCTIONS	
$\frac{d}{dx}\sin x = \cos x$	$\frac{d}{dx}\csc x = -\csc x \cot x$
$\frac{d}{dx}\cos x = -\sin x$	$\frac{d}{dx}\sec x = \sec x \tan x$
$\frac{d}{dx}\tan x = \sec^2 x$	$\frac{d}{dx}\cot x = -\csc^2 x$
$\frac{d}{dx}\arcsin x = \dfrac{1}{\sqrt{1 - x^2}}$	$\frac{d}{dx}\operatorname{arc\,csc} x = -\dfrac{1}{\lvert x \rvert \sqrt{x^2 - 1}}$
$\frac{d}{dx}\operatorname{arccccos} x = -\dfrac{1}{\sqrt{1 - x^2}}$	$\frac{d}{dx}\operatorname{arc\,sec} x = \dfrac{1}{\lvert x \rvert \sqrt{x^2 - 1}}$
$\frac{d}{dx}\arctan x = \dfrac{1}{1 + x^2}$	$\frac{d}{dx}\operatorname{arc\,cot} x = -\dfrac{1}{1 + x^2}$
$\frac{d}{dx}\ln x = \frac{1}{x}$	$\frac{d}{dx}e^x = e^x$

Example: Find the derivative of the function $y = 4e^{x^2} \sin x$.

Apply the appropriate rules (product and chain rules) to the function.

$$\frac{dy}{dx} = 4\left(\sin x \frac{d}{dx}e^{x^2} + e^{x^2}\frac{d}{dx}\sin x\right)$$

$$\frac{dy}{dx} = 4\left(\sin x\left[2xe^{x^2}\right] + e^{x^2}\cos x\right)$$

$$\frac{dy}{dx} = 8xe^{x^2}\sin x + 4e^{x^2}\cos x$$

Example: Find the derivative of the function $y = \dfrac{5}{e^{\sin x}}$.

Rewrite the function with a negative exponent and use the chain rule.

$$y = 5e^{-\sin x}$$

$$\frac{dy}{dx} = 5\frac{d}{dx}e^{-\sin x}$$

$$\frac{dy}{dx} = 5e^{-\sin x}\left[-\cos x\right]$$

$$\frac{dy}{dx} = -5e^{-\sin x}\cos x = -\frac{5\cos x}{e^{\sin x}}$$

Finding Slope of a Tangent Line at a Point

Using these properties of derivatives, the slopes (and therefore equations) of tangent lines can be found for a wide range of functions. The procedure simply involves finding the slope of the function at the given point using the derivative, then determining the equation of the line using point-slope form.

Example: Find the slope of the tangent line for the given function at the given point: $y = \frac{1}{x-2}$ at (3, 1).

Find the derivative of the function.

$$y' = \frac{d}{dx}(x - 2)^{-1}$$
$$y' = (-1)(x - 2)^{-2}(1) = -\frac{1}{(x - 2)^2}$$

Evaluate the derivative at $x = 3$:

$$y' = -\frac{1}{(3 - 2)^2} = -1$$

Thus, the slope of the function at the point is -1.

Example: Find the points at which the tangent to the curve $f(x) = 2x^2 + 3x$ is parallel to the line $y = 11x - 5$.

For the tangent line to be parallel to the given line, the only condition is that the slopes are equal. Thus, find the derivative of f, set the result equal to 11, and solve for x.

$$f'(x) = 4x + 3 = 11$$
$$4x = 8$$
$$x = 2$$

To find the y value of the point, simply substitute 2 into f.

$$f(2) = 2(2)^2 + 3(2) = 8 + 6 = 14$$

Thus, the tangent to f is parallel to $y = 11x - 5$ at the point (2, 14) only.

Example: Find the equation of the tangent line to $f(x) = 2e^{x^2}$ at $x = -1$.

To find the tangent line, a point and a slope are needed. The x value of the point is given; the y value can be found by substituting $x = -1$ into f.

$$f(-1) = 2e^{(-1)^2} = 2e$$

Thus, the point is (-1, 2e). The slope is found by substituting -1 into the derivative of f.

$$f'(x) = 2e^{x^2}(2x) = 4xe^{x^2}$$
$$f'(-1) = 4(-1)e^{(-1)^2} = -4e$$

Use the point-slope form of the line to determine the correct equation.

$$y - 2e = -4e(x - [-1])$$
$$y = 2e - 4ex - 4e = -4ex - 2e$$

Thus, the equation of the line tangent to f at $x = -1$ is $y = -4ex - 2e$.

Analyze the behavior of a function (e.g., *find relative maxima and minima, concavity)*; **solve problems involving related rates; solve applied minima-maxima problems**

Differential calculus can be a helpful tool in analyzing functions and the graphs of functions. Derivatives deal with the slope (or rate of change) of a function, and this information can be used to calculate the locations and values of extrema (maxima and minima) and inflection points, as well as to determine information concerning concavity.

Extrema

The concept of EXTREMA (maxima and minima) can be differentiated into local (or relative) and global (or absolute) extrema. For instance, consider the following function:

EXTREMA: the minimum and maximum values of a function

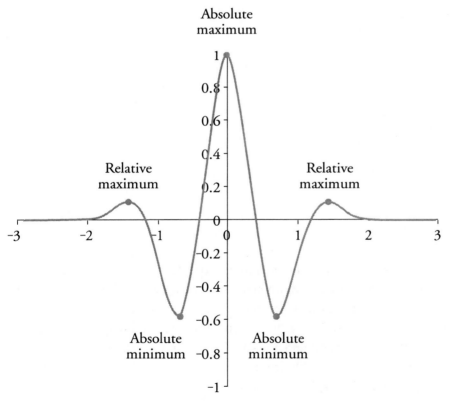

It is apparent that there are a number of peaks and valleys, each of which could, in some sense, be called a maximum or minimum. To allow for greater clarity, local and global extrema can be specified. For instance, the peak at $x = 0$ is the maximum for the entire function. Additionally, the valleys at about $x = \pm 0.7$

RELATIVE EXTREMA:
extreme values of a function over some limited interval

CRITICAL POINTS:
the points at which the derivative of a function is equal to zero

CRITICAL NUMBERS:
the critical numbers of a function are the x-values at which the derivative of the function is equal to zero.

The derivative of a function at an extremum is zero. However, not every point at which the derivative is zero is an extremum.

both correspond to an (equivalent) minimum for the entire function. These are absolute extrema. On the other hand, the peaks at about $x = \pm 1.4$ are each a maximum for the function within a specific area; thus, they are relative maxima. RELATIVE EXTREMA are extreme values of a function over some limited interval. The points at which the derivative of a function is equal to zero are called CRITICAL POINTS (the *x* values are called CRITICAL NUMBERS).

By inspection of any graph, it is apparent that all extrema (where the function is continuous on either side of the maximum or minimum point) are located at points where the slope of the function is zero. That is to say, the derivative of the function at an extremum is zero. It is not necessarily the case, however, that all points where the derivative of the function is zero correspond to extrema. Consider the function $y = x^3$, whose graph is shown below.

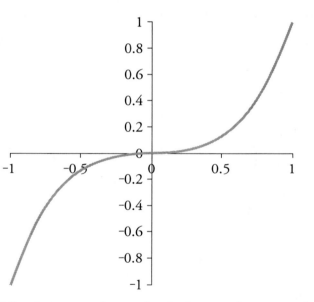

The derivative of y is $3x^2$, which is equal to zero only at $x = 0$. Nevertheless, the function y does not have an extremum at $x = 0$. The only cases for which critical points correspond to extrema are when the derivative of the function actually crosses the *x*-axis. These cases correspond to the function having a positive slope on one side of the critical point and a negative slope on the other. This is a requirement for an extremum. (Notice that, for the plot of $y = x^3$, the function has a positive slope on both sides of the critical point.)

A positive slope on the left side of a critical point and a negative slope on the right side indicate that the critical point is a maximum. If the slope is negative on the left and positive on the right, then the critical point corresponds to a minimum. If the slopes on either side are both positive or both negative, then there is no extremum at the critical point.

Extremum and the second derivative

Whether a critical point is an extremum can be determined using the second derivative f''. A critical point corresponds to a point at which the function f has zero slope. Thus, f' is zero at these points. As noted above, f has an extremum at the critical point only if f' crosses the x-axis. If f' is zero at a point but does not cross the x-axis, then that point is either a maximum or minimum of the function f', i.e., a critical number of f' ($f'' = 0$). As a result, if the critical number of f is also a critical number of f' (i.e., $f'' = 0$), the critical point does not correspond to an extremum of f. The procedure for finding extrema for $f(x)$ is thus as follows.

1. Calculate $f'(x)$.

2. Solve $f'(x) = 0$; the solutions of this equation are the critical numbers.

3. Calculate $f''(x)$.

4. Evaluate $f''(x)$ for each critical number c. If:

   a. $f''(c) = 0$, the critical point is not an extremum of f.

   b. $f''(c) > 0$, the critical point is a minimum of f.

   c. $f''(c) < 0$ the critical point is a maximum of f.

Example: Find the maxima and minima of $f(x) = 2x^4 - 4x^2$ on the closed interval $[-2, 1]$.

First, differentiate the function and set the result equal to zero.
$$\frac{df}{dx} = 8x^3 - 8x = 0$$

Next, solve by factoring to find the critical numbers.
$$8x(x^2 - 1) = 0$$
$$x(x - 1)(x + 1) = 0$$

The solutions for this equation, which are also the critical numbers, are $x = -1$, 0, and 1. For each critical number, it is necessary to determine whether the point corresponds to a maximum, a minimum, or neither.
$$\frac{d^2f}{dx^2} = 24x^2 - 8$$

Test each critical point by substituting into the result above.
$$f''(-1) = 24(-1)^2 - 8 = 24 - 8 = 16 \rightarrow \text{minimum}$$
$$f''(0) = 24(0)^2 - 8 = -8 \rightarrow \text{maximum}$$
$$f''(1) = 24(1)^2 - 8 = 24 - 8 = 16 \rightarrow \text{minimum}$$

The critical numbers correspond to the minima $(-1, -2)$ and $(1, -2)$, and to the maximum $(0, 0)$. The endpoint of the closed interval at $x = -2$ should also be tested to determine if it constitutes an extremum, as such may not be detectable using derivatives (the minimum at the endpoint $x = 1$ was detected, however). This endpoint corresponds to (-2, 16), which is the absolute maximum. Absolute minima exist at (-1, -2) and (1, -2), and a relative maximum exists at (0, 0).

Concavity

The second derivative of a function can also be viewed in terms of concavity. The first derivative reveals whether a curve is increasing or decreasing (increasing or decreasing) from the left to the right. In much the same way, the second derivative relates whether the curve is concave up (slope increasing) or concave down (slope decreasing). Curves that are concave up can be viewed as "collecting water"; curves that are concave down can be viewed as "dumping water."

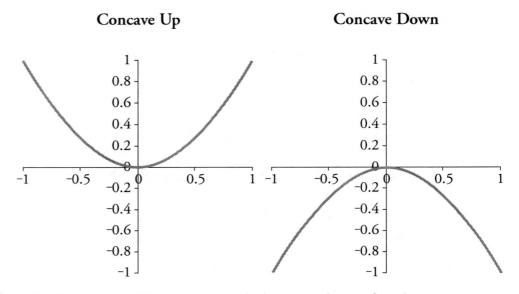

Concave Up | Concave Down

A POINT OF INFLECTION is a point at which a curve changes from being concave up to concave down (or vice versa). To find these points, find the critical numbers of the first derivative of the function (that is, solve the equation for which the second derivative of the function is set equal to zero). A critical number coincides with an inflection point if the curve is concave up on one side of the value and concave down on the other. The critical number is the x coordinate of the inflection point. To get the y coordinate, plug the critical number into the original function.

Example: Find the inflection points of f(x) = 2x − tan x over the interval
$-\frac{\pi}{2} < x < \frac{\pi}{2}$.

First, calculate the second derivative of f.

$$f''(x) = \frac{d^2 f(x)}{dx^2} = \frac{d}{dx}\left[\frac{d}{dx}(2x - \tan x)\right]$$

$$f''(x) = \frac{d}{dx}\left[2 - \sec^2 x\right] = -2\sec x \frac{d}{dx}\sec x$$

$$f''(x) = -2\sec x (\sec x \tan x) = -2\sec^2 x \tan x$$

Set the second derivative equal to zero and solve.

$$f''(x) = -2\sec^2 x \tan x = 0$$

The function is zero for either $\sec x = 0$ or $\tan x = 0$. Only $\tan x = 0$, however, has real solutions. This means that the inflection points are at $x = n\pi$, where $n = 0, 1, 2, \ldots$. Within the given interval, however, the only solution is $x = 0$. Substituting this value into the original equation yields the following:

$$f(0) = 2(0) - \tan 0 = 0 - 0 = 0$$

Thus, the inflection point for this function on the interval $-\frac{\pi}{2} < x < \frac{\pi}{2}$ is $(0, 0)$. The plot of the function is shown below, along with the associated inflection point. As hinted earlier, the inflection point can be seen graphically as the point at which the slope changes from an increasing value to a decreasing value (or vice versa).

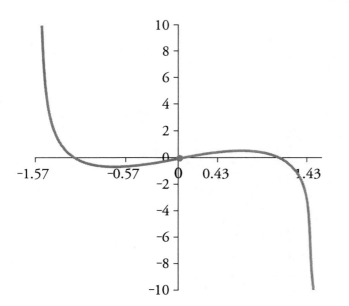

Example: Identify approximately the locations of the extrema (excluding the endpoints) and inflection points for the following graph.

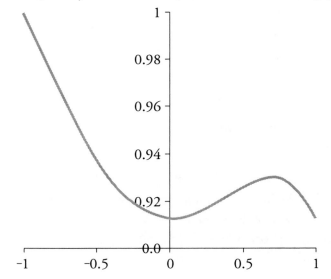

There are two obvious extrema in the graph: a minimum at about (0, .915) and a maximum at about (0.7, 0.93). These extrema are evidently relative extrema, since the function (at least apparently) has both larger and smaller values elsewhere. There is also an obvious concavity shift between the maximum and minimum. The inflection point is at about (0.35, 0.92). The extrema and inflection points are shown marked below.

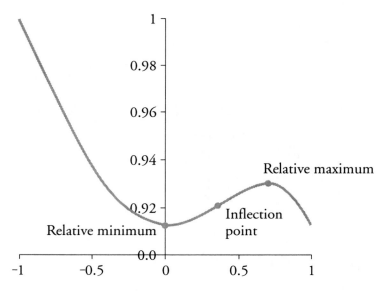

Optimization Problems

Extreme value problems, also known as max-min problems or optimization problems, entail using the first derivative to find values that either maximize or minimize some quantity, such as area, profit, or volume. The derivative is a critical tool in solving these types of problems. Follow these steps to solve an extreme value (optimization) problem.

1. Write an equation for the quantity to be maximized or minimized.

2. Use the other information in the problem to write secondary equations.

3. Use the secondary equations for substitutions, and rewrite the original equation in terms of only one variable.

4. Find the derivative of the primary equation (step 1) and the critical numbers of this derivative.

5. Substitute these critical numbers into the primary equation. The value that produces either the largest or smallest result can be used to find the solution.

Example: A manufacturer wishes to construct an open box from a square piece of metal by cutting squares from each corner and folding up the sides. The metal is 12 feet on each side. What are the dimensions of the squares to be cut out such that the volume of the box is maximized?

First, draw a figure that represents the situation. Assume that the squares to be cut from the metal have sides of length x. Noting that the metal has sides of length 12 feet, this leaves $12 - 2x$ feet remaining on each side after the squares are cut out.

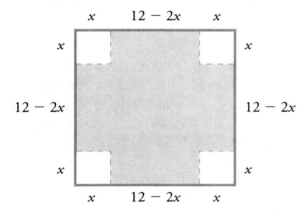

The volume $V(x)$ of the box formed when the sides are folded up is the following:

$$V(x) = x(12 - 2x)^2$$

Simplify and take the first derivative of the result.

$$V(x) = x(144 - 48x + 4x^2) = 4x^3 - 48x^2 + 144x$$
$$V'(x) = 12x^2 - 96x + 144$$

Set the first derivative to zero and solve by factoring.

$$V'(x) = 12x^2 - 96x + 144 = 0$$
$$(x - 6)(x - 2) = 0$$

The solutions are then $x = 2$ feet and $x = 6$ feet. Note that if $x = 6$ feet, the sides of the box become zero in width. This, therefore, is not a legitimate solution. Choose $x = 2$ feet as the solution that leads to the largest volume of the box.

Problems Involving Rectilinear Motion

If a particle (such as a car, bullet, or other object) is moving along a line, then the position of the particle can be expressed as a function of time.

The first derivative of the position function yields the velocity function.

The rate of change of position with respect to time is the velocity of the object; thus, the first derivative of the position function yields the velocity function for the particle. Substituting a value for time into this expression provides the instantaneous velocity of the particle at that time. The absolute value of the derivative is the speed (magnitude of the velocity) of the particle. A positive value for the velocity indicates that the particle is moving forward (that is, in the positive x direction); a negative value indicates the particle is moving backward (that is, in the negative x direction).

The second derivative of the position function (which is also the first derivative of the velocity function) yields the acceleration function.

The acceleration of the particle is the rate of change of the velocity. The second derivative of the position function (which is also the first derivative of the velocity function) yields the acceleration function. If a value for time produces a positive acceleration, the particle's velocity is increasing; if it produces a negative value, the particle's velocity is decreasing. If the acceleration is zero, the particle is moving at a constant speed.

Example: A particle moves along a line according to the equation $s(t) = 20 + 3t - 5t^2$, where s is in meters and t is in seconds. Find the position, velocity, and acceleration of the particle at t = 2 seconds.

To find the position, simply use $t = 2$ in the given position function. Note that the initial position of the particle is $s(0) = 20$ meters.

$$s(2) = 20 + 3(2) - 5(2)^2$$
$$s(2) = 20 + 6 - 20 = 6\text{m}$$

To find the velocity of the particle, calculate the first derivative of $s(t)$ and then evaluate the result for $t = 2$ seconds.

$$s'(t) = v(t) = 3 - 10t$$
$$v(2) = 3 - 10(2) = 3 - 20 = \text{-17m/s}$$

Finally, for the acceleration of the particle, calculate the second derivative of $s(t)$ (also equal to the first derivative of $v(t)$) and evaluate for $t = 2$ seconds.

$$s''(t) = v'(t) = a(t) = \text{-10m/s}^2$$

Since the acceleration function $a(t)$ is a constant, the acceleration is always -10m/s^2 (the velocity of the particle decreases every second by 10 meters per second).

Related Rate Problems

Some rate problems may involve functions with different parameters that are each dependent on time. In such a case, implicit differentiation may be required. Often times, related rate problems give certain rates in the description, thus eliminating the need to have specific functions of time for every parameter. Related rate problems are otherwise solved in the same manner as other similar problems.

Example: A spherical balloon is inflated such that its radius is increasing at a constant rate of 1 inch per second. What is the rate of increase of the volume of the balloon when the radius is 10 inches?

First, write the equation for the volume of a sphere in terms of the radius, r.

$$V(r) = \frac{4}{3}\pi r^3$$

Differentiate the function implicitly with respect to time, t, by using the chain rule.

$$\frac{dV(r)}{dt} = \frac{4}{3}\pi \frac{d}{dt}(r^3)$$

$$\frac{dV(r)}{dt} = \frac{4}{3}\pi (3r^2)\frac{dr}{dt} = 4\pi r^2 \frac{dr}{dt}$$

To find the solution to the problem, use the radius value $r = 10$ inches and the rate of increase of the radius $\frac{dr}{dt} = 1$in/sec. Calculate the resulting rate of increase of the volume, $\frac{dV(r)}{dt}$.

$$\frac{dV(10)}{dt} = 4\pi(10\text{in})^2\,1\text{in/sec} = 400\pi\text{in}^3/\text{sec} \approx 1257 \text{ in}^3/\text{sec}$$

The problem is thus solved.

SKILL 6.7 Demonstrate an understanding of and the ability to use the Mean Value Theorem and the Fundamental Theorem of Calculus

The Mean Value Theorem

The MEAN VALUE THEOREM states that there is some point c on the curve of any function f between $x = a$ and $x = b$ at which the derivative of f is equal to the slope of the secant line defined by these points. The slope m of the secant line is expressed as follows.

$$m = \frac{f(b) - f(a)}{b - a}$$

MEAN VALUE THEOREM: this theorem states that there is some point *c* on the curve of any function *f* between *x* = *a* and *x* = *b* at which the derivative of f is equal to the slope of the secant line defined by these points

To find the point or points at which the tangent line is parallel to the secant line formed by connecting points $(a, f(a))$ and $(b, f(b))$, set the derivative of f equal to m and solve for c. The Mean Value Theorem is thus expressed mathematically as follows.

$$f'(c) = \frac{f(b) - f(a)}{b - a}$$

The Mean Value Theorem is useful in instances where, for example, a problem refers to average rates of change.

Example: Prove that if the rate of change of a function is zero over an interval, the function is also constant over the interval.

Let the function be defined as $f(x)$, where the first derivative is $f'(x)$. If the rate of change of the function is zero over the interval, then $f'(x) = 0$ for all x on the interval. Apply the Mean Value Theorem for some $x = c$ between $x = a$ and $x = b$ for any values a and b in the interval:

$$f'(c) = 0 = \frac{f(b) - f(a)}{b - a}$$

Simplify:

$$0 = f(b) - f(a)$$
$$f(a) = f(b)$$

Thus, for any two values a and b in the interval at which the derivative of the function is zero, the function is constant. In other words, by the Mean Value Theorem, the function is constant over the interval.

The Fundamental Theorem of Calculus

The FUNDAMENTAL THEOREM OF CALCULUS relates differentiation with definite integration, which is fundamentally defined in terms of the Riemann sum. (For more information on integration and Riemann sums, see Skill 6.8.) According to the theorem, definite integration is the inverse of differentiation. The theorem is expressed below for the function $F(x)$, where $f(x) = F'(x)$ and where $f(x)$ is continuous on the interval $[a, b]$.

$$\int_a^b f(x)dx = F(b) - F(a)$$

The function $F(x)$ is also called an ANTIDERIVATIVE of $f(x)$, because the derivative of $F(x)$ is $f(x)$. Based on this theorem, it is clear that integrals can be evaluated without finding the limit of a Riemann sum as long as the antiderivative of a function can be determined. Thus, the key to evaluating definite integrals is knowing how to find the antiderivative of a function.

The definite integral can thus be interpreted in terms of antiderivatives. Note that the definite integral for the interval $[a, b]$ is the area under the curve $f(x)$ between

FUNDAMENTAL THEOREM OF CALCULUS: this theorem states that definite integration is the inverse of differentiation

ANTIDERIVATIVE: the function $F(x)$ is called an antiderivative of $f(x)$ if the derivative of $F(x)$ is $f(x)$

$x = a$ and $x = b$. The antiderivative, $F(c)$, is then the cumulative area under $f(x)$ between $x = 0$ and $x = c$. Thus, the difference between the antiderivative evaluated at b and the antiderivative evaluated at a is the definite integral of $f(x)$ between a and b.

The example graph below shows a function $f(x)$. The antiderivative $F(x)$ evaluated at $x = 1$ is the solid shaded area; the antiderivative evaluated at $x = 2$ is the striped area. The difference $F(2) - F(1)$ is the difference between the two areas (the non-overlapping striped region).

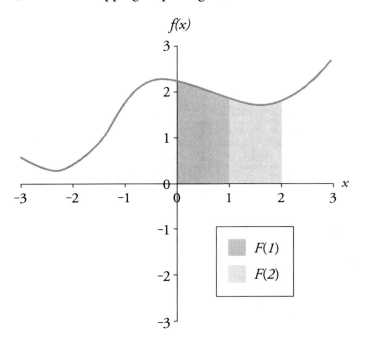

Demonstrate an intuitive understanding of integration as a limiting sum that can be used to compute area, volume, distance, or other accumulation processes

Riemann Sums

The formal definition of an integral is based on the Riemann sum. A RIEMANN SUM is the sum of the areas of a set of rectangles that is used to approximate the area under the curve of a function. Given a function f defined over some closed interval $[a, b]$, the interval can be divided into a set of n arbitrary partitions, each of length Δx_i. Within the limits of each partition, some value $x = c_i$ can be chosen such that Δx_i and $f(c_i)$ define the width and height (respectively) of a rectangle. The sum of the aggregate of all the rectangles defined in this manner over the interval $[a, b]$ is the Riemann sum.

RIEMANN SUM: the sum of the areas of a set of rectangles that is used to approximate the area under the curve of a function

Consider, for example, the function $f(x) = x^2 + 1$ over the interval $[0,1]$. The plot of the function is shown below.

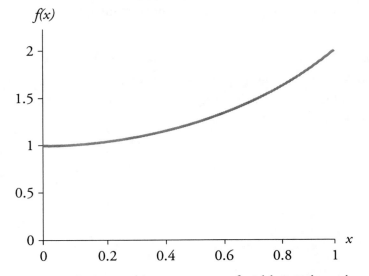

Partition the interval into segments of width 0.2 along the x-axis, and choose the function value $f(c_i)$ at the center of each interval. This function value is the height of the respective rectangle.

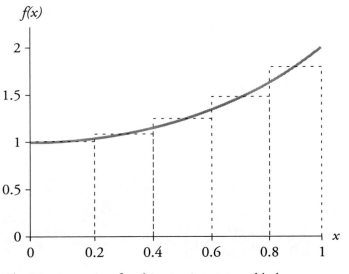

The Riemann sum for this case is expressed below.

$$\sum_{i=1}^{5} 0.2 f(0.2i - 0.1) = 1.33$$

This expression is the sum of the areas of all the rectangles shown above. This is an approximation of the area under the curve of the function (and a reasonably accurate one, as well—the actual area is $\frac{4}{3}$).

Generally, the Riemann sum for arbitrary partitioning and selection of the values c_i is the following:

$$\sum_{i=1}^{n} f(c_i)\Delta x_i$$

where c_i is within the closed interval defined by the partition Δx_i.

Definite Integrals

The DEFINITE INTEGRAL is defined as the limit of the Riemann sum as the widths of the partitions Δx_i go to zero (and, consequently, n goes to infinity). Thus, the definite integral can be expressed mathematically as follows:

$$\int_{a}^{b} f(x)dx = \lim_{\Delta x_m \to 0}\sum_{i=1}^{n} f(c_i)\Delta x_i$$

where Δx_m is the width of the largest partition. If the partitioning of the interval is such that each partition has the same width, then the definition can be written as follows:

$$\int_{a}^{b} f(x)dx = \lim_{\Delta x \to 0}\sum_{i=1}^{n} f(c_i)\Delta x$$

Note that $n = \frac{b-a}{\Delta x}$ in this case.

The definite integral, therefore, is the area under the curve of $f(x)$ over the interval $[a, b]$. By taking the limit of the Riemann sum, the number of rectangles used to find the area under the curve becomes infinite and, therefore, the error in the result goes to zero (since the width of each rectangle becomes infinitesimal).

Integrals of algebraic functions

Since we have outlined the formal definition of a definite integral, it is helpful to understand the process of deriving the integrals of algebraic functions based on this definition. The following example illustrates this process using the Riemann sum. The process can be summarized with the following basic steps.

1. Partition the interval into n segments of equal width

2. Substitute the value of the function into the Riemann sum using the x value at the center of each subinterval

3. Write the sum in closed form

4. Take the limit of the result as n approaches infinity

> **DEFINITE INTEGRAL:** the limit of the Riemann sum as the widths of the partitions Δx_i go to zero (and, consequently, n goes to infinity)

> *The definite integral, is the area under the curve of f(x) over the interval [a, b].*

Example: For f(x) = x², find the values of the Riemann sum over the interval [0, 1] using n subintervals of equal width, each evaluated at the right endpoint of each subinterval. Find the limit of the Riemann sum.

Take the interval $[0, 1]$ and subdivide it into n subintervals, each of length $\frac{1}{n}$.

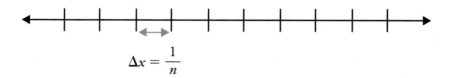

$$\Delta x = \frac{1}{n}$$

The endpoints of the ith subinterval are

$$\frac{i-1}{n} \quad \frac{i}{n}$$

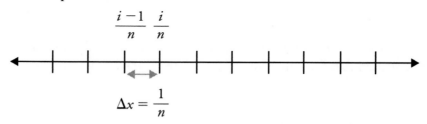

$$\Delta x = \frac{1}{n}$$

Let $x_i = \frac{i}{n}$ be the right endpoint. Draw a line of length $f(x_i) = (\frac{i}{n})^2$ at the right-hand endpoint.

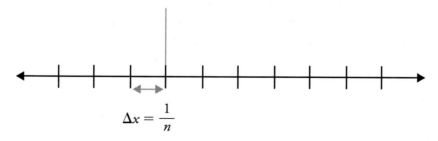

$$\Delta x = \frac{1}{n}$$

Draw a rectangle.

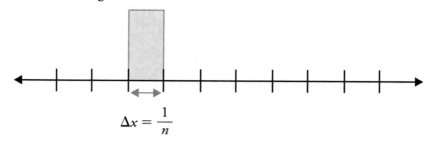

$$\Delta x = \frac{1}{n}$$

The area of this rectangle is $f(x)\Delta x$.

$$f(x)\Delta x = (\tfrac{i}{n})^2\tfrac{1}{n} = \tfrac{i^2}{n^3}$$

Now draw all *n* rectangles (drawing below not to scale).

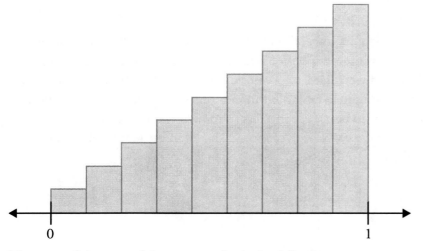

The sum of the area of these rectangles is the following.

$$\sum_{i=1}^{n} \frac{i^2}{n^3} = \frac{1}{n^3} \sum_{i=1}^{n} i^2$$

The sum can be evaluated as follows.

$$\frac{1}{n^3} \sum_{i=1}^{n} i^2 = \frac{1}{n^3} \frac{n(n+1)(2n+1)}{6}$$

This is the Riemann sum for *n* subdivisions of the interval [0, 1]. Finally, to evaluate the integral, take the limit as *n* approaches infinity.

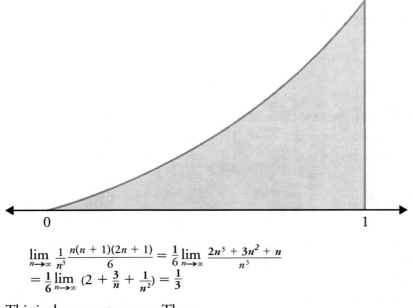

$$\lim_{n \to \infty} \frac{1}{n^3} \frac{n(n+1)(2n+1)}{6} = \frac{1}{6} \lim_{n \to \infty} \frac{2n^3 + 3n^2 + n}{n^3}$$
$$= \frac{1}{6} \lim_{n \to \infty} \left(2 + \frac{3}{n} + \frac{1}{n^2}\right) = \frac{1}{3}$$

This is the correct answer. Thus,

$$\int_0^1 x^2 \, dx = \frac{1}{3}$$

Understanding Definite Integrals

Geometrical interpretation

Geometrically, the definite integral is the area between the curve of the function $f(x)$ and the x-axis over some specified interval. Since, in general, $f(x)$ is not piecewise linear, the use of rectangles, trapezoids or other polygons (in finite numbers) is not sufficient to accurately calculate this area (unless additional mathematical machinery is brought to bear). For instance, although two triangles can approximate the area under the curve of the function shown in the graph below, they do not do so exactly.

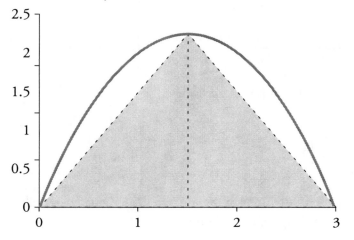

Numerical interpretation

Numerically, the definite integral is an area of a region defined by the product of a height and a width.

$$\int_{a}^{b} f(x)dx$$

In this case, the height is $f(x)$, and the width is dx. The height is continuously changing, so the width dx is infinitesimally small. Thus, the integral is a calculation of the product of the variable height and the constant width over the interval $[a, b]$.

Analytical interpretation

Analytically, as seen in the previous section, the definite integral is the limit of the Riemann sum as the number of subintervals (n) of a specific width (Δx) approaches infinity. Since it is apparent that larger rectangles generally provide less accuracy in the Riemann sum than do smaller rectangles, taking the limit as n approaches infinity is in fact a matter of increasing the accuracy of the result. In the limit, the Riemann sum is perfectly accurate. This concept is illustrated in the graphs below, where the increasing accuracy of the Riemann sum as n increases is apparent.

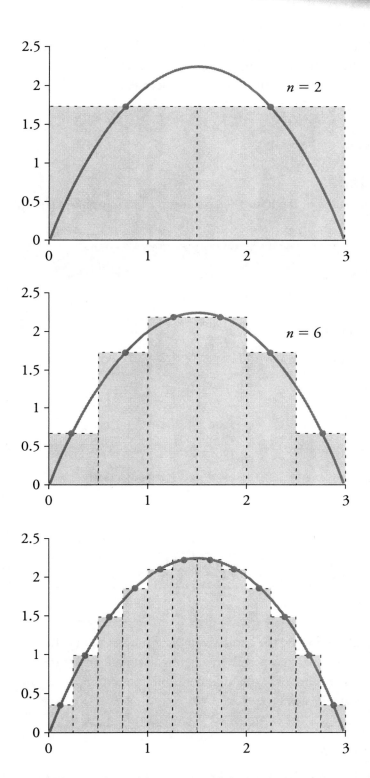

Again, notice how the accuracy of the area estimate using rectangles increases as n increases. This is the rationale behind the use of the limit for the Riemann sum, which yields the definite integral.

Thus, the limit of the Riemann sum increases the accuracy of the approximation to the area of a curve. In the limit, the accuracy is infinite. That is to say, the result is equal to the definite integral, which is the exact area under the curve on the specified interval.

$$\int_a^b f(x)\,dx = \lim_{\Delta x_m \to 0} \sum_{i=1}^{n} f(c_i)\Delta x_i$$

Basic Integration Rules

The following summarizes some of the basic rules for integration in terms of some common functions.

BASIC INTEGRATION RULES			
Integration Involving Constants	$\int 0\,dx = C$	$\int k\,dx = kx + C$	$\int kf(x)\,dx = k\int f(x)\,dx$
Integration of Sums or Differences of Functions	$\int [f(x) + g(x)]\,dx = \int f(x)\,dx + \int g(x)\,dx$		
	$\int [f(x) - g(x)]\,dx = \int f(x)\,dx - \int g(x)\,dx$		
Power Rule	$\int x^n\,dx = \frac{x^{n+1}}{n+1} + C$ for $n \neq -1$		
Trigonometric Functions	$\int \sin x\,dx = -\cos x + C$	$\int \cos x\,dx = \sin x + C$	
	$\int \tan x\,dx = \ln|\sec x| + C$	$\int \cot x\,dx = \ln|\sin x| + C$	
	$\int \csc x\,dx = \ln|\tan \frac{x}{2}| + C$	$\int \sec x\,dx = \ln|\tan [\frac{x}{2} + \frac{\pi}{4}]| + C$	
	$\int \sec^2 x\,dx = \tan x + C$	$\int \sec x \tan x\,dx = \sec x + C$	
	$\int \csc^2 x\,dx = -\cot x + C$	$\int \csc x \cot x\,dx = -\csc x + C$	
Logarithmic Functions	$\int \ln x\,dx = x\ln x - x + C$	$\int \frac{1}{x}\,dx = \ln|x| + C$	
Exponential Functions	$\int e^x\,dx = e^x + C$		

The above rules are helpful for finding the antiderivatives of functions, but they are far from complete, since they do not permit in any obvious manner integration of composite functions or functions with arguments other than simply x. To this end, several helpful strategies can be applied.

Integrating by u-Substitution

If a function is expressed in terms of another function (that is, if it is a composite function), then a change of variables permits integration through conversion of the expression into a form similar to a form given in the rules above.

Consider a composite function $f(g(x))$ in the context of the following integral:

$\int f(g(x))\ g'(x)dx$

An example of such a composite function might be $f(x) = (x + 1)^2$ or $f(x) = \sin(x^3)$. Assign $g(x)$ a new variable name, u. Then differentiate $g(x)$ in terms of x and rearrange the differentials.

$u = g(x)$

$\frac{dg(x)}{dx} = g'(x) = \frac{du}{dx}$

$du = g'(x)dx$

Use this result in the indefinite integration of the composite function:

$\int f(g(x))g'(x)dx = \int f(u)du$

With this simple substitution (sometimes called a u-substitution), the integral can be made to look like one of the general forms. It is sometimes necessary to experiment with different u-substitutions to find one that works (finding a u that allows complete elimination of x from the integral is not always trivial). Follow these steps for integration by substitution:

1. Select an appropriate value for u to perform the substitution

2. Differentiate u as shown above

3. Substitute u and du into the integral to eliminate x

4. Evaluate the integral

5. Substitute $g(x)$ back into the result to get the antiderivative

When dealing with definite integrals that require u-substitution, the only difference is that the limits of integration must be modified in accordance with the choice of u. Thus:

$\int_{a}^{b} f(g(x))g'(x)dx = \int_{g(a)}^{g(b)} f(u)du$

Example: Evaluate the following antiderivative: $\int 2\,x[\sin(x^2) + \cos(x^2)]dx$.

First, split the integral into two parts.

$\int 2\,x[\sin(x^2) + \cos(x^2)]dx = \int 2\,x\sin(x^2)\ dx + \int 2\,x\cos(x^2)\ dx$

Next, select an appropriate value for u. In this case, choose $u = x^2$. Then:

$du = 2x\ dx$

Rewrite the integral in terms of u.

$\int \sin(x^2)2x\ dx + \int \cos(x^2)2xdx = \int \sin u\,du + \int \cos u\,du$

This result is in a form for which the antiderivative can be found easily.

$\int \sin u\,du + \int \cos u\,du = -\cos u + \sin u + C$

Substitute the definition of u back into the result to get the antiderivative in terms of x.

$$-\cos u + \sin u + C = -\cos(x^2) + \sin(x^2) + C$$

Example: Evaluate the following antiderivative: $\int e^{\sin x} \cos x \, dx$.

Try choosing $u = \cos x$.

$$du = -\sin x \, dx$$

Substitute into the integral.

$$\int e^{\sin x} \cos x \, dx = -\int \frac{u e^{\sin x}}{\sin x} \, du$$

Note that there is no apparent way to eliminate x from the integral. Thus, this choice of u should be abandoned. Instead, try $u = \sin x$.

$$du = \cos x \, dx$$

Substitute into the integral, as before.

$$\int e^{\sin x} \cos x \, dx = \int e^u \, du$$

This choice of u was successful. Evaluate the antiderivative and substitute the definition of u back into the result.

$$\int e^u \, du = e^u = e^{\sin x}$$

Example: Evaluate the definite integral $\int \frac{1}{x \ln x} \, dx$ over the interval $[e, e^e]$.

Substitute using $u = \ln x$. Then, $du = \frac{1}{x} dx$.

$$\int \frac{1}{x \ln x} dx = \int \frac{1}{xu} x \, du = \int \frac{1}{u} du$$

Evaluate the integral and apply the limits of integration, which, using $u = \ln x$, lead to the interval $[\ln e, \ln e^e] = [1, e]$.

$$\int \frac{1}{u} du = \ln u \Big|_1^e$$
$$\ln u \Big|_1^e = \ln e - \ln 1 = 1 - 0 = 1$$

Integration by Parts

Another useful technique for evaluating complicated integrals is integration by parts. Since this method is itself complicated, it should only be used as a last resort if simpler methods of integration are not successful. Integration by parts requires two substitutions. To remember the formula for integration by parts, it is helpful to remember that it is based on the product rule of differentiation for two functions, u and v.

$$\frac{d}{dx}(uv) = u\frac{dv}{dx} + v\frac{du}{dx}$$

Naturally, then, integrating this result should return the product uv.

$$\int \frac{d}{dx}(uv) dx = \int d(uv) = uv$$

$$\int [u\frac{dv}{dx} + v\frac{du}{dx}] dx = \int u \, dv + \int v \, du$$

Rewrite the equation and rearrange to get the formula for integration by parts:

$uv = \int u\,dv + \int v\,du$

$\int u\,dv = uv - \int v\,du$

Thus, by identifying substitution functions for u and v, a method for integration is available. Proper selection of u and v is crucial to making this technique work. Use the following steps to perform integration by parts.

1. Choose dv as the most complicated part of the integral that can be integrated by itself

2. Choose u as the part of the integral that remains after the dv substitution is made. Preferably, the derivative of u should be simpler than u

3. Integrate dv to get v

4. Differentiate u to get du

5. Rewrite the integral in the form $\int u\,dv = uv - \int v\,du$

6. Integrate $\int v\,du$

7. If you cannot integrate $v\,du$, go back to the first step and try a different set of substitutions

Example: Find the antiderivative of the following function: $\int xe^{3x}dx$.

First, choose $dv = e^{3x}dx$ and $u = x$. Calculate du and v.

$dv = e^{3x}dx \qquad u = x$

$\int dv = \int e^{3x}dx \qquad du = dx$

$v = \dfrac{e^{3x}}{3}$

Substitute these results into the formula for integration by parts:

$\int u\,dv = \int xe^{3x}dx = uv - \int v\,du = \dfrac{xe^{3x}}{3} - \int \dfrac{e^{3x}}{3}dx$

The substitutions fit in this case, and the integration can now be performed easily.

$\int xe^{3x}dx = \dfrac{xe^{3x}}{3} - \int \dfrac{e^{3x}}{3}dx = \dfrac{xe^{3x}}{3} - \dfrac{e^{3x}}{9} + C$

$\int xe^{3x}dx = \dfrac{e^{3x}}{3}\left(x - \dfrac{1}{3}\right) + C$

This is the correct solution to the problem.

Example: Evaluate the following indefinite integral: $\int x \cos x\,dx$

Try choosing $u = x$ and $dv = \cos x\,dx$.

$du = dx \qquad\qquad \int dv = \int \cos x\,dx$

$\qquad\qquad\qquad\qquad v = \sin x$

Substitute into the formula for integration by parts:

$$\int u \, dv = \int x \cos x dx = uv - \int v \, du = x \sin x - \int \sin x dx$$

The choices of u and dv work, so the integral can be evaluated to find the result.

$$\int x \cos x \, dx = x \sin x + \cos x + C$$

Applications of Integrals

Area under a curve

Taking the integral of a function and evaluating it over some interval on x provides the *total area under the curve* (or, more formally, the *area bounded by the curve and the x-axis*). Thus, the areas of geometric figures can be determined when the figure can be cast as a function or set of functions in the coordinate plane. Remember, though, that regions above the x-axis have "positive" area and regions below the x-axis have "negative" area. It is necessary to account for these positive and negative values when finding the area under curves. The boundaries between positive and negative regions are delineated by the roots of the function. Follow these steps to find the total area under the curve:

1. Determine the interval or intervals on which the area under the curve is to be found. If portions of the function are negative, a given interval may need to be divided appropriately if all areas are to be considered positive.

2. Integrate the function.

3. Evaluate the integral once for each interval.

4. If any of the intervals evaluates to a negative number, reverse the sign (equivalently, take the absolute value of each integral).

5. Add the value of all the integrals to get the area under the curve.

Example: Find the area under the following function on the given interval: f(x) = sin x; [0,2π].

First, find the roots of the function on the interval.

$$f(x) = \sin x = 0$$
$$x = 0, \pi$$

The function $\sin x$ is positive over $[0, \pi]$ (since $\sin\frac{\pi}{2} = 1$) and negative over $[\pi, 2\pi]$ (since $\sin\frac{3\pi}{2} = -1$). Use these intervals for the integration to find the area A under the curve.

$$A = \int_0^{2\pi}|\sin x|dx = \left|\int_0^\pi \sin x \, dx\right| + \left|\int_\pi^{2\pi}\sin x \, dx\right|$$

$$A = \left|-\cos x\right|_0^\pi\right| + \left|-\cos x\right|_\pi^{2\pi}\right| = \left|-\cos \pi + \cos 0\right| + \left|-\cos 2\pi + \cos \pi\right|$$

$$A = \left|1 + 1\right| + \left|-1 - 1\right| = 2 + 2 = 4$$

Thus, the total area under the curve of $f(x) = \sin x$ on the interval $[0, 2\pi]$ is 4 square units.

Area between two curves

Finding the *area between two curves* is similar to finding the area under one curve. The general process involves integrating the absolute value of the difference between the two functions over the interval of interest. In some instances, it is necessary to find the intervals over which the difference is positive and over which the difference is negative. For the former, the integral can simply be taken with no modifications; for the latter, however, the result of the integral must be negated. To find the points at which the difference between the functions changes from positive to negative (or vice versa), simply set the functions equal to each other and solve. Take the absolute value of each portion of the integral (that is, each integral over a portion of the interval) and add all the parts. This yields the total area between the curves.

Example: Find the area of the regions bounded by the two functions on the indicated interval: $f(x) = x + 2$ and $g(x) = x^2$ on $[-2, 3]$.

The integral of interest is the following:

$$\int_{-2}^{3}|f(x) - g(x)|dx$$

To eliminate the need to use the absolute value notation inside the integral, find the values for which $f(x) = g(x)$.

$$f(x) = x + 2 = g(x) = x^2$$
$$x^2 - x - 2 = 0 = (x - 2)(x + 1)$$

The functions are then equal at $x = -1$ and $x = 2$. Perform the integration over the intervals defined by these values.

$$\int_{-2}^{3}|f(x) - g(x)|dx = \left|\int_{-2}^{-1}f(x) - g(x) \, dx\right| + \left|\int_{-1}^{2}f(x) - g(x) \, dx\right| + \left|\int_{2}^{3}f(x) - g(x) \, dx\right|$$

The antiderivative of $f(x) - g(x)$ is the following (ignoring the constant of integration).

$$\int [f(x) - g(x)]dx = \int (x + 2 - x^2)dx = \frac{x^2}{2} + 2x - \frac{x^3}{3}$$

Evaluate over the intervals above.

$$\int_{-2}^{3}|f(x) - g(x)|dx = \left|\left[\frac{x^2}{2} + 2x - \frac{x^3}{3}\right]_{-2}^{-1}\right| + \left|\left[\frac{x^2}{2} + 2x - \frac{x^3}{3}\right]_{-1}^{2}\right| + \left|\left[\frac{x^2}{2} + 2x - \frac{x^3}{3}\right]_{2}^{3}\right|$$

$$\left|\left[\frac{x^2}{2} + 2x - \frac{x^3}{3}\right]_{-2}^{-1}\right| = \left|(\frac{1}{2} - 2 + \frac{1}{3}) - (\frac{4}{2} - 4 + \frac{8}{3})\right| = \left|-\frac{7}{6} - \frac{2}{3}\right| = \frac{11}{6}$$

$$\left|\left[\frac{x^2}{2} + 2x - \frac{x^3}{3}\right]_{-1}^{2}\right| = \left|(\frac{4}{2} + 4 - \frac{8}{3}) - (\frac{1}{2} - 2 + \frac{1}{3})\right| = \left|\frac{10}{3} + \frac{7}{6}\right| = \frac{27}{6}$$

$$\left|\left[\frac{x^2}{2} + 2x - \frac{x^3}{3}\right]_{2}^{3}\right| = \left|(\frac{9}{2} + 6 - \frac{27}{3}) - (\frac{4}{2} + 4 - \frac{8}{3})\right| = \left|\frac{3}{2} - \frac{10}{3}\right| = \frac{11}{6}$$

The sum of these individual parts is $\frac{49}{6}$.

Volumes of solids of revolution

An area bounded by a curve (or curves) and revolved about a line is called a SOLID OF REVOLUTION. To find the volume of such a solid, the disc method (called the washer method if the solid has an empty interior of some form) works in most instances. Imagine slicing through the solid perpendicular to the line of revolution. The cross section should resemble either a disc or a washer. The washer method involves finding the sum of the volumes of all "washers" that compose the solid, using the following general formula:

$$V = \pi(r_1^2 - r_2^2)t$$

where V is the volume of the washer, r_1 and r_2 are the interior and exterior radii, and t is the thickness of the washer.

SOLID OF REVOLUTION: an area bounded by a curve (or curves) and revolved about a line

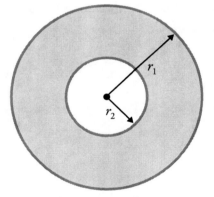

Depending on the situation, the radius is the distance from the line of revolution to the curve; or if there are two curves involved, the radius is the difference between the two functions. The thickness is dx if the line of revolution is parallel to the x-axis and dy if the line of revolution is parallel to the y-axis. The integral is then the following, where dV is the differential volume of a washer.

$$\int dV = \int \pi(r_1^2 - r_2^2)dt$$
$$V = \pi\int(r_1^2 - r_2^2)dt$$

It is assumed here that r_1 is the outer radius and r_2 is the inner radius. For the disc method, where only one radius is needed, $r_2 = 0$.

Example: Find the volume of the solid of revolution made by revolving f(x) = 9 − x² about the x-axis on the interval [0,4].

This problem can be solved using the disc method. First, note that the radius is $9 - x^2$ and the thickness of the disc is dx. Write the appropriate integral as follows.

$$V = \pi \int_0^4 (9 - x^2)^2 \, dx$$

Next, expand the radius term and evaluate the integral.

$$V = \pi \int_0^4 (81 - 18x^2 + x^4) \, dx$$
$$V = \pi [81x - \tfrac{18}{3}x^3 + \tfrac{1}{5}x^5]_0^4$$
$$V = \pi [81(4) - \tfrac{18}{3}(4)^3 + \tfrac{1}{5}(4)^5]$$
$$V = \pi [324 - 384 + 204.8] = 144.8\pi \approx 454.9$$

The volume is thus approximately 454.9 cubic units.

Arc Length

Finding the arc length of a curve is another useful application of integration. The ARC LENGTH is the distance traversed by a curve over a given interval. Geometrically, the distance d between two points (x_1, y_1) and (x_2, y_2) is given by the following formula.

$$d = \sqrt{(x_2 - x_1)^2 + (y_2 - y_1)^2}$$

ARC LENGTH: the distance traversed by a curve over a given interval

If the points are only an infinitesimal distance apart (*ds*, which is the differential arc length), then the above expression can be written as follows in differential form:

$$ds = \sqrt{dx^2 + dy^2}$$

Factor out the *dx* term:

$$ds = \sqrt{1 + \left(\frac{dy}{dx}\right)^2} \, dx$$

But $\frac{dy}{dx}$ is simply the derivative of a function $y(x)$ (which can be expressed as $f(x)$ instead). Thus, the integral of the above expression over the interval [*a*, *b*] yields the formula for the arc length.

$$\int ds = = \int_a^b \sqrt{1 + [f'(x)]^2} \, dx$$

Example: Find the distance traversed by the function f(x) = ln (cos x) on the interval [-\frac{\pi}{4}, \frac{\pi}{4}].

Use the formula for arc length *s*, applying trigonometric identities as appropriate.

$$s = \int \sqrt{1 + [\tfrac{d}{dx}\ln(\cos x)]^2} \, dx = \int \sqrt{1 + \left[\frac{\sin x}{\cos x}\right]^2} \, dx$$
$$s = \int \sqrt{1 + [\tan x]^2} \, dx = \int \sqrt{1 + \tan^2 x} \, dx = \int \sqrt{\sec^2 x} \, dx$$
$$s = \int \sec x \, dx$$

Evaluate the integral over the limits of integration.

$$s = \int_{-\pi/4}^{\pi/4} \sec x \, dx = \ln(\sec x + \tan x)\big|_{-\pi/4}^{\pi/4}$$

$$s = \ln(\sec \tfrac{\pi}{4} + \tan \tfrac{\pi}{4}) - \ln(\sec [-\tfrac{\pi}{4}] + \tan [\tfrac{\pi}{4}])$$

$$s = \ln(\sqrt{2} + 1) - \ln(\sqrt{2} - 1) \approx 1.763$$

The result is approximately 1.763 units.

Linear motion

Integral calculus, in addition to differential calculus, is a powerful tool for analysis of problems involving linear motion. The derivative of the position (or displacement) function is the velocity function, and the derivative of a velocity function is the acceleration function. As a result, the antiderivative of an acceleration function is a velocity function, and the antiderivative of a velocity function is a position (or displacement) function. Solving word problems of this type involves converting the information given into an appropriate integral expression. To find the constant of integration, use the conditions provided in the problem (such as an initial displacement, velocity, or acceleration).

The antiderivative of an acceleration function is a velocity function, and the antiderivative of a velocity function is a position (or displacement) function.

Example: A particle moves along the x-axis with acceleration $a(t) = 3t - 1 \frac{cm}{sec^2}$. At time $t = 4$ seconds, the particle is moving to the left at 3 cm per second. Find the velocity of the particle at time $t = 2$ seconds.

Evaluate the antiderivative of the acceleration function $a(t)$ to get the velocity function $v(t)$ along with the unknown constant of integration C.

$$v(t) = \int a(t)dt = \int (3t - 1)dt$$
$$v(t) = \frac{3t^2}{2} - t + C$$

Use the condition that at time $t = 4$ seconds, the particle has a velocity of -3 cm/sec.

$$v(4) = \frac{3(4)^2}{2} - 4 + C = -3$$
$$\frac{48}{2} - 4 + C = -3$$
$$C = -3 + 4 - 24 = -23 \tfrac{cm}{sec}$$

Now evaluate $v(t)$ at time $t = 2$ seconds to get the solution to the problem.

$$v(t) = \frac{3t^2}{2} - t - 23 \tfrac{cm}{sec}$$
$$v(2) = \frac{3(2)^2}{2} - 2 - 23 \tfrac{cm}{sec} = 6 - 25 \tfrac{cm}{sec} = -19 \tfrac{cm}{sec}$$

Example: Find the displacement function of a particle whose acceleration is described by the equation a(t) = 3sin 2t. Assume that the particle is initially motionless at the origin.

Find the antiderivative of the acceleration function $a(t)$ to get the velocity function $v(t)$.

$$v(t) = \int 3 \sin 2t \, dt = -3\tfrac{1}{2}\cos 2t + C$$

Note that the initial velocity is zero; thus:

$$v(0) = 0 = -\tfrac{3}{2} \cos 2(0) + C = -\tfrac{3}{2} + C$$

$$C = \tfrac{3}{2}$$

$$v(t) = \tfrac{3}{2}(1 - \cos 2t)$$

Find the antiderivative of the velocity function to get the displacement function $s(t)$.

$$s(t) = \int \tfrac{3}{2}(1 - \cos 2t) dt = \tfrac{3}{2}(t - \tfrac{1}{2}\sin 2t) + C'$$

The initial position is at the origin, so C' can be found.

$$s(0) = 0 = \tfrac{3}{2}(0 - \tfrac{1}{2}\sin 2(0)) + C'$$

$$s(0) = 0 = \tfrac{3}{2}(0 - 0) + C'$$

$$C' = 0$$

$$s(t) = \tfrac{3}{2}(t - \tfrac{1}{2}\sin 2t)$$

This last result is the solution to the problem. A necessary (but not sufficient) check of the answer is to differentiate $s(t)$ twice and compare with $a(t)$.

$$s'(t) = \tfrac{3}{2}(1 - \cos 2t)$$

$$s''(t) = 3 \sin 2t = a(t)$$

SKILL 6.9 Determine the limits of sequences and simple infinite series

See Competency 10

DOMAIN IV
DATA ANALYSIS AND STATISTICS AND PROBABILITY

PERSONALIZED STUDY PLAN

PAGE	COMPETENCY AND SKILL	KNOWN MATERIAL/ SKIP IT
183	**7: Data analysis and statistics**	☐
	7.1: Organize data into a suitable form	☐
	7.2: Know and find the appropriate uses of common measures of central tendency and dispersion	☐
	7.3: Analyze data to determine what type of function would most likely model that particular phenomenon; use the regression feature of the calculator; interpret the regression coefficients, correlation, and residuals in context	☐
	7.4: Understand and apply normal distributions and their characteristics	☐
	7.5: Understand sample statistics and sampling distributions	☐
	7.6: Understand various studies and which inferences can legitimately be drawn from each	☐
	7.7: Know the characteristics of well-defined studies	☐
202	**8: Probability**	☐
	8.1: Understand the concepts of sample space and probability distribution	☐
	8.2: Understand the concepts of conditional probability, independent events and the probability of a compound event	☐
	8.3: Compute and interpret the expected value of random variables	☐
	8.4: Use simulations to construct empirical probability distributions	☐

COMPETENCY 7
DATA ANALYSIS AND STATISTICS

Methods of data analysis and statistics can be applied to both discrete and continuous distributions of data. Although the specific formulas and expressions may vary slightly, the general concepts are largely the same.

> **FREQUENCY DISTRIBUTION:** divides a set of data into classes or intervals

---

SKILL Organize data into a suitable form (e.g., construct a histogram and use it
7.1 in the calculation of probabilities)

> **FREQUENCY:** the number of occurrences of a data point in a data set

Displaying Statistical Data
The data obtained from sampling may be categorical (e.g., yes or no responses) or numerical. In both cases, results are displayed using a variety of graphical techniques. Geographical data is often displayed superimposed on maps.

> **RELATIVE FREQUENCY:** the frequency divided by the total number of data points

Histograms
The most common form of graphical display used for numerical data obtained from random sampling is the histogram. A trend line can be superposed on a histogram to observe the general shape of the distribution. In some cases, the trend line may also be fitted to a probability density function.

> *The relative frequency of a data point represents the probability of occurrence of that value.*

If the data set is large, it may be expressed in compact form as a FREQUENCY DISTRIBUTION. The number of occurrences of each data point is the FREQUENCY of that value. The RELATIVE FREQUENCY is defined as the frequency divided by the total number of data points. Since the sum of the frequencies equals the number of data points, the relative frequencies add up to 1. The relative frequency of a data point, therefore, represents the probability of occurrence of that value. Thus, a distribution consisting of relative frequencies is known as a PROBABILITY DISTRIBUTION. The CUMULATIVE FREQUENCY of a data point is the sum of the frequencies from the beginning up to that point.

> **PROBABILITY DISTRIBUTION:** a distribution consisting of relative frequencies

> **CUMULATIVE FREQUENCY:** the sum of the frequencies from the beginning up to that point

A histogram is used to display a discrete frequency distribution graphically. It shows the counts of data in different ranges, the center of the data set, the spread of the data, and whether there are any outliers. It also shows whether the data has a single mode or more than one.

> *A histogram is used to display a discrete frequency distribution graphically.*

Example: The table below shows the summary of some test results, where people scored points ranging from 0 to 45. The total range of points has been divided into bins 0–5, 6–10, 11–15, and so on. The frequency for the first bin (labeled 5) is the number of people who scored points ranging from 0 to 5; the frequency for the second bin (labeled 10) is the number of people who scored points ranging from 6 to 10; and so on.

Points	Frequency	Cumulative Frequency	Relative Frequency
5	1	1	0.009
10	4	5	0.035
15	12	17	0.105
20	22	39	0.193
25	30	69	0.263
30	25	94	0.219
35	13	107	0.114
40	6	113	0.053
45	1	114	0.009

The histogram of the probability distribution is given below:

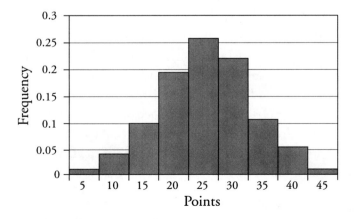

The probability distribution can be used to calculate the probability of a particular test score occurring in a certain range. For instance, the probability of a test score lying between 15 and 30 is given by the sum of the areas (assuming width of 1) of the three middle bins in the histogram above:

$$0.193 + 0.263 + 0.219 = 0.675$$

Bar graphs

Bar graphs are used to compare various quantities using bars of different lengths.

Example: A class had the following grades: 4 A's, 9 B's, 8 C's, 1 D, 3 F's. Graph these on a bar graph.

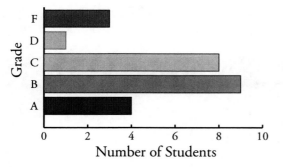

> Bar graphs are used to compare various quantities using bars of different lengths.

Line graphs

Line graphs are used to show trends, often over a period of time.

Example: Graph the following information using a line graph.

> Line graphs are used to show trends, often over a period of time.

THE NUMBER OF NATIONAL MERIT FINALISTS/SCHOOL YEAR						
School	**90-91**	**91-92**	**92-93**	**93-94**	**94-95**	**95-96**
Central	3	5	1	4	6	8
Wilson	4	2	3	2	3	2

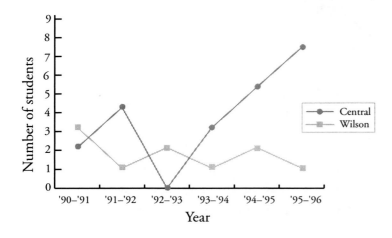

Circle graphs (pie charts)

Circle graphs or pie charts show the relationships of various parts of a data set to each other and to the whole.

Circle graphs or pie charts show the relationships of various parts of a data set to each other and to the whole. Each part is shown as a percentage of the total and occupies a proportional sector of the circular area. To make a circle graph, total all the information that is to be included on the graph. Determine the central angle to be used for each sector of the graph using the following formula:

$$\frac{\text{information}}{\text{total information}} \times 360° = \text{degrees in central} \angle$$

Lay out the central angles according to these sizes, label each section and include its percentage.

Example: Graph this information on a circle graph:

MONTHLY EXPENSES	
Rent	$400
Food	$150
Utilities	$75
Clothes	$75
Church	$100
Misc.	$200

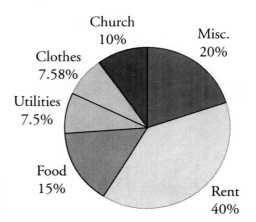

Scatter plots

Scatter plots compare two characteristics of the same group of things or people and usually consist of a large body of data. They show how much one variable is affected by another.

Scatter plots compare two characteristics of the same group of things or people and usually consist of a large body of data. They show how much one variable is affected by another. The relationship between the two variables is their

CORRELATION. The closer the data points come to making a straight line when plotted, the closer the correlation.

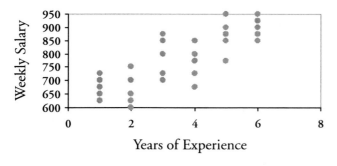

CORRELATION: the relationship between two variables when comparing statistical data

SKILL
7.2 **Know and find the appropriate uses of common measures of central tendency** *(e.g., population mean, sample mean, median, mode)* **and dispersion** *(e.g., range, population standard deviation, sample standard deviation, population variance, sample variance)*

Statistics for Discrete Distributions

Mean, Median, and Mode

The mean, median, and mode are measures of central tendency (i.e., the average or typical value) in a data set. They can be defined both for discrete and continuous data sets. For discrete data, the MEAN is the average of the data items, or the value obtained by adding all the data values and dividing by the total number of data items. For a data set of n items with data values $x_1, x_2, x_3, \ldots, x_n$, the mean is given by

$$\bar{x} = \frac{x_1 + x_2 + x_3 + \ldots + x_n}{n}$$

MEAN: for discrete data, the value obtained by adding all the data values and then dividing by the total number of values

The WEIGHTED AVERAGE is the mean of a set of data in which each individual datum has an associated probability or weight. For data values $x_1, x_2, x_3, \ldots, x_n$, with associated probabilities (or weights) $p(x_1), p(x_2), p(x_3), \ldots, p(x_n)$, the mean value is

$$\bar{x} = x_1 p(x_1) + x_2 p(x_2) + x_3 p(x_3) + \ldots + x_n p(x_n) = \sum_i x_i p(x_i)$$

This is the most general definition of the mean.

WEIGHTED AVERAGE: the mean of a set of data in which each individual datum has an associated probability or weight

The MEDIAN is found by putting the data in order from smallest to largest and selecting the value in the middle (or the average of the two values in the middle if the number of data items is even). The MODE is the most frequently occurring datum. There can be more than one mode in a data set.

MEDIAN: this is found by putting the data in order from smallest to largest and selecting the value in the middle

MODE: the most frequently occurring datum

Example: Find the mean, median, and mode of the test scores listed below:

85	77	65
92	90	54
88	85	70
75	80	69
85	88	60
72	74	95

Mean: sum of all scores ÷ number of scores = 78

Median: Put the numbers in order from smallest to largest. Pick the middle number.

54 60 65 69 70 72 74 75 $\boxed{77\ 80}$ 85 85 85 88 88 90 92 95

Two values are in the middle.

Therefore, the median is average of the two numbers in the middle, or 78.5.
The mode is the most frequent number, or 85.

Range, variance, and standard deviation

The RANGE is a measure of variability that is calculated by subtracting the smallest value from the largest value in a set of discrete data.

The VARIANCE and STANDARD DEVIATION are measures of the "spread" of data around the mean. It is noteworthy that descriptive statistics involving such parameters as variance and standard deviation can be applied to a set of data that spans the entire population (population parameters, typically represented using Greek symbols) or to a set of data that only constitutes a portion of the population (sample statistics, typically represented by Latin letters).

When making informal inferences about a population based on sample statistics, it is important to ensure that the sample is collected in a manner that adequately represents the population (see the discussion of surveys and sampling below). The confidence in an inference based on sample statistics can increase when, for instance, the size of the sample space approaches that of the population, or when the sampling approach is designed to take into account known aspects of the population. Insofar as the sample represents the population, sample statistics approach (and can be equal to, in some cases) population parameters.

The mean of a set of data, whether for a population (μ) or for a sample ($\overline{x}$), uses the formula discussed above and can be represented as either a set of individual data or as a set of data with associated frequencies. The variance and standard deviation for the population differ slightly from those of a sample. The population variance (σ^2) and the population standard deviation (σ) are as follows.

$$\sigma^2 = \tfrac{1}{n} \Sigma (x_i - \mu)^2$$
$$\sigma = \sqrt{\sigma^2}$$

RANGE: this is found by subtracting the smallest data value from the largest

VARIANCE: a measure of the "spread" of data about the mean

STANDARD DEVIATION: also a measure of the "spread" of data about the mean; the standard deviation is the square root of the variance

For a sample, the data does not include the entire population. As a result, it should be expected that the sample data might not be perfectly representative of the population. To account for this shortcoming in the sample variance (s^2) and standard deviation (s), the sum of the squared differences between the data and the mean is divided by ($n - 1$) instead of just n. This increases the variance and standard deviation slightly, which in turn increases slightly the data spread to account for the possibility that the sample may not accurately represent the population.

$$s^2 = \frac{1}{n-1} \Sigma \, (x_i - \overline{x})^2$$

$$s = \sqrt{s^2}$$

Example: Calculate the range, variance, and standard deviation for the following data set: {3, 3, 5, 7, 8, 8, 8, 10, 12, 21}.

The range is simply the largest data value minus the smallest. In this case, the range is $21 - 3 = 18$.

To calculate the variance and standard deviation, first calculate the mean. If it is not stated whether a data set constitutes a population or sample, assume it is a population. (In this case, if the data were labeled as "ages of the 10 people in a room," this would be a population. If the data were labeled "ages of males at a crowded circus event," the data would be a sample.)

$$\mu = \frac{3 + 3 + 5 + 7 + 8 + 8 + 8 + 10 + 12 + 21}{10} = 8.5$$

Use this mean to calculate the variance.

$$\sigma^2 = \frac{1}{10} \Sigma \, (x_i - 8.5)^2$$

$$\sigma^2 = \frac{1}{10} \{(3 - 8.5)^2 + (3 - 8.5)^2 + (5 - 8.5)^2 + \ldots + (21 - 8.5)^2\}$$

$$\sigma^2 = \frac{246.5}{10} = 24.65$$

The standard deviation is

$$\sigma = \sqrt{\sigma^2} = \sqrt{24.65} \approx 4.96$$

Statistics for Continuous Distributions

The *range* for a continuous data distribution is the same as that for a discrete distribution: the largest value minus the smallest value. Calculation of the mean, variance, and standard deviation are similar, but slightly different. Since a continuous distribution does not permit a simple summation, integrals must be used.

PROBABILITY DENSITY FUNCTION: the integral of the probability density function over a certain range gives the probability of a data point being in that range of values

A large data set of continuous data is often represented using a probability distribution expressed as a PROBABILITY DENSITY FUNCTION. The integral of the probability density function over a certain range gives the probability of a data point being in that range of values. The integral of the probability density function over the whole range of values is equal to 1.

The *mean* value for a distribution of a variable x represented by a probability density function $f(x)$ is given by

$$\int_{-\infty}^{+\infty} xf(x)\,dx$$

(Compare this with its discrete counterpart $\bar{x} = \Sigma\, x_i f_i'$).

The *median* is the upper bound for which the integral of the probability density function is equal to 0.5; i.e., if $\int_{-\infty}^{a} f(x)\,dx = 0.5$, then a is the median of the distribution.

The *mode* is the maximum value or values of the probability density function within the range of the function.

If a distribution is skewed to the right, the mean is greater than the median. If a distribution is skewed to the left, the mean is smaller than the median.

As mentioned before, the mean and median are very close together for symmetric distributions. If a distribution is skewed to the right, the mean is greater than the median. If a distribution is skewed to the left, the mean is smaller than the median.

Example: Find the mean, median, and mode for the distribution given by the probability density function

$$f(x) = \begin{cases} 4x(1 - x^2) & 0 \le x \le 1 \\ 0 & \text{otherwise} \end{cases}$$

$$\text{Mean} = \int_{0}^{1} 4x^2(1 - x^2)\,dx = \frac{4x^3}{3}\Big|_{0}^{1} - \frac{4x^5}{5}\Big|_{0}^{1} = \frac{4}{3} - \frac{4}{5} = \frac{20 - 12}{15} = \frac{8}{15} = 0.53$$

If $x = a$ is the median, then

$$\int_{0}^{a} 4x(1 - x^2)\,dx = 0.5$$
$$\rightarrow \frac{4x^2}{2}\Big|_{0}^{a} - \frac{4x^4}{4}\Big|_{0}^{a} = 0.5$$
$$\rightarrow 2a^2 - a^4 = 0.5$$
$$\rightarrow 2a^4 - 4a^2 + 1 = 0$$

Solving for a yields

$$a^2 = \frac{4 \pm \sqrt{16 - 8}}{4} = 1 \pm \frac{2\sqrt{2}}{4} = 1 - \frac{\sqrt{2}}{2} \text{ (to keep } x \text{ within the range 0 to 1)}$$

$$a = \sqrt{1 - \frac{1}{\sqrt{2}}} = 0.54$$

The mode is obtained by taking the derivative of the probability density function and setting it to zero as shown below. (Notice that the second derivative is negative at $x = 0.58$, and, hence, this is clearly a maximum.)

$$\frac{d}{dx}(4x - 4x^3) = 4 - 12x^2 = 0$$

$$\rightarrow 12x^2 = 4$$

$$\rightarrow x^2 = \frac{1}{3}$$

$$\rightarrow x = \frac{1}{\sqrt{3}} = 0.58$$

The variance σ^2 also has an integral form, and has a form similar to that of a discrete distribution.

$$\sigma^2 = \int_{-\infty}^{\infty} (x - \mu)^2 f(x)dx$$

The standard deviation σ is simply

$$\sigma = \sqrt{\sigma^2}$$

Example: Calculate the standard deviation of a data distribution function f(x), where

$$f(x) = \begin{cases} 0 & x < -1 \\ -2x^2 + 2 & -1 \leq x \leq 1 \\ 0 & x > 1 \end{cases}$$

First calculate the mean of the function. Since the function is zero except between 1 and -1, the integral can likewise be evaluated from -1 to 1. (*For further discussion of integrals, see Skill 6.8.*)

$$\mu = \int_{-1}^{1} (-2x^2 + 2)xdx$$

$$\mu = -2\int_{-1}^{1} (x^3 - x)dx$$

$$\mu = -2 \left[\frac{x^4}{4} - \frac{x^2}{2}\right]_{x=-1}^{x=1}$$

$$\mu = -2 \left\{ \left[\frac{(1)^4}{4} - \frac{(1)^2}{2}\right] - \left[\frac{(-1)^4}{4} - \frac{(-1)^2}{2}\right] \right\} = 0$$

The mean can also be seen clearly by the fact that the graph of the function $f(x)$ is symmetric about the y-axis, indicating that its center (or mean) is at $x = 0$. Next, calculate the variance of f.

$$\sigma^2 = \int_{-1}^{1} (x - 0)^2 (-2x^2 + 2)dx = -2\int_{-1}^{1} x^2(x^2 - 1)dx$$

$$\sigma^2 = -2\int_{-1}^{1} (x^4 - x^2)dx$$

$$\sigma^2 = -2\left[\frac{x^5}{5} - \frac{x^3}{3}\right]_{x=-1}^{x=1} = -2\left\{\left[\frac{(1)^5}{5} - \frac{(1)^3}{3}\right] - \left[\frac{(-1)^5}{5} - \frac{(-1)^3}{3}\right]\right\}$$

$$\sigma^2 = -2\left\{\frac{1}{5} - \frac{1}{3} - \left(-\frac{1}{5}\right) + \left(-\frac{1}{3}\right)\right\} = -2\left(\frac{2}{5} - \frac{2}{3}\right)$$

$$\sigma^2 = \frac{8}{15} \approx 0.533$$

The standard deviation is

$$\sigma = \sqrt{\sigma^2} = \sqrt{\frac{8}{15}} \approx 0.730$$

SKILL Analyze data from specific situations to determine what type of
7.3 function *(e.g., linear, quadratic, exponential)* would most likely model
that particular phenomenon; use the regression feature of the
calculator to determine curve of best fit; interpret the regression
coefficients, correlation, and residuals in context

Choosing a Regression Model

> *There are two basic aspects of regression: selection of an appropriate curve that best fits the data and quantification of the "goodness of fit" of that curve.*

It is often helpful to use regression to construct a more general trend or distribution based on sample data. To select an appropriate model for the regression, a representative set of data must be examined. It is often helpful, in this case, to plot the data and review it visually on a graph. In this manner, it is relatively simple to select a general class of functions (linear, quadratic, exponential, etc.) that might be used to model the data. There are two basic aspects of regression: selection of an appropriate curve that best fits the data and quantification of the "goodness of fit" of that curve. For instance, if a line can be constructed that passes through every data point of a distribution, then that line is a perfect fit to the data (and, obviously, linear regression is an appropriate choice for the model). If the distribution of data points seems to bear no particular resemblance to the line, then linear regression is probably not a wise choice, and a quantification of the goodness of fit should reflect this fact.

The following discussion summarizes least squares linear regression analysis. The same principles can be applied to other forms of regression (such as quadratic or exponential).

The Method of Least Squares

Given a set of data, a curve approximation can be fitted to the data by using the METHOD OF LEAST SQUARES. The best-fit curve, defined by the function $f(x)$, is assumed to approximate a set of data with coordinates (x_i, y_i) by minimizing the sum of squared differences between the curve and the data. Mathematically, the sum of these squared differences (errors) can be written as follows for a data set with n points.

> **METHOD OF LEAST SQUARES:** used to approximately fit a curve to a particular data set by minimizing the sum of squared differences between the curve and the data

$$S = \sum_{i=1}^{n} [f(x_i) - y_i]^2$$

Thus, the best-fit curve approximation to a set of data (x_i, y_i) is $f(x)$ such that S is minimized.

Shown below is a set of data and a linear function that approximates it. The vertical distances between the data points and the line are the errors that are squared and summed to find S.

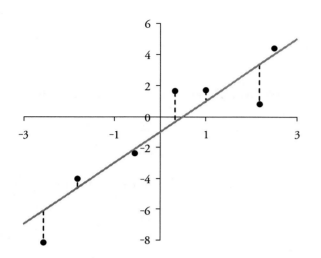

Linear Least Squares Regression

If the curve $f(x)$ that is used to approximate a set of data by minimizing the sum of squared errors (or RESIDUALS), S, is linear, then $f(x)$ is called a least squares regression line. The process of determining $f(x)$ is called LINEAR LEAST SQUARES REGRESSION. In this case, $f(x)$ has the following form:

$$f(x) = ax + b$$

Given a set of data $\{(x_1, y_1), (x_2, y_2), (x_3, y_3), \ldots, (x_n, y_n)\}$, the sum S for linear regression is the following.

$$S = \sum_{i=1}^{n} [ax_i + b - y_i]^2$$

To find $f(x)$, it is necessary to find a and b. This can be done by minimizing S. Since S is a function of both a and b, S must be minimized through the use of partial derivatives. (A partial derivative is exactly the same as a full derivative, except that all variables other than the one being differentiated are treated as constants. Partial derivatives often use the symbol ∂ in place of d.) Therefore, find the partial derivative with respect to a and the partial derivative with respect to b.

$$\frac{\partial S}{\partial a} = \frac{\partial}{\partial a} \sum_{i=1}^{n} [ax_i + b - y_i]^2 \quad \frac{\partial S}{\partial b} = \frac{\partial}{\partial b} \sum_{i=1}^{n} [ax_i + b - y_i]^2$$

$$\frac{\partial S}{\partial a} = \sum_{i=1}^{n} 2x_i [ax_i + b - y_i] \quad \frac{\partial S}{\partial b} = \sum_{i=1}^{n} 2[ax_i + b - y_i]$$

Set these equal to zero. This yields a system of equations that can be solved to find a and b. Although the algebra is somewhat involved, it is not conceptually difficult. The results are given below.

$$a = \frac{n\sum\limits_{i=1}^{n} x_i y_i - \sum\limits_{i=1}^{n} x_i \sum\limits_{i=1}^{n} y_i}{n\sum\limits_{i=1}^{n} x_i^2 - [\sum\limits_{i=1}^{n} x_i]^2}$$

Note that the average x value for the data (which is the sum of all x values divided by n) and the average y value for the data (which is the sum of all y values divided by n) can be used to simplify the expression. The average x value is defined as $\bar{x}$,

RESIDUALS: the difference between an observed data value and the value predicted by a regression model

LINEAR LEAST SQUARES REGRESSION: fitting a data set to a linear function by using the method of least squares.

A partial derivative is exactly the same as a full derivative, except that all variables other than the one being differentiated are treated as constants. Partial derivatives often use the symbol ∂ in place of d.

and the average y value is defined as $\overline{y}$.

$$a = \frac{\sum\limits_{i=1}^{n} x_i y_i - n\overline{xy}}{\sum\limits_{i=1}^{n} x_i^2 - n\overline{x}^2}$$

Since the expression for b is complicated, it suffices to the above expression for b in terms of a.

$$b = \frac{1}{n} \left(\sum\limits_{i=1}^{n} y_i - a \sum\limits_{i=1}^{n} x_i \right)$$
$$b = \overline{y} - a\overline{x}$$

Thus, given a set of data, the linear least squares regression line can be found by calculating a and b as shown above.

Correlation coefficient

The CORRELATION COEFFICIENT, r, can be used as a measure of the quality of $f(x)$ as a fit to the data set. The value of r ranges from zero (for a poor fit) to one (for a good fit). The correlation coefficient formula is given below.

> **CORRELATION COEFFICIENT:** a value between 0 and 1 that measures how well a particular model "fits" a particular set of data

$$r^2 = \frac{[\sum\limits_{i=1}^{n} x_i y_i - \frac{1}{n} \sum\limits_{i=1}^{n} x_i \sum\limits_{i=1}^{n} y_i]^2}{[\sum\limits_{i=1}^{n} x_i^2 - \frac{1}{n}(\sum\limits_{i=1}^{n} x_i)^2][\sum\limits_{i=1}^{n} y_i^2 - \frac{1}{n}(\sum\limits_{i=1}^{n} y_i)^2]}$$

$$r^2 = \frac{(\sum\limits_{i=1}^{n} x_i y_i - n\overline{xy})^2}{(\sum\limits_{i=1}^{n} x_i^2 - n\overline{x}^2)(\sum\limits_{i=1}^{n} y_i^2 - n\overline{y}^2)}$$

Example: A company has collected data comparing the ages of its employees to their respective incomes (in thousands of dollars). Find the line that best fits the data (using a least squares approach). Also calculate the correlation coefficient for the fit. The data is given below in the form of (age, income).

{(35, 42), (27, 23), (54, 43), (58, 64), (39, 51), (31, 40)}

The data are plotted in the graph below.

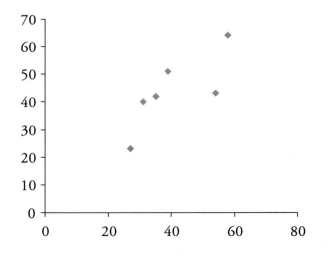

Note that there are six pieces of data. It is helpful to first calculate the following sums:

$$\sum_{i=1}^{6} x_i = 35 + 27 + 54 + 58 + 39 + 31 = 244$$

$$\sum_{i=1}^{6} y_i = 42 + 23 + 43 + 64 + 51 + 40 = 263$$

$$\sum_{i=1}^{6} x_i y_i = 35(42) + 27(23) + 54(43) + 58(64) + 39(51) + 31(40) = 11354$$

$$\sum_{i=1}^{6} x_i^2 = 35^2 + 27^2 + 54^2 + 58^2 + 39^2 + 31^2 = 10716$$

$$\sum_{i=1}^{6} y_i^2 = 42^2 + 23^2 + 43^2 + 64^2 + 51^2 + 40^2 = 12439$$

Based on these values, the average x and y values are given below.

$$\bar{x} = \frac{244}{6} \approx 40.67$$

$$\bar{y} = \frac{263}{6} \approx 43.83$$

To find the equation of the least squares regression line, calculate the values of a and b.

$$a = \frac{\sum_{i=1}^{n} x y_i - n\bar{x}\bar{y}}{\sum_{i=1}^{n} x_i^2 - n\bar{x}^2} = \frac{11354 - 6\,(40.67)\,(43.83)}{10716 - 6\,(40.67)^2} \approx 0.832$$

$$b = \bar{y} - a\bar{x} = 43.83 - 0.832\,(40.67) = 9.993$$

Thus, the equation of the least squares regression line is

$$f(x) = 0.832x + 9.993$$

This result can be displayed on the data graph to ensure that there are no egregious errors in the result.

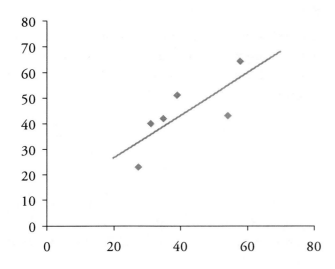

The regression line in the graph above appears to do a good job of approximating the trend of the data. To quantify how well the line fits the data, calculate the correlation coefficient using the formula given above.

$$r^2 = \frac{(11354 - 6\,(40.67)\,(43.83))^2}{(10716 - 6\,(40.67)^2)(12439 - 6\,(43.83)^2)}$$

$$r^2 = \frac{(658.603)^2}{(791.707)(912.587)} = 0.600$$

$$r = 0.775$$

Thus, the fit to the data is reasonably good.

Calculators and Regression

Modern handheld calculators, especially graphing calculators, often have built-in tools for handling regression. After entering the data (in the form of lists, for instance), the calculator's regression functions can be employed. It is usually best to test several different functions (if no particular model is obviously appropriate) and to compare the associated residual or correlation coefficient values for each function. For instance, it may be best to test a data set using both linear and exponential models. By comparing the correlation coefficient, the better-fitting curve can be determined. In this case, the closer the value is to unity, the better the fit. Of course, it is necessary to know the features of a particular calculator, as well as its limitations, to accurately employ regression functions.

SKILL 7.4 **Understand and apply normal distributions and their characteristics** *(mean, standard deviation)*

The Normal Distribution

NORMAL DISTRIBUTION: the probability distribution associated with most sets of real-world data; also called a bell curve

A NORMAL DISTRIBUTION (frequently called a bell curve) is the probability distribution associated with most sets of real-world data. A normal distribution has a continuous random variable X with mean μ and variance σ^2. The normal distribution has the following form.

$$f(x) = \frac{1}{\sigma\sqrt{2\pi}}\, e^{-\frac{1}{2}\left(\frac{x-\mu}{\sigma}\right)^2}$$

The total area under the normal curve is 1. Thus,

$$\int_{-\infty}^{\infty} f(x)\,dx = 1$$

Since the area under the curve of this function is 1, the distribution can be used to determine probabilities through integration. If a continuous random variable x follows the normal distribution, then the probability that x has a value between a and b is

$$P(a < X \le b) = \int_{a}^{b} f(x)\,dx = F(b) - F(a)$$

Since this integral is difficult to evaluate analytically, tables of values are often used. Often, however, the tables use the integral

$$\frac{1}{\sqrt{2\pi}}\int_a^b e^{-\frac{t^2}{2}}\, dt = F(b) - F(a)$$

To use this form, simply convert x values to t values using

$$t = \frac{x_i - \mu}{\sigma}$$

where x_i is a particular value for the random variable X. This formula is often called the Z-SCORE.

> **Z-SCORE:** this score gives the number of standard deviations between a data value x and the mean of the x distribution

Example: Albert's Bagel Shop's morning customer load follows a normal distribution, with mean (average) 50 and standard deviation 10. Determine the probability that the number of customers on a particular morning will be less than 42.

First, convert to a form that allows use of normal distribution tables:

$$t = \frac{x - \mu}{\sigma} = \frac{42 - 50}{10} = -0.8$$

Next, use a table to find the probability corresponding to the z-score. The actual integral in this case is

$$P(X < 42) = \frac{1}{\sqrt{2\pi}} \int_{-\infty}^{-0.8} e^{-\frac{t^2}{2}}\, dt$$

The table gives a value for $x = 0.8$ of 0.7881. To find the value for $x < -0.8$, subtract this result from 1.

$$P(X < 42) = 1 - 0.7881 = 0.2119$$

This means that there is about a 21.2% chance that there will be fewer than 42 customers in a given morning.

Example: The scores on Mr. Rogers' statistics exam follow a normal distribution with mean 85 and standard deviation 5. A student is wondering about the probability that she will score between a 90 and a 95 on her exam.

To compute $P(90 < x < 95)$, first compute the z-scores for each raw score.

$$z_{90} = \frac{90 - 85}{5} = 1$$
$$z_{95} = \frac{95 - 85}{5} = 2$$

Use the tables to find $P(1 < z < 2)$. To do this, subtract as follows.

$$P(1 < z < 2) = P(z < 2) - P(z < 1)$$

The table yields

$$P(1 < z < 2) = 0.9772 - 0.8413 = 0.1359$$

It can then be concluded that there is a 13.6% chance that the student will score between a 90 and a 95 on her exam.

The Binomial Distribution

The binomial distribution is a probability distribution for discrete random variables and is expressed as follows.

$$f(x) = \binom{n}{x} p^x q^{n-x}$$

where a sequence of n trials of an experiment are performed and where p is the probability of "success" and q is the probability of "failure." The value x is the number of times the experiment yields a successful outcome. Notice that this probability function is the product of p^x (the probability of successful outcomes in x trials) and q^{n-x} (the probability of unsuccessful outcomes in the remainder of the trials). The factor $\binom{n}{x}$ indicates that the x successful trials can be chosen $\binom{n}{x}$ ways (combinations) from the n total trials. (In other words, the successful trials may occur at different points in the sequence.)

Example: A loaded coin has a probability 0.6 of landing heads up. What is the probability of getting three heads in four successive tosses?

Use the binomial distribution. In this case, p is the probability of the coin landing heads up, and $q = 1 - p$ is the probability of the coin landing tails up. Also, the number of "successful" trials (heads up) is 3. Then,

$$f(3) = \binom{4}{3} (0.6)^3 (1 - 0.6)^{4-3}$$

$$f(3) = \frac{4!}{3! \, (4 - 3)!} (0.6)^3 (0.4)^1$$

$$f(3) = \frac{24}{6(1)} (0.216) (0.4) = 0.3456$$

Thus, there is a 34.56% chance that the loaded coin will land heads up three out of four times.

The Exponential Distribution

The exponential distribution is for continuous random variables and has the following form.

$$f(x) = \lambda e^{-\lambda x}$$

Here, $x \geq 0$. The parameter λ is called the rate parameter. For instance, the exponential distribution is often applied to failure rates. If a certain device has a failure rate of λ failures per hour, then the probability that a device has failed at time T hours is

$$P(T) = \lambda \int_0^T e^{-\lambda t} \, dt = -\lambda \frac{1}{\lambda} e^{-\lambda t} \Big|_0^T = -[e^{-\lambda T} - e^0] = 1 - e^{-\lambda T}$$

Example: Testing has revealed that a newly designed widget has a failure rate of 1 per 5,000 hours of use. What is the probability that a particular part will be operational after one year.

Use the formula given above for the exponential distribution.

$$P \text{ (1 year)} = 1 - e^{-\lambda(1 \text{ year})}$$

Write λ in terms of failures per year.

$$\lambda = \frac{1 \text{ failure}}{5,000 \text{ hours}} \left(\frac{24 \text{ hours}}{1 \text{ day}}\right)\left(\frac{365 \text{ days}}{1 \text{ year}}\right) = 1.752 \frac{\text{failures}}{\text{year}}$$

Then

$$P \text{ (1 year)} = 1 - e^{-1.752(1)} = 1 - 0.173 = 0.827$$

Thus, there is an 82.7% probability that the device will not be operational after one year of continual use and a 17.3% probability that it will be operational after a year.

SKILL 7.5 Understand how sample statistics reflect the values of population parameters, and use sampling distributions as the basis for informal inference

Statistical studies typically involve a large number of people or a large pool of data known as the POPULATION. In most cases, it is impractical or impossible to collect data from every member, and therefore a representative sample has to be chosen. The process of selecting a sample must be undertaken with extreme care to ensure that it truly represents a population. Different methods of sampling are discussed in *Skill 7.7*.

In addition to deciding what kind of sample will be selected, one must also select the sample statistic to be used. Different sample statistics can be used to estimate a particular population parameter. In order to estimate a population mean, for instance, one can use the sample median or the sample mean. One way to evaluate whether a sample statistic accurately reflects the value of a population parameter is by studying the characteristics of a sampling distribution. For a study that involves a sample of size n, for example, different samples of the same size and same type will produce slightly different values for the same statistic. A SAMPLE STATISTIC, therefore, is a random variable that follows a probability distribution. Informal inferences about the shape, symmetry, mean, and variance of this sampling distribution can help in selection of the appropriate sampling statistic or estimator.

POPULATION: in a statistical study, a large number of people or a large pool of data

SAMPLE STATISTIC: a random variable that follows a probability distribution

UNBIASED ESTIMA-TOR: a sample statistic that accurately reflects a population parameter

For an UNBIASED ESTIMATOR, i.e., a sample statistic that accurately reflects a population parameter, the sampling distribution mean is equal to the estimated population parameter and the distribution is centered at the population parameter. The shape of the sample distribution approaches a normal distribution as the sample size increases. Since consistency between samples is desired in the choice of an estimator, a smaller standard deviation indicates a better estimator.

SKILL 7.6 Understand the differences among various kinds of studies and which types of inferences can legitimately be drawn from each

See Skill 7.7

SKILL 7.7 Know the characteristics of well-defined studies, including the role of randomization in surveys and experiments

Surveys and Sampling

In cases where the number of events or individuals is too large to collect data on each one, scientists collect information from only a small percentage. This is known as SAMPLING or SURVEYING. If sampling is done correctly, it should give the investigator nearly the same information he would have obtained by testing the entire population. The survey must be carefully designed, considering both the sampling technique and the size of the sample.

SAMPLING OR SUR-VEYING: when scientists collect information from only a small percentage of a numbers of events or individuals because the data pool is too large

There are a variety of sampling techniques, both random and nonrandom. Random sampling is also known as probability sampling, since the methods of probability theory can be used to ascertain the odds that the sample is representative of the whole population. Statistical methods may be used to determine how large a sample is necessary to give an investigator a specified level of certainty (95% is a typical confidence interval). Conversely, if an investigator has a sample of certain size, those same statistical methods can be used to determine how confident one can be that the sample accurately reflects the whole population.

A truly random sample must choose events or individuals without regard to time, place, or result. Simple random sampling is ideal for populations that are relatively homogeneous with respect to the data being collected.

In some cases an accurate representation of distinct sub-populations requires stratified random sampling or quota sampling. For instance, if men and women are likely to respond very differently to a particular survey, the total sample population can be separated into these two subgroups and then a random group of respondents selected from each subgroup. This kind of sampling not only provides balanced representation of different subgroups, it also allows comparison of data between subgroups.

Stratified sampling is sometimes proportional; i.e., the number of samples selected from each subgroup reflects the fraction of the whole population represented by the subgroup.

Sometimes compromises must be made to save time, money, or effort. For instance, when conducting a phone survey, calls are typically made only in a certain geographical area and at a certain time of day. This is an example of cluster random sampling. There are three stages to cluster or area sampling:

1. The target population is divided into many regional clusters (groups).

2. A few clusters are randomly selected for study.

3. A few subjects are randomly chosen from within a cluster.

Systematic random sampling involves the collection of a sample at defined intervals (for instance, every tenth part to come off a manufacturing line). Here, it is assumed that the population is ordered randomly and that there is no hidden pattern that may compromise the randomness of the sampling.

Nonrandom sampling is also known as nonprobability sampling. Convenience sampling is the method of choosing items arbitrarily and in an unstructured manner from the frame. Purposive sampling targets a particular section of the population. Snowball sampling (e.g., having survey participants recommend others) and expert sampling are other types of nonrandom sampling. Obviously, nonrandom samples are far less representative of the whole population than random ones. They may, however, be the only methods available or may meet the needs of a particular study.

COMPETENCY 8
PROBABILITY

> **SKILL Understand the concepts of sample space and probability**
> **8.1 distribution, and construct sample spaces and distributions in**
> **simple cases**

Elements of Probability

The PROBABILITY of an outcome, given a RANDOM EXPERIMENT (a structured, repeatable experiment for which the outcome cannot be predicted or, alternatively, for which the outcome is dependent on "chance"), is the relative frequency of the outcome. The RELATIVE FREQUENCY of an outcome is the fraction or percentage of times an experiment yields that outcome for a very large (ideally, infinite) number of trials. For instance, if a "fair" coin is tossed a very large number of times, then the relative frequency of a "heads-up" outcome is 0.5, or 50% (that is, one out of every two trials, on average, should be heads up). The probability is this relative frequency.

In probability theory, the SAMPLE SPACE is a list of all possible outcomes of an experiment. For example, the sample space of tossing two coins is the set {HH, HT, TT, TH}, where H is heads and T is tails, and the sample space of rolling a six-sided die is the set {1, 2, 3, 4, 5, 6}. When conducting experiments with a large number of possible outcomes, it is important to determine the size of the sample space. The size of the sample space can be determined by using the fundamental counting principles and the rules of combinations and permutations (*see Skill 10.1*).

A RANDOM VARIABLE is a function that corresponds to the outcome of some experiment or event, which is in turn dependent on "chance." For instance, the result of a tossed coin is a random variable: the outcome is either heads or tails, and each outcome has an associated probability. A DISCRETE VARIABLE is one that can only take on certain specific values. For instance, the number of students in a class can only be a whole number (e.g., 15 or 16, but not 15.5). A CONTINUOUS VARIABLE, such as the weight of an object, can take on a continuous range of values.

The probabilities for the possible values of a random variable constitute the PROBABILITY DISTRIBUTION for that random variable. Probability distributions can be discrete, as with the case of the tossing of a coin (there are only two possible

PROBABILITY: given a random experiment, the relative frequency of an outcome

RANDOM EXPERIMENT: a structured, repeatable experiment for which the outcome cannot be predicted

RELATIVE FREQUENCY: the fraction or percentage of times an experiment yields that outcome for a very large number of trials

SAMPLE SPACE: a list of all possible outcomes of an experiment

RANDOM VARIABLE: a function that corresponds to the outcome of some experiment or event

distinct outcomes), or they can be continuous, as with the outside temperature at a given time of day. In the latter case, the probability is represented as a continuous function over a range of possible temperatures, and finite probabilities can only be measured in terms of ranges of temperatures rather than specific temperatures. That is to say, for a continuous distribution, it is not meaningful to say "the probability that the outcome is x"; instead, only "the probability that the outcome is between x and $\triangle x$" is meaningful. (Note that if each potential outcome in a continuous distribution has a non-zero probability, then the sum of all the probabilities would be greater than 1, since there are an infinite number of potential outcomes.)

Example: Find the sample space and construct a probability distribution for tossing a six-sided die (with numbers 1 through 6) for which even numbers are twice as likely as odd numbers to come up on a given roll (assume the even numbers are equally likely and the odd numbers are equally likely).
The sample space is simply the set of all possible outcomes that can arise in a given trial. For this die, the sample space is {1, 2, 3, 4, 5, 6}. To construct the associated probability distribution, note first that the sum of the probabilities must equal 1. Let the probability of rolling an odd number (1, 3, or 5) be x; the probability of rolling an even number (2, 4, or 6) is then $2x$.

$$1 = p(1) + p(2) + p(3) + p(4) + p(5) + p(6) = 3x + 6x = 9x$$
$$x = \frac{1}{9}$$

The probability distribution can be shown as a histogram below.

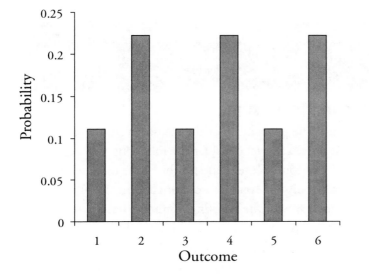

The sum of the probabilities for all the possible outcomes of a discrete distribution (or the integral of the continuous distribution over all possible values) must be equal to unity. The expected value of a probability distribution is the same

EXPECTED VALUE: a measure of the central tendency or average value for a random variable with a given probability distribution

as the mean value of a probability distribution. The EXPECTED VALUE is thus a measure of the central tendency or average value for a random variable with a given probability distribution.

A BERNOULLI TRIAL is an experiment whose outcome is random and can be either of two possible outcomes, which are called "success" or "failure." Tossing a coin would be an example of a Bernoulli trial. The probability of success is represented by p, with the probability of failure being $q = 1 - p$. Bernoulli trials can be applied to any real-life situation in which there are only two possible outcomes. For example, concerning the birth of a child, the only two possible outcomes for the sex of the child are male or female.

BERNOULLI TRIAL: an experiment whose outcome is random and can be either of two possible outcomes, which are called "success" or "failure"

Probability can also be expressed in terms of odds. ODDS are defined as the ratio of the number of favorable outcomes to the number of unfavorable outcomes. The sum of the favorable outcomes and the unfavorable outcomes should always equal the total possible outcomes.

ODDS: the ratio of the number of favorable outcomes to the number of unfavorable outcomes

For example, given a bag of 12 red marbles and 7 green marbles, compute the odds of randomly selecting a red marble.

Odds of red $= \frac{12}{7}$

Odds of not getting red $= \frac{7}{12}$

In the case of flipping a coin, it is equally likely that a head or a tail will be tossed. The odds of tossing a head are 1:1. This is called even odds.

SKILL **Understand the concepts of conditional probability and**
8.2 **independent events; understand how to compute the probability of**
a compound event

Dependent and Independent Events

DEPENDENT EVENTS occur when the probability of the second event depends on the outcome of the first event. For example, consider the following two events: the home team wins the semifinal round (event *A*) and the home team wins the final round (event *B*). The probability of event *B* is contingent on the probability of event *A*. If the home team fails to win the semifinal round, it has a zero probability of winning in the final round. On the other hand, if the home team wins the semifinal round, then it may have a finite probability of winning in the final round. Symbolically, the probability of event *B* given event *A* is written $P(B|A)$.

DEPENDENT EVENTS: events that occur when the probability of the second event depends on the outcome of the first event

The CONDITIONAL PROBABILITY can be calculated according to the following definition (the symbol ∩ means "and," ∪ means "or," and $P(x)$ means "the probability of x"):

$$P(B|A) = \frac{P(A \cap B)}{P(A)}$$

Consider a pair of dice: one red and one green. First the red die is rolled, followed by the green die. It is apparent that these events do not depend on each other, since the outcome of the roll of the green die is not affected by the outcome of the roll of the red die. Thus the events are INDEPENDENT EVENTS. The total probability of two independent events can be found by multiplying the separate probabilities.

$$P(A \cap B) = P(A)P(B)$$
$$P(A \cap B) = \left(\tfrac{1}{6}\right)\left(\tfrac{1}{6}\right) = \tfrac{1}{36}$$

Replacement

In many instances, events are not independent. Suppose a jar contains 12 red marbles and 8 blue marbles. If a marble is selected at random and then replaced, the probability of picking a certain color is the same in the second trial as it is in the first trial. If the marble is *not* replaced, then the probability of picking a certain color is *not* the same in the second trial, because the total number of marbles is decreased by 1. This is an illustration of conditional probability. If R_n signifies selection of a red marble on the nth trial and B_n signifies selection of a blue marble on the nth trial, then the probability of selecting a red marble in two trials *with replacement* is

$$P(R_1 \cap R_2) = P(R_1)P(R_2) = \left(\tfrac{12}{20}\right)\left(\tfrac{12}{20}\right) = \tfrac{144}{400} = 0.36$$

The probability of selecting a red marble in two trials *without replacement* is

$$P(R_1 \cap R_2) = P(R_1)P(R_2|R_1) = \left(\tfrac{12}{20}\right)\left(\tfrac{11}{19}\right) = \tfrac{132}{380} \approx 0.347$$

Example: A car has a 75% probability of traveling 20,000 miles without breaking down. It has a 50% probability of traveling 10,000 additional miles without breaking down if it first makes it to 20,000 miles without breaking down. What is the probability that the car reaches 30,000 miles without breaking down?

Let event A be that the car reaches 20,000 miles without breaking down.

$$P(A) = 0.75$$

Event B is that the car travels an additional 10,000 miles without breaking down (assuming it didn't break down for the first 20,000 miles). Since event B is contingent on event A, write the probability as follows:

$$P(B|A) = 0.50$$

CONDITIONAL PROBABILITY: the probability that event B will occur, given that event A has occurred

INDEPENDENT EVENTS: when the probability of a second event occurring does not depend on the probability of the first event occurring

The total probability of two independent events can be found by multiplying the separate probabilities.

Use the conditional probability formula to find the probability that the car travels 30,000 miles $(A \cap B)$ without breaking down.

$$P(B|A) = \frac{P(A \cap B)}{P(A)}$$
$$0.50 = \frac{P(A \cap B)}{0.75}$$
$$P(A \cap B) = (0.50)(0.75) = 0.375$$

Thus, the car has a 37.5% probability of traveling 30,000 consecutive miles without breaking down.

SKILL 8.3 Compute and interpret the expected value of random variables in simple cases (e.g., fair coins, expected winnings, expected profit)

As mentioned in *Skill 8.1*, the expected value of a random variable is the mean value of the probability distribution. In the case of discrete variables such as coin toss outcomes, one can think of it as a weighted average.

For instance, for a regular six-sided die, where each outcome is equally probable, the expected value on a roll is a simple average and is given by

$(1 + 2 + 3 + 4 + 5 + 6)/6 = 21/6 = 3.5$

For the die for which even numbers are twice as likely to come up on a roll as odd numbers (see example in *Skill 8.1*), on the other hand, the probability of each odd number coming up is 1/9, and the probability of each even number coming up is 2/9. Hence, the expected value of one roll of this die is given by

$(1 + 3 + 5)(1/9) + (2 + 4 + 6)(2/9) = 33/9 = 3.67$

The higher probability of the numbers with relatively greater value is reflected in the increase in the expected value compared to the regular die.

Example: A fair coin is tossed three times. What is the expected value of the total number of heads?

Consider the different ways in which a coin can be tossed three times:

HHH, HHT, HTH, THH, TTH, HTT, THT, TTT

Notice that the probability of getting zero heads is 1/8, one head is 3/8, two heads is 3/8, and three heads is 1/8.

Hence the expected value for the number of heads is

$(1/8)(0) + (3/8)(1) + (3/8)(2) + (1/8)(3) = 12/8 = 1.5$

SKILL 8.4 Use simulations to construct empirical probability distributions and to make informal inferences about the theoretical probability distribution

Probability Simulations

Simulations of random events or variables can be helpful in making informal inferences about theoretical probability distributions. Although simulations can involve use of physical situations that bear some similarity to the situation of interest, oftentimes simulations involve computer modeling.

Pseudorandom numbers

One of the crucial aspects of modeling probability using a computer program is the need for a random number that can be used to "randomize" the aspect of the program that corresponds to the event or variable. Although there is no function on a computer that can provide a truly random number, most programming languages have some function designed to produce a pseudorandom number. A PSEUDORANDOM NUMBER is not truly random, but it is sufficiently unpredictable that it can be used as a random number in many contexts.

Pseudorandom numbers can serve as the basis for simulation of rolling a die, flipping a coin, selecting an object from a collection of different objects, and a range of other situations. If, for instance, the pseudorandom number generator produces a number between 0 and 1, simply divide up that range in accordance with the probabilities of each particular outcome. (For instance, assign 0 to 0.5 as heads and 0.5 to 1 as tails for the flip of a fair coin.) By performing a number of simulated trials and tallying the results, empirical probability distributions can be created.

Ideally, as the number of trials goes to infinity, the empirical probability distribution should approach the theoretical distribution. As a result, by performing a sufficiently large number of trials (this number must be at least somewhat justified for the particular situation), one should be able to make informal inferences based on the data. Such inferences, however, must take into account the limitations of the computer, such as the inability to perform an infinite number of trials in finite time and the numerical inaccuracies that are an inherent part of computer programming.

> **PSEUDORANDOM NUMBER:** a number that is not truly random but that is sufficiently unpredictable that it can be used as a random number in many contexts

DOMAIN V
MATRIX ALGEBRA AND DISCRETE MATHEMATICS

PERSONALIZED STUDY PLAN

KNOWN MATERIAL/ SKIP IT

PAGE	COMPETENCY AND SKILL	
211	**9: Matrix algebra**	☐
	9.1: Understand vectors and matrices	☐
	9.2: Scalar multiply, add, subtract, and multiply vectors and matrices; find inverses of matrices	☐
	9.3: Use matrix techniques to solve systems of linear equations	☐
	9.4: Use determinants to reason about inverses of matrices and solutions to systems of equations	☐
	9.5: Understand and represent translations, reflections, rotations, and dilations of objects	☐
225	**10: Discrete mathematics**	☐
	10.1: Solve basic problems that involve counting techniques; use counting techniques to understand various situations	☐
	10.2: Find values of functions defined recursively and understand how recursion can be used to model various phenomena	☐
	10.3: Determine whether a binary relation on a set is reflexive, symmetric, or transitive	☐
	10.4: Use finite and infinite arithmetic and geometric sequences and series to model simple phenomena	☐
	10.5: Understand the relationship between discrete and continuous representations	☐
	10.6: Use difference equations, vertex-edge graphs, trees, and networks to model and solve problems	☐

COMPETENCY 9
MATRIX ALGEBRA

Vectors and matrices are tools that simplify certain types of calculations. Both vectors and matrices are useful for solving systems of equations and for modeling physical phenomena that display the characteristic of direction in addition to magnitude, such as velocity, force, and momentum.

> **SKILL Understand vectors and matrices as systems that have some of the**
> **9.1 same properties as the real number system** *(e.g., identity, inverse, and commutativity under addition and multiplication)*

Vectors

A **VECTOR** is any quantity that has magnitude (or length) and direction. For instance, unlike temperature (which is just a scalar), velocity is a vector because it has magnitude (speed) and direction (the direction of travel). Because vectors do not have specified locations, they can be translated as long as their direction and magnitude remain the same. A vector is often written in the same form as a point; for instance, a vector can be written as (x_1, y_1, z_1). In this case, the direction and magnitude of the vector are defined by a ray that starts at the origin and terminates at the point (x_1, y_1, z_1).

VECTOR: any quantity that has a magnitude (or length) and direction

Because vectors do not have specified locations, they can be translated as long as their direction and magnitude remain the same.

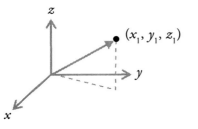

As noted before, however, the vector is not confined to the location shown above. The magnitude of a vector is simply the distance from the origin to the point (x_1, y_1, z_1). If $\vec{A} = (x_1, y_1, z_1)$, then the magnitude is written as $|\vec{A}|$.

$$|\vec{A}| = \sqrt{x_1^2 + y_1^2 + z_1^2}$$

Note that the direction of a vector can be written as a unit vector $\vec{u}$ of length 1, such that

$$\vec{A} = \vec{u}|\vec{A}|$$

Vectors obey the laws of associativity, commutativity, identity, and additive inverses:

$$\vec{A} + (\vec{B} + \vec{C}) = (\vec{A} + \vec{B}) + \vec{C}$$
$$\vec{A} + \vec{B} = \vec{B} + \vec{A}$$
$$\vec{A} + 0 = \vec{A}$$
$$\vec{A} + (-\vec{A}) = 0$$

As such, vectors have some of the same properties as real numbers.

Matrices

Matrices are slightly more complicated than vectors, and operations involving matrices likewise require more subtle analysis. In fact, vectors can simply be viewed as a type of matrix. Like vectors, matrices obey some of the same rules and principles as do real numbers; in other cases, however, such as commutativity, matrices and real numbers differ.

MATRIX: an ordered set of numbers written in rectangular form

A MATRIX is an ordered set of numbers written in rectangular form. An example matrix is shown below.

Since this matrix has 3 rows and 3 columns, it is called a 3×3 matrix. The element in the second row of the third column would be denoted as $3_{2,3}$. In general, a matrix with r rows and c columns is an $r \times c$ matrix.

In general, a matrix with r rows and c columns is an $r \times c$ matrix.

Matrix addition and subtraction obey the rules of associativity, commutativity, identity, and additive inverse.

$$\overline{A} + (\overline{B} + \overline{C}) = (\overline{A} + \overline{B}) + \overline{C}$$
$$\overline{A} + \overline{B} = \overline{B} + \overline{A}$$
$$\overline{A} + 0 = \overline{A}$$
$$\overline{A} + (-\overline{A}) = 0$$

SKILL **Scalar multiply, add, subtract, and multiply vectors and matrices;**
9.2 **find inverses of matrices**

Addition, Subtraction, and Scalar Multiplication of Vectors

Addition and subtraction of two vectors $\vec{A} = (x_1, y_1, z_1)$ and $\vec{B} = (x_2, y_2, z_2)$ can be performed by adding or subtracting corresponding components of the vectors.

$$\vec{A} + \vec{B} = (x_1 + x_2, y_1 + y_2, z_1 + z_2)$$
$$\vec{A} - \vec{B} = (x_1 - x_2, y_1 - y_2, z_1 - z_2)$$

Geometrically, addition involves placing the tail of $\vec{B}$ on the head of $\vec{A}$, as shown below. The result is a vector that starts from the tail of $\vec{A}$ and ends at the head of $\vec{B}$.

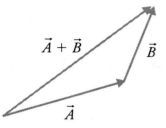

Subtraction of two vectors involves the same process, except that the direction of $\vec{B}$ must be reversed.

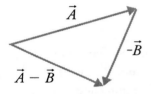

Multiplication of a vector by a scalar simply involves multiplying each component by the scalar.

$$c\vec{A} = (cx_1, cy_1, cz_1)$$

Geometrically, this operation extends the length of the vector by a factor c.

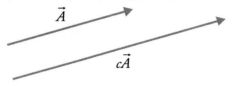

Vector Multiplication

Vector multiplication takes two forms: the DOT PRODUCT (or scalar product) and the CROSS PRODUCT (or vector product). The dot product is calculated by multiplying corresponding components of two vectors. The operator for this product is typically a small dot (·).

$$\vec{A} \cdot \vec{B} = x_1 x_2 + y_1 y_2 + z_1 z_2$$

Notice that the dot product yields a single scalar value. Also note that the magnitude of a vector can be written in terms of the dot product.

$$|\vec{A}| = \sqrt{\vec{A} \cdot \vec{A}}$$

> **DOT PRODUCT:** the product of two vectors is found by multiplying corresponding components of the vectors; the result is a scalar

Geometrically, the dot product is a projection of one vector onto another.

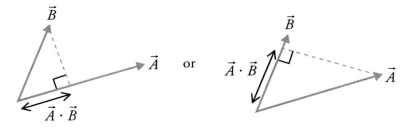

It can be shown that the dot product of two vectors is equivalent to the following:

$$\vec{A} \cdot \vec{B} = |\vec{A}| |\vec{B}| \cos \theta$$

It is clear, both from the geometric and the algebraic definitions of the dot product, that if two vectors are perpendicular, then their dot product is zero.

> *If two vectors are perpendicular, then their dot product is zero.*

The cross product of two vectors, typically symbolized by a "×" operator, yields a third vector. The cross product is defined as follows.

$$\vec{A} \times \vec{B} = (y_1 z_2 - y_2 z_1, z_1 x_2 - z_2 x_1, x_1 y_2 - x_2 y_1)$$

> **CROSS PRODUCT:** a third vector that is perpendicular to both original vectors (that is to the plane formed by the two original vectors)

Geometrically, the CROSS PRODUCT of $\vec{A}$ and $\vec{B}$ is a third vector that is perpendicular to both $\vec{A}$ and $\vec{B}$ (that is, to the plane formed by $\vec{A}$ and $\vec{B}$), with the direction defined by the so-called right-hand screw rule. If a right-hand screw is turned in the direction from $\vec{A}$ to $\vec{B}$, the direction in which the screw advances is the direction of the cross product.

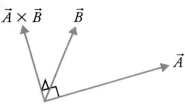

The magnitude of $\vec{A} \times \vec{B}$ is the area of the parallelogram defined by $\vec{A}$ and $\vec{B}$.

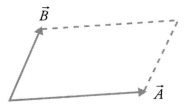

The magnitude of the cross product can also be written as follows.

$$|\vec{A} \times \vec{B}| = |\vec{A}| |\vec{B}| \sin \theta$$

> *If two vectors are parallel, their cross product is zero.*

From both the algebraic and geometric definitions of the cross product, it is apparent that if two vectors are parallel, their cross product is zero.

Multiplication of vectors, either by the dot product or cross product, obeys the rule of distibutivity, where $*$ symbolizes either $\cdot$ or $\times$.

$$\vec{A} * (\vec{B} + \vec{C}) = \vec{A} * \vec{B} + \vec{A} * \vec{C}$$

Only the dot product obeys commutativity, however. There is a similar rule for cross products, though.

$$\vec{A} \cdot \vec{B} = \vec{B} \cdot \vec{A}$$
$$\vec{A} \times \vec{B} = -\vec{B} \times \vec{A}$$

Example: Find the cross product $\vec{a} \times \vec{b}$, *where* $\vec{a} = (-1, 4, 2)$ *and* $\vec{b} = (3, -1, 4)$.

Use the expression given to calculate the cross product.

$$\vec{a} \times \vec{b} = (4 \cdot 4 - (-1) \cdot 2, 2 \cdot 3 - 4 \cdot (-1), (-1) \cdot (-1) - 3 \cdot 4)$$
$$\vec{a} \times \vec{b} = (16 + 2, 6 + 4, 1 - 12) = (18, 10, -11)$$

Example: Find the following for $\vec{a} = (1, 2, 3)$, $\vec{b} = (2, 3, 1)$ *and* $c = 2$: $c(\vec{a} \cdot \vec{b})$.

First, find the dot product; then multiply. Note that the result must be a scalar.

$$c(\vec{a} \cdot \vec{b}) = 2[1(2) + 2(3) + 3(1)] = 2[11] = 22$$

Addition, Subtraction, and Multiplication of Matrices

Matrices can be added or subtracted only if their dimensions are the same. To add (subtract) compatible matrices, simply add (subtract) the corresponding elements, as with the example below for 2×2 matrices.

$$\begin{pmatrix} a_{11} & a_{12} \\ a_{21} & a_{22} \end{pmatrix} + \begin{pmatrix} b_{11} & b_{12} \\ b_{21} & b_{22} \end{pmatrix} = \begin{pmatrix} a_{11} + b_{11} & a_{12} + b_{12} \\ a_{21} + b_{21} & a_{22} + b_{22} \end{pmatrix}$$

Multiplication of matrices is more complicated, except for the case of multiplication by a scalar. The product of a matrix and a scalar is found by multiplying each element of the matrix by the scalar.

$$c \begin{pmatrix} a_{11} & a_{12} \\ a_{21} & a_{22} \end{pmatrix} = \begin{pmatrix} ca_{11} & ca_{12} \\ ca_{21} & ca_{22} \end{pmatrix}$$

Multiplication of two matrices is only defined if the number of columns in the first matrix is equal to the number of rows in the second matrix. Matrix multiplication is not necessarily commutative. Given an $n \times m$ matrix ($\overline{A}$) multiplied by an $m \times p$ matrix ($\overline{B}$) (multiplied in that order), the product is an $n \times p$ matrix. Each element C_{ij} in the product matrix is equal to the sum of each element in the

Multiplication of two matrices is only defined if the number of columns in the first matrix is equal to the number of rows in the second matrix.

ith row of the $n \times m$ matrix multiplied by each corresponding element in the jth column of the $m \times p$ matrix. Thus, each element C_{ij} of the product matrix $\overline{AB}$ is equal to the following, where $\overline{AB} = \overline{C}$:

$$C_{ij} = \sum_{k=1}^{m} A_{ik}B_{kj}$$

Consider the following example.

$$\begin{pmatrix} 1 & 2 & 3 \\ 4 & 5 & 6 \end{pmatrix}\begin{pmatrix} 7 \\ 8 \\ 9 \end{pmatrix}$$

The solution is found as follows.

$$\begin{pmatrix} 1 & 2 & 3 \\ 4 & 5 & 6 \end{pmatrix}\begin{pmatrix} 7 \\ 8 \\ 9 \end{pmatrix} = \begin{pmatrix} (1)(7) + (2)(8) + (3)(9) \\ (4)(7) + (5)(8) + (6)(9) \end{pmatrix} = \begin{pmatrix} 50 \\ 122 \end{pmatrix}$$

Matrix multiplication obeys the rules of associativity and distributivity, but not commutativity.

$$\overline{A}(\overline{BC}) = (\overline{AB})\overline{C}$$
$$\overline{A}(\overline{B} + \overline{C}) = \overline{AB} + \overline{AC}$$
$$(B + \overline{C})\overline{A} = \overline{BA} + \overline{CA}$$

Example: Determine the product $\overline{AB}$ of the following matrices.

$$\overline{A} = \begin{pmatrix} -1 & 2 & 8 \\ 4 & -3 & 7 \\ 0 & 1 & 4 \end{pmatrix} \quad \overline{B} = \begin{pmatrix} 0 & 5 & 0 \\ 7 & -2 & -1 \\ -8 & 0 & 3 \end{pmatrix}$$

The product AB is a 3×3 matrix. The first column of AB is the dot product of the first column of B with each row of A.

$$\overline{AB} = \begin{pmatrix} -1 & 2 & 8 \\ 4 & -3 & 7 \\ 0 & 1 & 4 \end{pmatrix}\begin{pmatrix} 0 & 5 & 0 \\ 7 & -2 & -1 \\ -8 & 0 & 3 \end{pmatrix} = \begin{pmatrix} 0 + 14 - 64 & \cdot & \cdot \\ -21 - 56 & \cdot & \cdot \\ 7 - 32 & \cdot & \cdot \end{pmatrix}$$

The other columns of AB are found using the same approach for the other columns of B.

$$\overline{AB} = \begin{pmatrix} -50 & -9 & 22 \\ -77 & 26 & 24 \\ -25 & -2 & 11 \end{pmatrix}$$

SKILL **Use matrix techniques to solve systems of linear equations**
9.3

For information on finding the determinants of matrices, see Skill 9.4.

Solving Systems of Equations Using Matrices

When given a system of equations, such as

$$ax + by = e$$
$$cx + dy = f$$

the matrix equation is written in the following form.

$$\begin{pmatrix} a & b \\ c & d \end{pmatrix} \begin{pmatrix} x \\ y \end{pmatrix} = \begin{pmatrix} e \\ f \end{pmatrix}$$

The same general pattern follows for n equations in n variables. (The result is an $n \times n$ matrix with a variable vector and a constant vector, each with n entries.) The solution is found using the inverse of the matrix of coefficients. The inverse of a 2 $\times$ 2 matrix can be written as follows ($|A|$ is the determinant of the 2 $\times$ 2 matrix A with elements a, b, c, d; see Skill 9.4 for determinants):

$$A^{-1} = \frac{1}{|A|} \begin{pmatrix} d & -b \\ -c & a \end{pmatrix}$$

Then,

$$\begin{pmatrix} a & b \\ c & d \end{pmatrix}^{-1} \begin{pmatrix} a & b \\ c & d \end{pmatrix} \begin{pmatrix} x \\ y \end{pmatrix} = \begin{pmatrix} x \\ y \end{pmatrix} = \begin{pmatrix} a & b \\ c & d \end{pmatrix}^{-1} \begin{pmatrix} e \\ f \end{pmatrix}$$

The solution set defined by the variable vector can then be found by performing the matrix multiplication on the right of the above equation.

$$\begin{pmatrix} x \\ y \end{pmatrix} = \frac{1}{|A|} \begin{pmatrix} d & -b \\ -c & a \end{pmatrix} \begin{pmatrix} e \\ f \end{pmatrix} = \frac{1}{|A|} \begin{pmatrix} ed - bf \\ af - ce \end{pmatrix}$$

Solving systems of equations with many variables can involve the more complicated tasks of finding the determinant and inverse of large matrices.

Note that if the determinant of a matrix is zero, then the matrix is called SINGULAR. In such cases, a unique solution to the system of equations does not exist.

SINGULAR: occurs when the determinant of a matrix is zero

Gauss elimination

If a matrix larger than 2 $\times$ 2 must be inverted, then Gauss elimination can be used to find the solution. The approach for this technique first involves augmenting the matrix with the constant vector. Using the above example, the augmented matrix is

$$\left(\begin{array}{cc|c} a & b & e \\ c & d & f \end{array} \right)$$

The goal of Gauss elimination is to perform row operations such that the coefficient matrix becomes the identity matrix:

$$\begin{pmatrix} 1 & 0 & \cdots \\ 0 & 1 & \cdots \\ \vdots & \vdots & \ddots \end{pmatrix}$$

For the example matrix above, first divide the first row by a.

$$\left(\begin{array}{cc|c} 1 & \frac{b}{a} & \frac{e}{a} \\ & d & f \end{array} \right)$$

Next, subtract c times the first row from the second row.

$$\left(\begin{array}{cc|c} 1 & \frac{b}{a} & \frac{e}{a} \\ 0 & d - \frac{cb}{a} & f - \frac{ec}{a} \end{array} \right)$$

The process can be continued until the result is found, which is

$$\left(\begin{array}{cc|c} 1 & 0 & \frac{ed - bf}{|A|} \\ 0 & 1 & \frac{af - ce}{|A|} \end{array} \right)$$

Example: Write the matrix equation of the following system of equations and solve for x and y.

$3x - 4y = 2$

$2x + y = 5$

$$\begin{pmatrix} 3 & -4 \\ 2 & 1 \end{pmatrix} \begin{pmatrix} x \\ y \end{pmatrix} = \begin{pmatrix} 2 \\ 5 \end{pmatrix} \qquad \text{Definition of matrix equation.}$$

$$\begin{pmatrix} x \\ y \end{pmatrix} = \frac{1}{11} \begin{pmatrix} 1 & 4 \\ -2 & 3 \end{pmatrix} \begin{pmatrix} 2 \\ 5 \end{pmatrix} \qquad \text{Multiply by the inverse of the coefficient matrix.}$$

$$\begin{pmatrix} x \\ y \end{pmatrix} = \frac{1}{11} \begin{pmatrix} 22 \\ 11 \end{pmatrix} \qquad \text{Matrix multiplication.}$$

$$\begin{pmatrix} x \\ y \end{pmatrix} = \begin{pmatrix} 2 \\ 1 \end{pmatrix} \qquad \text{Scalar multiplication.}$$

The solution is then $x = 2$ and $y = 1$.

Use determinants to reason about inverses of matrices and solutions to systems of equations

Determinants

Associated with every square matrix is a number called its determinant. The determinant of a matrix is typically denoted using straight brackets; thus, the determinant of matrix A is $|A|$. Use these formulas to calculate determinants.

$$\begin{vmatrix} a & b \\ c & d \end{vmatrix} = ad - bc$$

$$\begin{vmatrix} a_1 & b_1 & c_1 \\ a_2 & b_2 & c_2 \\ a_3 & b_3 & c_3 \end{vmatrix} = (a_1 b_2 c_3 + b_1 c_2 a_3 + c_1 a_2 b_3) - (a_3 b_2 c_1 + b_3 c_2 a_1 + c_3 a_2 b_1)$$

The second formula is found by repeating the first two columns and then using the diagonal lines to find the value of each expression as shown below:

$$\begin{vmatrix} a_1 & b_1 & c_1 \\ a_2 & b_2 & c_2 \\ a_3 & b_3 & c_3 \end{vmatrix} \begin{matrix} a_1 & b_1 \\ a_2 & b_2 \\ a_3 & b_3 \end{matrix}$$
$$= (a_1 b_2 c_3 + b_1 c_2 a_3 + c_1 a_2 b_3) - (a_3 b_2 c_1 + b_3 c_2 a_1 + c_3 a_2 b_1)$$

Example: Find the value of the determinant of $\begin{pmatrix} 4 & -8 \\ 7 & 3 \end{pmatrix}$.

Use the formula for calculating the determinant.

$$\begin{vmatrix} 4 & -8 \\ 7 & 3 \end{vmatrix} = (4)(3) - (-8)(7) = 12 + 56 = 68$$

For information on using determinants to find the inverse of a 2 × 2 matrix, see Skill 9.3.

Applications of Matrices

Matrices are often used to solve systems of equations. They are also used by physicists, mathematicians, and biologists to organize and study data such as population growth, and they are used in finance for such purposes as investment growth and portfolio analysis. Matrices are easily translated into computer code in high-level programming languages and can be easily expressed in electronic spreadsheets.

The following is an example of using a matrix to solve a simple financial problem. A company has two stores. The incomes and expenses (in dollars) for the two stores, for three months, are shown in the matrices.

April	Income	Expenses
Store 1	190,000	170,000
Store 2	100,000	110,000

May	Income	Expenses
Store 1	210,000	200,000
Store 2	125,000	120,000

June	Income	Expenses
Store 1	220,000	215,000
Store 2	130,000	115,000

The owner wants to know what his first-quarter income and expenses were, so he adds the three matrices.

1st Quarter   Income   Expenses

Store 1

Store 2

$$\begin{bmatrix} 620{,}000 & 585{,}000 \\ 355{,}000 & 345{,}000 \end{bmatrix}$$

Then, to find the profit for each store:

Profit for Store 1 = \$620,000 − \$585,000 = \$35,000

Profit for Store 2 = \$355,000 − \$345,000 = \$10,000

SKILL 9.5 **Understand and represent translations, reflections, rotations, and dilations of objects in the plane by using sketches, coordinates, vectors, and matrices**

Planar Transformations Using Vectors and Matrices

The different types of transformations of geometric figures in the plane, such as translations, rotations, reflections, and dilations, are discussed in Skill 3.7. Often, however, it can be helpful to represent these transformations (especially when the transformations are complicated or when multiple sequential transformations are to be performed) using vectors and matrices.

Points in a geometric figure, such as vertices, can be treated as a vector with two elements—(x_1, y_1), for instance—that specify the location of the point in some coordinate system. Consider the example below.

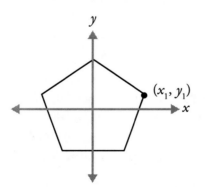

Given that each point on the figure is represented by an ordered pair, a 2×2 matrix can be used to perform the transformation. For any given transformation, a particular 2×2 matrix $\overline{T}$ can be determined that transforms all the points in the correct manner.

Reflections

Consider a reflection about the *x*-axis. This transformation results in the following:

$$(x, y) \to (x, {}^-y)$$

The result of this transformation is shown below for the pentagon given in the diagram above.

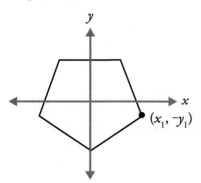

A matrix $\overline{T}$ can be constructed that performs this transformation.

$$\overline{T} = \begin{pmatrix} 1 & 0 \\ 0 & -1 \end{pmatrix}$$

Thus:

$$\overline{T} \begin{pmatrix} x \\ y \end{pmatrix} = \begin{pmatrix} 1 & 0 \\ 0 & -1 \end{pmatrix} \begin{pmatrix} x \\ y \end{pmatrix} = \begin{pmatrix} x \\ -y \end{pmatrix}$$

A similar transformation matrix can be constructed for reflections about the *y*-axis or about an arbitrary line (although this latter case is significantly more difficult).

Translations

For a translation, it is sufficient to simply construct a vector that is added to each point (x, y) in the figure. This vector is composed of a length for the translation in the *x* direction and a length for the translation in the *y* direction. For instance, to translate a figure a distance *a* in the positive *x* direction and a distance *b* in the negative *y* direction, use a vector $(a, {}^-b)$. The result is shown below for the pentagon.

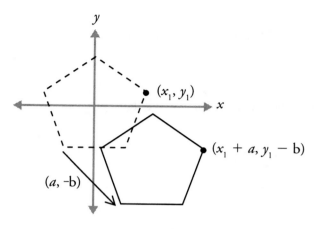

Algebraically, the transformation for the transformed figure in terms of the points (x, y) on the original figure is the following for a general translation (c, d):

$$\begin{pmatrix} x \\ y \end{pmatrix} + \begin{pmatrix} c \\ d \end{pmatrix}$$

Rotations

Rotations are slightly more complicated transformations. Consider a rotation around the origin of a point specified as (x_1, y_1).

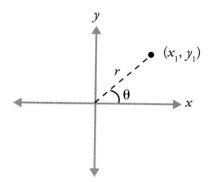

Using polar coordinates (*see Skill 4.5 for more on polar coordinates*), the point can likewise be represented as a distance r from the origin and an angle θ from the x-axis.

$$r = \sqrt{x_1^2 + y_1^2}$$
$$\theta = \arctan\frac{y_1}{x_1}$$

A rotation around the origin simply involves, in this case, changing θ but holding r constant. Consider a rotation α in the counterclockwise direction.

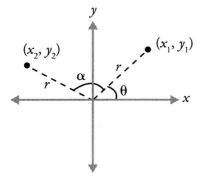

The coordinates of the new point (x_2, y_2) are then the following:

$$x_2 = r \cos (\alpha + \theta)$$
$$y_2 = r \sin (\alpha + \theta)$$

Use the sum formulas for trigonometric functions (*see Skill 4.4*) to expand and then simplify these expressions.

$$x_2 = r (\cos \alpha \cos \theta - \sin \alpha \sin \theta) = (r \cos \theta) \cos \alpha - (r \sin \theta) \sin \alpha$$
$$y_2 = r (\sin \alpha \cos \theta + \cos \alpha \sin \theta) = (r \cos \theta) \sin \alpha + (r \sin \theta) \cos \alpha$$

But $r \cos \theta$ is simply x_1, and r $\sin \theta$ is simply y_1.

$$x_2 = x_1 \cos \alpha - y_1 \sin \alpha$$
$$y_2 = x_1 \sin \alpha + y_1 \cos \alpha$$

Clearly, these two equations can be written in matrix form. Thus, a rotation of point (x_1, y_1) about the origin by angle α can be expressed as follows.

$$\begin{pmatrix} x_2 \\ y_2 \end{pmatrix} = \begin{pmatrix} \cos \alpha & -\sin \alpha \\ \sin \alpha & \cos \alpha \end{pmatrix} \begin{pmatrix} x_1 \\ y_1 \end{pmatrix}$$

This result can be tested using simple cases. For instance, consider a point $(1, 0)$ rotated by π radians.

$$\begin{pmatrix} x_2 \\ y_2 \end{pmatrix} = \begin{pmatrix} \cos \pi & -\sin \pi \\ \sin \pi & \cos \pi \end{pmatrix} \begin{pmatrix} 1 \\ 0 \end{pmatrix} = \begin{pmatrix} -1 & 0 \\ 0 & -1 \end{pmatrix} \begin{pmatrix} 1 \\ 0 \end{pmatrix} = \begin{pmatrix} -1 \\ 0 \end{pmatrix}$$

This result makes intuitive sense. To rotate a figure, simply rotate a set of representative points (such as the vertices); then reconnect them after the rotation. In cases in which a point of rotation is chosen that is not the origin, a change of coordinates to make the origin and the point of rotation coincide may simplify the problem and eliminate the need to handle complicated transformation matrices.

Dilations

Dilations involve a change in the distance r from some point (such as the origin), rather than a change in the angle θ. As with rotations, it is sometimes convenient to perform a change of coordinates so that the center of dilation and the origin of the coordinate system coincide. In such a case, a dilation simply involves multiplying both coordinates of each point in the figure by the dilation factor. Consider the pentagon used above with a dilation factor of 2. For each point (x, y) on the pentagon, the corresponding point (x', y') on the dilated pentagon is simply the following:

$$\begin{pmatrix} x' \\ y' \end{pmatrix} = d \begin{pmatrix} x \\ y \end{pmatrix}$$

where, in this case, the dilation factor d is 2. The result of the dilation is shown below for the pentagon.

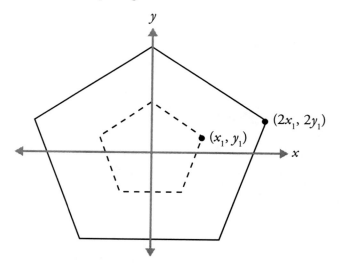

Compound transformations

Compound transformations can be made by simply concatenating several transformation operators (whether a multiplicative matrix, a multiplicative constant, or an additive vector).

Example: Find the formula for a transformation involving first a rotation of α counterclockwise around the origin, then a dilation by a factor of 4, then a translation in the positive y direction by 2, and then a clockwise rotation by α.

To solve this problem, consider a point (x, y) on the plane. To rotate counterclockwise by α, use the rotation matrix.

$$\begin{pmatrix} x' \\ y' \end{pmatrix} = \begin{pmatrix} \cos \alpha & -\sin \alpha \\ \sin \alpha & \cos \alpha \end{pmatrix} \begin{pmatrix} x \\ y \end{pmatrix}$$

The dilation simply involves multiplication by a factor of 4.

$$\begin{pmatrix} x'' \\ y'' \end{pmatrix} = 4 \begin{pmatrix} x' \\ y' \end{pmatrix}$$

The translation can be represented as follows.

$$\begin{pmatrix} x''' \\ y''' \end{pmatrix} = \begin{pmatrix} x'' \\ y'' \end{pmatrix} + \begin{pmatrix} 0 \\ 2 \end{pmatrix}$$

The final result requires use of the rotation matrix for $-\alpha$.

$$\begin{pmatrix} \bar{x} \\ \bar{y} \end{pmatrix} = \begin{pmatrix} \cos\alpha & \sin\alpha \\ -\sin\alpha & \cos\alpha \end{pmatrix} \begin{pmatrix} x''' \\ y''' \end{pmatrix}$$

Rewriting the equation in full yields

$$\begin{pmatrix} \bar{x} \\ \bar{y} \end{pmatrix} = \begin{pmatrix} \cos\alpha & \sin\alpha \\ -\sin\alpha & \cos\alpha \end{pmatrix} \left\{ 4 \begin{pmatrix} \cos\alpha & -\sin\alpha \\ \sin\alpha & \cos\alpha \end{pmatrix} \begin{pmatrix} x \\ y \end{pmatrix} + \begin{pmatrix} 0 \\ 2 \end{pmatrix} \right\}$$

Using this formula, any point or set of points can be transformed in the manner specified by the question.

COMPETENCY 10
DISCRETE MATHEMATICS

Discrete mathematics involves such areas as graphs and trees, binary relations, sequences and series, and recursive or iterative functions. In addition, application of counting principles to problems involving permutations and combinations can also fall into the category of discrete mathematics.

> SKILL 10.1 **Solve basic problems that involve counting techniques, including the multiplication principle, permutations, and combinations; use counting techniques to understand various situations** (e.g., number of ways to order a set of objects, to choose a subcommittee from a committee, to visit n cities)

Fundamental Counting Principles

The following discussion uses the symbols $\cap$ to mean "and," $\cup$ to mean "or," and $P(x)$ to mean "the probability of x." Also, $N(x)$ means "the number of ways that x can occur."

ADDITION PRINCIPLE OF COUNTING: states that if A and B are arbitrary events, then $N(A \cup B) = N(A) + N(B) - N(A \cap B)$

The ADDITION PRINCIPLE OF COUNTING states that if A and B are arbitrary events, then

$$N(A \cup B) = N(A) + N(B) - N(A \cap B)$$

Furthermore, if A and B are MUTUALLY EXCLUSIVE EVENTS, then

$$N(A \cup B) = N(A) + N(B)$$

Correspondingly, the probabilities associated with arbitrary events are

$$P(A \cup B) = P(A) + P(B) - P(A \cap B)$$

For mutually exclusive events,

$$P(A \cup B) = P(A) + P(B)$$

MUTUALLY EXCLUSIVE EVENTS: events that cannot occur together or have no outcomes in common

Example: In how many ways can you select a black card or a jack from an ordinary deck of playing cards?

Let B denote selection of a black card and let J denote selection of a jack. Then, since half the cards (26) are black and four are jacks,

$$N(B) = 26$$
$$N(J) = 4$$

Also, since a card can be both black and a jack (the jack of spades and the jack of clubs),

$$N(B \cap J) = 2$$

Thus, the solution is

$$N(B \cup J) = N(B) + N(J) - N(B \cap J) = 26 + 4 - 2 = 28$$

Example: A travel agency offers 40 possible trips: 14 to Asia, 16 to Europe, and 10 to South America. In how many ways can you select a trip to Asia or Europe through this agency?

Let A denote selection of a trip to Asia and let E denote selection of a trip to Europe. Since these are mutually exclusive events, then

$$N(A \cup E) = N(A) + N(E) = 14 + 16 = 30$$

Therefore, there are 30 ways you can select a trip to Asia or Europe.

The MULTIPLICATION PRINCIPLE OF COUNTING FOR DEPENDENT EVENTS states that if A and B are arbitrary events, then the number of ways that A and B can occur in a two-stage experiment is given by

$$N(A \cap B) = N(A)N(B \mid A)$$

MULTIPLICATION PRINCIPLE OF COUNTING FOR DEPENDENT EVENTS: states that if A and B are arbitrary events, then the number of ways that A and B can occur in a two-stage experiment is given by $N(A \cap B) = N(A)N(B|A)$ where $N(B|A)$ is the number of ways B can occur given that A has already occurred

where $N(B \mid A)$ is the number of ways B can occur given that A has already occurred. If A and B are mutually exclusive events, then

$$N(A \cap B) = N(A)N(B)$$

Also, the probabilities associated with arbitrary events are

$$P(A \cap B) = P(A)P(B|A)$$

For mutually exclusive events,

$$P(A \cap B) = P(A)P(B)$$

Example: In how many ways can two jacks from an ordinary deck of 52 cards be drawn in succession if the first card is not replaced into the deck before the second card is drawn (that is, without replacement)?

This is a two-stage experiment. Let A be selection of a jack in the first draw and let B be selection of a jack in the second draw. It is clear that

$$N(A) = 4$$

If the first card drawn is a jack, however, then there are only three remaining jacks remaining for the second draw. Thus, drawing two cards without replacement means the events A and B are dependent, and

$$N(B|A) = 3$$

The solution is then

$$N(A \cap B) = N(A)N(B|A) = (4)(3) = 12$$

Example: How many six-letter code "words" can be formed if repetition of letters is not allowed?

Since these are code words, a word does not have to be in the dictionary; for example, abcdef could be a code word. Since the experiment requires choosing each letter without replacing the letters from previous selections, the experiment has six stages.

Repetition is not allowed; thus, there are 26 choices for the first letter, 25 for the second, 24 for the third, 23 for the fourth, 22 for the fifth, and 21 for the sixth. Therefore, if A is the selection of a six-letter code word without repetition, then

$$N(A) = (26)(25)(24)(23)(22)(21) = 165,765,600$$

There are over 165 million ways to choose a six-letter code word with six unique letters.

Finite Probability

Using the fundamental counting principles described above, finite probability problems can be solved. Generally, finding the probability of a particular event or set of events involves dividing the number of ways the particular event can take place by the total number of possible outcomes for the experiment. Thus, by appropriately counting these possible outcomes using the above rules, probabilities can be determined.

Example: Determine the probability of rolling three even numbers on three successive rolls of a six-sided die.

This is a three-stage experiment. First, determine the total number of possible outcomes for three rolls of a die. For each roll,

$N(\text{roll}) = 6$

There are three possible even rolls for a die: 2, 4 and 6.

$N(\text{even}) = 3$

The probability of rolling an even number on any particular roll is then

$P(\text{even}) = \frac{N(\text{even})}{N(\text{roll})} = \frac{3}{6} = \frac{1}{2}$

For three successive rolls, use the multiplication rule for mutually exclusive events.

$P(3 \text{ even rolls}) = P(\text{even})^3 = (\frac{1}{2})^3 = \frac{1}{8} = 0.125$

Thus, the probability of rolling three successive even numbers using a six-sided die is 0.125.

Permutations and Combinations

A PERMUTATION is the number of possible arrangements of n items, without repetition, where order of selection is important.

A COMBINATION is the number of possible arrangements of n items, without repetition, where order of selection is not important.

Example: If any two numbers are selected from the set {1, 2, 3, 4}, list the possible permutations and combinations.

Combinations	Permutations
12, 13, 14, 23, 24, 34: six ways	12, 21, 13, 31, 14, 41, 23, 32, 24, 42, 34, 43: twelve ways

Note that the list of permutations includes 12 and 21 as separate possibilities since the order of selection is important. In the case of combinations, however, the order of selection is not important and, therefore, 12 is the same combination as 21. Hence, 21 is not listed separately as a possibility.

The number of permutations and combinations may also be found by using the formulae given below.

The number of possible permutations in selecting r objects from a set of n is given by

$_nP_r = \frac{n!}{(n-r)!}$ The notation nPr is read "the number of permutations of n objects taken r at a time."

PERMUTATION: the number of possible arrangements of n items, without repetition, where order of selection is important

COMBINATION: the number of possible arrangements of n items, without repetition, where order of selection is not important

In our example, two objects are being selected from a set of four.

$$_4P_2 = \frac{4!}{(4-2)!}$$ Substitute known values.

$$_4P_2 = 12$$

The number of possible combinations in selecting r objects from a set of n is given by

$$_nC_r = \frac{n!}{(n-r)!r!}$$ The number of combinations when r objects are selected from n objects.

In our example,

$$_4C_2 = \frac{4!}{(4-2)!2!}$$ Substitute known values.

$$_4C_2 = 6$$

Objects arranged in a row

It can be shown that $_nP_n$, the number of ways n objects can be arranged in a row, is equal to $n!$. We can think of the problem as n positions being filled, one at a time. The first position can be filled in n ways using any one of the n objects. Since one of the objects has already been used, the second position can be filled only in $n - 1$ ways. Similarly, the third position can be filled in $n - 2$ ways, and so on. Hence, the total number of possible arrangements of n objects in a row is given by

$$_nP_n = n(n-1)(n-2)........1 = n!$$

Example: Five books are placed in a row on a bookshelf. In how many different ways can they be arranged?

The number of possible ways in which 5 books can be arranged in a row is $5! = 1 \times 2 \times 3 \times 4 \times 5 = 120$.

The formula given above for $_nP_r$, *the number of possible permutations of* r *objects selected from* n *objects,* can also be proven in a similar manner. If r positions are filled by selecting from n objects, the first position can be filled in n ways, the second position can be filled in $n - 1$ ways, and so on (as shown before). The rth position can be filled in $n - (r - 1) = n - r + 1$ ways. Hence,

$$_nP_r = n(n-1)(n-2).....(n-r+1) = \frac{n!}{(n-r)!}$$

The formula for the *number of possible combinations of* r *objects selected from* n, $_nC_r$, may be derived by using the above two formulae. For the same set of r objects, the number of permutations is $r!$. All of these permutations, however, correspond to the same combination. Hence,

$$_nC_r = \frac{_nP_r}{r!} = \frac{n!}{(n-r)!r!}$$

Objects arranged in a ring

The number of permutations of n objects in a ring is given by $(n - 1)!$. This can be demonstrated by considering the fact that the number of permutations of n objects in a row is $n!$. When the objects are placed in a ring, moving every object one place to its left will result in the same arrangement. Moving each object two places to its left will also result in the same arrangement. We can continue this kind of movement up to n places to get the same arrangement. Thus the count $n!$ is n times too many when the objects are arranged in a ring. Hence, the number of permutations of n objects in a ring is given by $\frac{n!}{n} = (n - 1)!$.

Example: There are 20 people at a meeting. Five of them are selected to lead a discussion. How many different combinations of five people can be selected from the group? If the five people are seated in a row, how many different seating permutations are possible? If the five people are seated around a circular table, how many possible permutations are there?

The number of possible combinations of 5 people selected from the group of 20 is

$$_{20}C_5 = \frac{20!}{15!5!} = \frac{16 \times 17 \times 18 \times 19 \times 20}{1 \times 2 \times 3 \times 4 \times 5} = \frac{1860480}{120} = 15504$$

The number of possible permutations of the five seated in a row is

$$_{20}P_5 = \frac{20!}{15!} = 16 \times 17 \times 18 \times 19 \times 20 = 1860480$$

The number of possible permutations of the five seated in a circle is

$$\frac{_{20}P_5}{5} = \frac{20!}{5 \times 15!} = \frac{16 \times 17 \times 18 \times 19 \times 20}{5} = 372096$$

Sets containing like objects

If the set of n objects contains some objects that are exactly alike, the number of permutations will again be different than $n!$. For instance, if n_1 of the n objects are exactly alike, then switching those objects among themselves will result in the same arrangement. Since we already know that n_1 objects can be arranged in $n_1!$ ways, n! must be reduced by a factor of $n_1!$ to get the correct number of permutations. Thus, the number of permutations of n objects of which n_1 are exactly alike is given by $\frac{n!}{n_1!}$. Generalizing this, *we can say that the number of different permutations of* n *objects of which* n_1 *are alike,* n_2 *are alike, ...,* n_j *are alike, is*

$$\frac{n!}{n_1!\, n_2!... n_j!} \text{ where } n_1 + n_2 ..... + n_j = n$$

Example: A box contains 3 red, 2 blue, and 5 green marbles. If all the marbles are taken out of the box and arranged in a row, how many different permutations are possible?

The number of possible permutations is

$$\frac{10!}{3!2!5!} = \frac{6 \times 7 \times 8 \times 9 \times 10}{6 \times 2} = 2520$$

SKILL **Find values of functions defined recursively and understand how**
10.2 **recursion can be used to model various phenomena; translate**
between recursive and closed-form expressions for a function

Iteration and Recursive Patterns and Relations

A RECURRENCE RELATION is an equation that defines a sequence recursively; in other words, each term of the sequence is defined as a function of the preceding terms. For instance, the formula for the balance of an interest-bearing savings account after t years, which is given in a later section in closed form (that is, explicit form), can be expressed recursively as follows.

$$A_t = A_{t-1} \left(1 + \frac{r}{n}\right)^n \text{ where } A_0 = P \text{ which is the initial principal invested.}$$

Here, r is the annual interest rate and n is the number of times the interest is compounded per year. Mortgage and annuity parameters can also be expressed in recursive form. Calculation of a past or future term by applying a recursive formula multiple times is called ITERATION.

Sequences of numbers can be defined by iteratively applying a recursive pattern. For instance, the Fibonacci sequence is defined as follows.

$$F_i = F_{i-1} + F_{i-2} \quad \text{where } F_0 = 0 \text{ and } F_1 = 1$$

Applying this recursive formula gives the sequence $\{0, 1, 1, 2, 3, 5, 8, 13, 21, \ldots\}$.

It is sometimes difficult or impossible to write recursive relations in explicit or closed form. In such cases, especially when computer programming is involved, the recursive form can still be helpful. When the elements of a sequence of numbers or values depend on one or more previous values, then it is possible that a recursive formula could be used to summarize the sequence.

If a value or number from a later point in the sequence (that is, other than the beginning) is known and it is necessary to find previous terms, then the indices of the recursive relation can be adjusted to find previous values instead of later ones. Consider, for instance, the Fibonacci sequence.

$$F_i = F_{i-1} + F_{i-2}$$
$$F_{i+2} = F_{i+1} + F_i$$
$$F_i = F_{i+2} - F_{i+1}$$

Thus, if any two consecutive numbers in the Fibonacci sequence are known, then the previous numbers of the sequence can be found (in addition to the later numbers).

RECURRENCE RELA-TION: an equation that defines a sequence recursively; in other words, each term of the sequence is defined as a function of the preceding terms

ITERATION: the process of calculating a past or future term by applying a recursive formula multiple times

Example: Write a recursive formula for the following sequence: {2, 3, 5, 9, 17, 33, 65, …}.

By inspection, it can be seen that each number in the sequence is equal to twice the previous number, less 1. If the numbers in the sequence are indexed such that, for the first number, $i = 1$, and so on, then the recursion relation is the following.

$$N_i = 2N_{i-1} - 1$$

Example: If a recursive relation is defined by $N_i = N_{i-1}^2$ and the fourth term is 65,536, what is the first term?

Adjust the indices of the recursion and then solve for N_i.

$$N_{i+1} = N_i^2$$
$$N_i = \sqrt{N_{i+1}}$$

Use this relationship to backtrack to the first term.

$$N_3 = \sqrt{N_4} = \sqrt{65,536} = 256$$
$$N_2 = \sqrt{N_3} = \sqrt{256} = 16$$
$$N_1 = \sqrt{N_2} = \sqrt{16} = 4$$

The first term of the sequence is thus 4.

Converting between Recursive and Closed Forms

It is helpful in some situations to convert between the recursive form and closed form of a function. Given a closed-form representation of a function, the recursive form can be found by writing out the corresponding series or sequence and then determining a pattern or formula that accurately represents that series or sequence. Consider, for instance, the mortgage principal formula in recursive form:

$$A_i = A_{i-1}(1 + \tfrac{r}{n}) - M \qquad \text{where } A_0 = P$$

Here, A_i is the remaining principal on the mortgage after the ith payment, r is the annual interest rate, which is compounded n times annually, and M is the monthly payment. The initial value P is the original loan amount for the mortgage. To obtain a closed-form expression for this recursive formula, first write out the terms of the corresponding sequence.

$$A_0 = P$$
$$A_1 = P(1 + \tfrac{r}{n}) - M$$
$$A_2 = A_1(1 + \tfrac{r}{n}) - M = P(1 + \tfrac{r}{n})^2 - M(1 + \tfrac{r}{n}) - M$$
$$A_3 = A_2(1 + \tfrac{r}{n}) - M = P(1 + \tfrac{r}{n})^3 - M(1 + \tfrac{r}{n})^2 - M(1 + \tfrac{r}{n}) - M$$

This pattern continues until $i = k$, where k is the total number of payments in the mortgage term. Note that the term A_k can be written as follows, where $z = 1 + \tfrac{r}{n}$:

$$A_k = Pz^k - M\{z^{k-1} + z^{k-2} + ...z^2 + z + 1\}$$

But the expression in the curly brackets is simply a geometric series, which can be written in closed form as

$$z^{k-1} + z^{k-2} + ...z^2 + z + 1 = \frac{1-z^k}{1-z}$$

Thus, the closed form expression for the principle remaining after k payments on the mortgage is

$$A_k = Pz^k - M\frac{1-z^k}{1-z} \qquad \text{where } z = 1 + \frac{r}{n}$$

The process for converting from closed form to recursive form is similar (it is essentially the reverse of the process described above). Simply write out the terms, determine the pattern and then write the ith value in terms of the $(i-1)^{st}$ or $(i+1)^{st}$ value.

SKILL 10.3 **Determine whether a binary relation on a set is reflexive, symmetric, or transitive; determine whether a relation is an equivalence relation**

Binary Relations

A BINARY RELATION ON A SET is a set of ordered pairs (a, b), where both a and b are elements of a particular set. A binary relation R may be defined on a set such that each ordered pair (a, b) obeys aRb. For instance, consider the relation "is less than," where R can be expressed as the symbol "$<$." The binary relation on the set of real numbers is then the set of ordered pairs (a, b) such that $a < b$.

> **BINARY RELATION ON A SET:** a set of ordered pairs (a, b), where both a and b are elements of a particular set

Reflexive binary relations

A binary relation on a set may or may not be reflexive, symmetric, or transitive. A binary relation R on a set S is REFLEXIVE if aRa is true for every a in set S.

Example: Determine if the binary relation "is a factor of" (or "divides") on the set of natural numbers (1, 2, 3,...) is reflexive.

This relation is reflexive only if each number is a factor of itself. Let a be one of the natural numbers; note the following:

$$\frac{a}{a} = 1$$

> **REFLEXIVE:** a binary relation R on a set S is reflexive if aRa is true for every a in set S

Thus, each natural number a is a factor of itself. Thus, aRa, where R represents "is a factor of," is always true. The relation is thus reflexive.

Symmetric binary relations

A binary relation R on a set S is SYMMETRIC if both aRb and bRa are true (or both are false), where a and b are elements of S.

> **SYMMETRIC:** a binary relation R on a set S is symmetric if both aRb and bRa are true (or both are false), where a and b are elements of S

Example: Determine if the binary relation $\geq$ on the set of integers is symmetric.

It is sufficient to show one counterexample to prove that the relation is not symmetric. Consider the integers 1 and 2.

$1 \geq 2$ True

$2 \geq 1$ False

Thus, the relation is not symmetric.

Transitive binary relations

A binary relation R on a set S is TRANSITIVE if, for any a, b, and c belonging to S, aRc is true as long as aRb and bRc are true.

Example: Determine if the relation $>$ on the set of real numbers is transitive.

Consider real numbers a, b and c. If $a > b$ and $b > c$, it follows that $a > c$. Thus, the relation is transitive.

Equivalence relations

EQUIVALENCE RELA-TION: a binary relation is an equivalence relation if it is simultaneously reflexive, symmetric, and transitive

A binary relation is an EQUIVALENCE RELATION if it is simultaneously reflexive, symmetric, and transitive. For instance, equality (represented by the "$=$" symbol) is an equivalence relation, since for a, b, and c in a set (such as the real numbers), all three properties apply.

> **SKILL 10.4** **Use finite and infinite arithmetic and geometric sequences and series to model simple phenomena** *(e.g., compound interest, annuity, growth, decay)*

Sequences and Series

A sequence is a set of numbers; a series is the sum of the terms of a sequence.

Sequences and series can take on a vast range of different forms and patterns. Sequences and series are essentially two different representations of a set of numbers: a sequence is the set of numbers, and a series is the sum of the terms of the sequence. That is, a sequence such as

$a_1, a_2, a_3, \ldots$

has a corresponding series S such that

$S = a_1 + a_2 + a_3 + \ldots$

Two of the most common forms of series are the arithmetic and geometric series, both of which are discussed below.

Arithmetic series

A finite series of numbers for which the difference between successive terms is constant is called an ARITHMETIC SERIES. An arithmetic series with n terms can be expressed as follows, where a and d are constants. (The constant a is the first term, and d is the difference between successive terms.)

$$a + (a + d) + (a + 2d) + (a + 3d) + \ldots (a + [n - 1]d)$$

To derive the general formula, examine the series sum for several small values of n.

n	Sum
1	a
2	$2a + d$
3	$3a + 3d$
4	$4a + 6d$
5	$5a + 10d$
6	$6a + 15d$
. . .	. . .
n	$na + d\sum\limits_{i=1}^{n-1} i$

The result in the table for n terms is found by examining the pattern of the previous series. All that is necessary, then, is to determine a closed expression for the summation.

By inspection, it can be seen that the product of n and $(n + 1)$, divided by 2, is the expression for the sum of $1 + 2 + 3 + 4 + 5 + \ldots + n$. Then:

$$\sum\limits_{i=1}^{n} i = \tfrac{1}{2}n(n + 1)$$

An simple derivation of this relationship may be made as follows:

$$S_n = 1 + 2 + 3 + \ldots\ldots\ldots + n$$

Writing the terms in reverse order:

$$S_n = n + (n - 1) + (n - 2) + \ldots\ldots\ldots + 1$$

Adding the two expressions for S_n term by term, we get
$$2S_n = (1 + n) + (2 + n - 1) + (3 + n - 2) + ... (n + 1)$$
$$= (1 + n) + (1 + n) + (1 + n) + ... (n + 1)$$
$$= n(n + 1)$$
Therefore, $S_n = \frac{n(n + 1)}{2}$

For the general case (with first term a and common difference d), therefore, the sum for a series with n terms is given by
$$na + d \sum_{i=1}^{n-1} i = na + d\frac{(n - 1)(n)}{2} = \frac{1}{2}n(2a + d(n - 1))$$

Often times, closed formulas for series such as the arithmetic series must be found by inspection, as a more rigorous derivation is difficult. The result can be proven using mathematical induction, however.

Example: Calculate the sum of the series 1 + 5 + 9 + ... + 57.

This is an arithmetic series, as the difference between successive terms, d, is constant ($d = 4$). Determine the total number of terms by subtracting the first term from the last term, dividing by d, and adding 1.
$$n = \frac{57 - 1}{4} + 1 = \frac{56}{4} + 1 = 14 + 1 = 15$$

That this approach works can be seen by testing simple examples. For instance, if the series is $1 + 5 + 9$, then
$$n = \frac{9 - 1}{4} + 1 = \frac{8}{4} + 1 = 2 + 1 = 3$$

There are indeed three terms in this simple series. Next, apply the formula, noting that $a = 1$.
$$\frac{1}{2}n[2a + d(n - 1)] = \frac{1}{2}(15)[2(1) + (4)(15 - 1)]$$
$$= \frac{15}{2}[2 + 4(14)] = \frac{15}{2}(58) = 435$$

Thus, the answer is 435.

Geometric series

GEOMETRIC SERIES:
a series whose successive terms are related by a common factor

A GEOMETRIC SERIES is a series whose successive terms are related by a common factor (rather than the common difference of the arithmetic series). Assuming that a is the first term of the series and r is the common factor, the general n-term geometric series can be written as follows.
$$a + ar + ar^2 + ar^3 + ... + ar^{n - 1}$$

The geometric series can also be written using sum notation.
$$a + ar + ar^2 + ... + ar^{n - 1} = \sum_{i=0}^{n-1} ar^i$$

To derive the closed-form expression for this finite series, let the sum for n terms be defined as S_n. Multiply S_n by r.

$$S_n = a + ar + ar^2 + ... + ar^{n-1}$$
$$rS_n = ar + ar^2 + ar^3 + ... + ar^n$$

Note that if a is added to this new series, the result is the sum S_{n+1}, which has $n + 1$ terms.

$$a + rS_n = a + ar + ar^2 + ar^3 + ... + ar^n = S_{n+1}$$

But S_{n+1} is simply $S_n + ar^n$, so the above expression can be written solely in terms of S_n.

$$a + rS_n = S_{n+1} = S_n + ar^n$$

Rearrange the result to obtain a simple formula for the geometric series.

$$a + rS_n = S_n + ar^n$$
$$a - ar^n = S_n - rS_n$$
$$a(1 - r^n) = S_n(1 - r)$$
$$S_n = a\frac{1 - r^n}{1 - r}$$

Infinite geometric series

The infinite geometric series is the limit of S_n as n approaches infinity.

$$a + ar + ar^2 + ... = \lim_{n\to\infty} a\frac{1 - r^n}{1 - r}$$

Three cases are of interest: $r \geq 1$, $r \leq -1$, and $-1 < r < 1$. To determine the limit in each case, first apply L'Hopital's rule.

$$\lim_{n\to\infty} a\frac{1 - r^n}{1 - r} = a\lim_{n\to\infty} \frac{\frac{d}{dr}(1 - r^n)}{\frac{d}{dr}(1 - r)} = a\lim_{n\to\infty} \frac{-nr^{n-1}}{-1}$$

$$\lim_{n\to\infty} a\frac{1 - r^n}{1 - r} = a\lim_{n\to\infty} nr^{n-1}$$

Thus, it can be seen that if r is either 1 or -1, the limit goes to infinity due to the factor n. The same reasoning applies if r is greater than 1 or less than -1. For $-1 < r < 1$, rearrange the original form of the limit.

$$\lim_{n\to\infty} a\frac{1 - r^n}{1 - r} = a\frac{1 - r^\infty}{1 - r}$$

Since the magnitude of r is less than 1, r^∞ must be zero. This yields a closed form for the infinite geometric series, which converges only if $-1 < r < 1$.

$$a + ar + ar^2 + ... = \frac{a}{1 - r}$$

Example: Evaluate the following series: $1 + \frac{1}{2} + \frac{1}{4} + \frac{1}{8} + ...$.

Note that this series is an infinite geometric series with $a = 1$ and $r = \frac{1}{2}$ (or 0.5).

Use the formula to evaluate the series.

$$1 + \frac{1}{2} + \frac{1}{4} + \frac{1}{8} + \ldots = \frac{a}{1-r} = \frac{1}{1-0.5} = \frac{1}{0.5} = 2$$

The answer is thus 2.

Modeling Phenomena with Sequences and Series

Arithmetic and geometric sequences and series can be used to model various phenomena and are especially useful for financial mathematics. Compound interest, annuities, and mortgages can all be modeled using sequences and series. Growth and decay problems, such as those that arise in physics and other sciences, can also be modeled using sequences and series.

Compound interest

Compound interest can be modeled by deriving a general formula for the total amount of money available after a principal deposit P has accrued interest at rate of r (a decimal) compounded n times annually for t years. The same sequence-based approach to modeling compound interest is illustrative and can be applied in a similar manner to the various aspects of annuities and mortgages as well. Interest is compounded n times per year, so, after each interval, the total balance accrues interest at a rate $\frac{r}{n}$. For the first instance,

$$A_1 = P + \frac{r}{n}P = P(1 + \frac{r}{n})$$

In the second instance,

$$A_2 = A_1 + \frac{r}{n}A_1 = A_1(1 + \frac{r}{n})$$

The pattern continues. Note that if the expression is written out fully, then:

$$A_2 = A_1(1 + \frac{r}{n}) = P(1 + \frac{r}{n})^2$$

The pattern that emerges from this approach can be expressed generally for a sequence with n terms:

$$A_n = P(1 + \frac{r}{n})^n$$

A_n is the total amount (principal plus accrued interest) after one year. Thus, for t years, the total balance is the following.

$$A = P(1 + \frac{r}{n})^{nt}$$

If the interest is compounded continuously, then the formula becomes the limit of the above expression as n approaches infinity.

$$A = \lim_{n \to \infty} [P(1 + \frac{r}{n})^{nt}]$$

By rearranging this expression, a simpler form of the limit can be found.

$$A = P \lim_{n \to \infty} [(1 + \frac{1}{n/r})^{n/r}]^{rt} = P \lim_{n/r \to \infty} [(1 + \frac{1}{n/r})^{n/r}]^{rt}$$

Evaluating the limit reveals the balance after t years with continuously compounded interest.

$$A = Pe^{rt}$$

Example: Calculate the interest accrued after 3 years for $1,000 in a savings account that compounds the interest monthly at an annual rate of 3%.

Use the formula derived above, where $t = 3$, $n = 12$, $P = 1,000$, and $r = 0.03$.

$$A = P(1 + \tfrac{r}{n})^{nt} = \$1000(1 + \tfrac{0.03}{12})^{(12)(3)} = \$1000(1.0025)^{36}$$
$$A = \$1094.05$$

Thus, the total interest accrued is $94.05.

Example: What is the total balance after 5 years in a savings account with an annual continuously compounded interest rate of 1% if the initial deposit is $500?

Use the expression for continuously compounded interest, substituting all the relevant information described in the problem.

$$A = Pe^{rt} = \$500e^{(0.01)(5)} = \$500e^{0.05}$$
$$A = \$525.64$$

SKILL **Understand the relationship between discrete and continuous**
10.5 **representations and how they can be used to model various phenomena**

Discrete and Continuous Representations

An understanding of discrete representations versus continuous representations is helpful in a number of areas, including electronics, signal processing, and calculus. As the name indicates, a continuous representation of a function or phenomenon applies to a continuous range of values. For instance, an analog electronic signal can have any arbitrary voltage value (perhaps within some defined upper and lower bounds). Also, the set of real numbers can be viewed as a continuous representation, since, between any two values in the set, there is always another value that is also in the set. A discrete representation, on the other hand, involves a set of discrete values. A digital electronic signal is discrete in that it can only hold certain discrete voltage levels. A binary digital signal, for example, can only have a high voltage (5 volts, for instance) or a low voltage (0 volts, for instance). In mathematics, the set of integers can be viewed as a discrete representation, since there are integers between which no other values in the set exist. (That is, there are no values in the set between n and $n + 1$, where n is an integer.)

A continuous representation of a function or phenomenon applies to a continuous range of values. A discrete representation, on the other hand, involves a set of discrete values.

Representations of functions

Functions can have discrete or continuous representations as well. Consider the function f defined below.

$$f(x) = x^2$$

This function can be represented in a continuous manner by considering the domain to be the set of real numbers. In this case, the range is also continuous, and the graph of the function, shown below, is likewise a continuous curve.

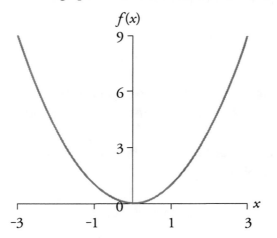

This function can be represented in a discrete manner by considering the domain to be the set of integers instead of the set of real numbers. The range of the function is then a subset of the integers. The graph of the function, which is shown below, is similar in form to the above graph, but it is defined only at certain values (corresponding to the integers).

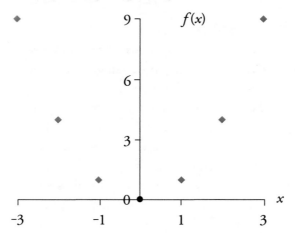

The function f described above might have a domain that corresponds to time, distance, or any number of other units. Note that the discrete function closely represents the continuous function as long as the sampling rate (or the distance between successive values in the domain) is sufficiently high (or low).

Real-life limitations

Since most measurements cannot be taken in a continuous manner (even computer-controlled systems are limited to a finite number of measurements per time interval), representations of continuous phenomena in nature must be constructed (ultimately) from discrete measurements. Thus, although the height of a projectile might be represented as a continuous function, the measurements that lead to a representation of a projectile's height are fundamentally discrete. Considering the other direction, if a discrete model is to be constructed from a continuous model, the primary task is limitation or conversion of the continuous range of values to a discrete set of values, as was done for the function f given above.

> **SKILL 10.6** **Use difference equations, vertex-edge graphs, trees, and networks to model and solve problems**

Difference Equations

A DIFFERENCE EQUATION is a discrete analog for a differential equation, with "differences" being analogous to derivatives. For a sequence of numbers $\{a_n\}$, the first difference is defined as

$$d(a_n) = a_n - a_{n-1}$$

The second difference is given by

$$d^2(a_n) = d(a_n) - d(a_{n-1}) = a_n - 2a_{n-1} + a_{n-2}$$

Subsequent differences are defined in a similar fashion.

A diference equation is an equation composed of a discrete variable a_n and its differences of different orders. It is clear from the above definitions that a difference equation is nothing but a recurrence relation, and many people use the two terms interchangeably. For information on recurrence relations and their solutions, *see Skill 10.2.*

Graphs

A GRAPH is a set of points (or nodes) and lines (or edges) that connect some subset of these points. A FINITE GRAPH has a limited number of both nodes and edges. An example graph follows. Note that not all of the nodes in a graph need be connected to other nodes.

> **DIFFERENCE EQUATION:** a discrete analog for a differential equation, with "differences" being analogous to derivatives

> **GRAPH:** a set of points (or nodes) and lines (or edges) that connect some subset of these points

> **FINITE GRAPH:** a graph with a limited number of both nodes and edges

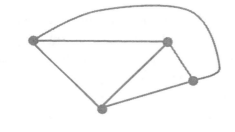

The edges of a graph may or may not have a specified direction or orientation; also, the edges (and nodes) may or may not have some assigned label or value. For instance, a graph representing airline flight paths might include nodes that represent cities and edges the represent the direction and distance of the paths between the cities.

Trees

TREE: a graph that does not include any closed loops or unconnected nodes

FINITE TREE: a tree with a limited number of edges and nodes

A TREE is a graph that does not include any closed loops. In addition, a tree has no unconnected nodes (separate nodes or groups of connected nodes constitute a separate tree—groups of several trees are called a forest). In addition, the edges that connect the nodes of a tree do not have a direction or orientation. A FINITE TREE, like a finite graph, has a limited number of edges and nodes. The graph shown above is not a tree, but it takes the form of a tree with a few alterations:

Networks

NETWORK: a graph (directed or undirected) in which each edge is assigned a positive real number in accordance with a specific function

A NETWORK is a graph (directed or undirected) in which each edge is assigned a positive real number in accordance with a specific function. The function may correspond to the distance between two points on a map, for instance.

Solving Problems Using Trees and Graphs

Trees and graphs can be used to represent a wide variety of types of information. They can also be useful tools for solving problems that involve maps, hierarchies, directories, structures, communications networks and a range of other objects.

Example: Find the shortest path between points A and B on the following directed graph.

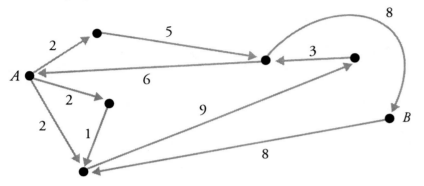

Taking careful note of the direction of the edges, find the possible routes through the graph from *A* to *B*. Only two paths are possible; choose the path with the smallest sum of the values along the associated edges.

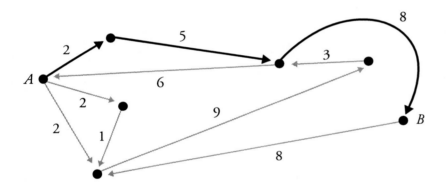

The total distance for the shortest path is 2 + 5 + 8 = 15.

SAMPLE TEST

SAMPLE TEST

Directions: Read each item and select the best response.

(Easy) (Skill 1.3)

1. Find the LCM of 27, 90, and 84.

   A. 90

   B. 3,780

   C. 204,120

   D. 1,260

(Average) (Skill 1.2)

2. Which of the following sets is closed under division?

   I) {½, 1, 2, 4}

   II) {-1, 1}

   III) {-1, 0, 1}

   A. I only

   B. II only

   C. III only

   D. I and II

(Average) (Skill 1.4)

3. What would be the total cost of a suit for $295.99 and a pair of shoes for $69.95 including 6.5% sales tax?

   A. $389.73

   B. $398.37

   C. $237.86

   D. $315.23

(Average) (Skill 1.3)

4. Which of the following is always composite if x is odd, y is even, and both x and y are greater than or equal to 2?

   A. $x + y$

   B. $3x + 2y$

   C. $5xy$

   D. $5x + 3y$

(Rigorous) (Skill 1.8)

5. Find the length of the major axis of $x^2 + 9y^2 = 36$.

   A. 4

   B. 6

   C. 12

   D. 8

(Average) (Skill 1.5)

6. Which graph represents the solution set for $x^2 - 5x > -6$?

   A.

   B.

   C.

   D.

(Easy) (Skill 1.5)

7. What is the equation of the graph shown below?

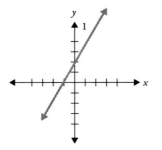

  A. $2x + y = 2$

  B. $2x - y = -2$

  C. $2x - y = 2$

  D. $2x + y = -2$

(Rigorous) (Skill 1.8)

8. Which equation represents a circle with a diameter whose endpoints are (0, 7) and (0, 3)?

  A. $x^2 + y^2 + 21 = 0$

  B. $x^2 + y^2 - 10y + 21 = 0$

  C. $x^2 + y^2 - 10y + 9 = 0$

  D. $x^2 - y^2 - 10y + 9 = 0$

(Average) (Skill 1.3)

9. What is the smallest number that is divisible by 3 and 5 and leaves a remainder of 3 when divided by 7?

  A. 15

  B. 18

  C. 25

  D. 45

(Rigorous) (Skill 1.5)

10. Solve for x: $18 = 4 + |2x|$

  A. {-11, 7}

  B. {-7, 0, 7}

  C. {-7, 7}

  D. {-11, 11}

(Average) (Skill 2.1)

11. The mass of a Chips Ahoy cookie is about:

  A. 1 kilogram

  B. 1 gram

  C. 15 grams

  D. 15 milligrams

(Average) (Skill 2.1)

12. Given that M is a mass, V is a velocity, A is an acceleration and T is a time, what type of unit corresponds to the overall expression $\frac{AMT}{V}$?

  A. Mass

  B. Time

  C. Velocity

  D. Acceleration

(Easy) (Skill 2.2)

13. Which word best describes a set of measured values that are all very similar but that all deviate significantly from the expected result?

  A. Perfect

  B. Precise

  C. Accurate

  D. Appropriate

(Average) (Skill 2.1)

14. The term "cubic feet" indicates which kind of measurement?

    A. Volume

    B. Mass

    C. Length

    D. Distance

(Easy) (Skill 3.6)

15. Find the surface area of a box that is 3 feet wide, 5 feet tall, and 4 feet deep.

    A. 47 sq. ft.

    B. 60 sq. ft.

    C. 94 sq. ft.

    D. 188 sq. ft.

(Average) (Skill 3.6)

16. Find the height of a box with surface area of 94 sq. ft. with a width of 3 feet and a depth of 4 feet.

    A. 3 ft.

    B. 4 ft.

    C. 5 ft.

    D. 6 ft.

(Average) (Skill 3.6)

17. Given a 30 meter by 60 meter garden with a circular fountain with a 5 meter radius, calculate the area of the portion of the garden not occupied by the fountain.

    A. 1,721 m²

    B. 1,879 m²

    C. 2,585 m²

    D. 1,015 m²

(Rigorous) (Skill 3.6)

18. If the area of the base of a cone is tripled, the volume will be

    A. the same as the original

    B. 9 times the original

    C. 3 times the original

    D. 3 p times the original

(Rigorous) (Skill 3.6)

19. Find the area of the figure pictured below.

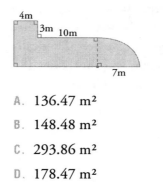

    A. 136.47 m²

    B. 148.48 m²

    C. 293.86 m²

    D. 178.47 m²

(Rigorous) (Skill 3.6)

20. Compute the area of the shaded region, given a radius of 5 meters. Point O is the center.

    A. 7.13 cm²

    B. 7.13 m²

    C. 78.5 m²

    D. 19.63 m²

(Rigorous) (Skill 5.4)

21. The length of a picture frame is 2 inches greater than its width. If the area of the frame is 143 square inches, what is its width?

   A. 11 inches

   B. 13 inches

   C. 12 inches

   D. 10 inches

(Easy) (Skill 3.1)

22. When you begin by assuming that the conclusion of a theorem is false, then show through a sequence of logically correct steps that you contradict an accepted fact, this is known as:

   A. Inductive reasoning

   B. Direct proof

   C. Indirect proof

   D. Exhaustive proof

(Rigorous) (Skill 3.6)

23. Determine the area of the shaded region of the trapezoid in terms of x and y.

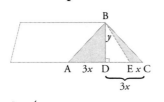

   A. $4xy$

   B. $2xy$

   C. $3x^2y$

   D. There is not enough information given

(Average) (Skill 3.1)

24. Which theorem can be used to prove $\triangle BAK \cong \triangle MKA$?

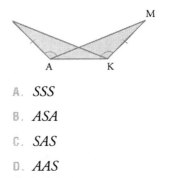

   A. SSS

   B. ASA

   C. SAS

   D. AAS

(Average) (Skill 3.3)

25. Choose the correct statement concerning the median and altitude in a triangle.

   A. The median and altitude of a triangle may be the same segment

   B. The median and altitude of a triangle are always different segments

   C. The median and altitude of a right triangle are always the same segment

   D. The median and altitude of an isosceles triangle are always the same segment

(Average) (Skill 3.7)

26. Compute the distance from $(-2, 7)$ to the line $x = 5$.

   A. -9

   B. -7

   C. 5

   D. 7

(Average) (Skill 3.2)

27. **Which of the following statements about a trapezoid is incorrect?**

    A. It has one pair of parallel sides

    B. The parallel sides are called bases

    C. If the two bases are the same length, the trapezoid is called isosceles

    D. The median is parallel to the bases

(Rigorous) (Skill 3.7)

28. **Given $K(-4, y)$ and $M(2, -3)$ with midpoint L(x, 1), determine the values of x and y.**

    A. $x = -1, y = 5$

    B. $x = 3, y = 2$

    C. $x = 5, y = -1$

    D. $x = -1, y = -1$

(Rigorous) (Skill 3.2)

29. **What is the degree measure of an interior angle of a regular 10-sided polygon?**

    A. 18°

    B. 36°

    C. 144°

    D. 54°

(Rigorous) (Skill 3.4)

30. **What is the measure of minor arc AD, given measure of arc PS is 40° and $m < K = 10°$?**

    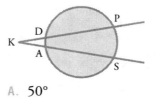

    A. 50°

    B. 20°

    C. 30°

    D. 25°

(Easy) (Skill 4.1)

31. **The cosine function is equivalent to:**

    A. $\dfrac{1}{\text{sine}}$

    B. $\dfrac{1}{\text{tangent}}$

    C. $\dfrac{\text{sine}}{\text{tangent}}$

    D. $\dfrac{\text{cotangent}}{\text{sine}}$

(Easy) (Skill 4.3)

32. **Which of the following is a Pythagorean identity?**

    A. $\sin^2 \theta - \cos^2 \theta = 1$

    B. $\sin^2 \theta + \cos^2 \theta = 1$

    C. $\cos^2 \theta - \sin^2 \theta = 1$

    D. $\cos^2 \theta - \tan^2 \theta = 1$

(Average) (Skill 4.1)

33. Determine the measures of angles *A* and *B*.

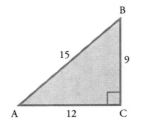

A. $A = 30°$, $B = 60°$

B. $A = 60°$, $B = 30°$

C. $A = 53°$, $B = 37°$

D. $A = 37°$, $B = 53°$

(Average) (Skill 4.3)

34. Which expression is not identical to sin *x*?

A. $\sqrt{1 - \cos^2 x}$

B. $\tan x \cos x$

C. $1/\csc x$

D. $1/\sec x$

(Average) (Skill 4.5)

35. Determine the rectangular coordinates of the point with polar coordinates (5, 60°).

A. (0.5, 0.87)

B. (−0.5, 0.87)

C. (2.5, 4.33)

D. (25, 150°)

(Rigorous) (Skill 4.3)

36. Which expression is equivalent to $1 - \sin^2 x$?

A. $1 - \cos^2 x$

B. $1 + \cos^2 x$

C. $1/\sec x$

D. $1/\sec^2 x$

(Rigorous) (Skill 4.1)

37. For an acute angle *x*, $\sin x = 0.6$. What is cot *x*?

A. $\frac{5}{3}$

B. 0.75

C. 1.33

D. 1

(Rigorous) (Skill 5.4)

38. Which of the following is a factor of the expression $9x^2 + 6x - 35$?

A. $3x - 5$

B. $3x - 7$

C. $x + 3$

D. $x - 2$

(Rigorous) (Skill 5.4)

39. Which of the following is a factor of $6 + 48m^3$?

A. $(1 + 2m)$

B. $(1 - 8m)$

C. $(1 + m - 2m)$

D. $(1 - m + 2m)$

(Average) (Skill 5.4)

40. State the domain of the function
$f(x) = \frac{3x - 6}{x^2 - 25}$.

   A. $x \neq 2$

   B. $x \neq 5, -5$

   C. $x \neq 2, -2$

   D. $x \neq 5$

(Average) (Skill 5.4)

41. Solve for x by factoring:
$2x^2 - 3x - 2 = 0$

   A. $x = (-1, 2)$

   B. $x = (0.5, -2)$

   C. $x = (-0.5, 2)$

   D. $x = (1, -2)$

(Average) (Skill 5.5)

42. Given $f(x) = 3x - 2$ and $g(x) = x^2$,
determine $g(f(x))$.

   A. $3x^2 - 2$

   B. $9x^2 + 4$

   C. $9x^2 - 12x + 4$

   D. $3x^3 - 2$

(Easy) (Skill 5.4)

43. Which of the following is equivalent to
$\sqrt[b]{x^a}$?

   A. $x^{a/b}$

   B. $x^{b/a}$

   C. $a^{x/b}$

   D. $b^{x/a}$

(Average) (Skill 5.4)

44. How does the function $y = x^3 + x^2 + 4$
behave from $x = 1$ to $x = 3$?

   A. Increasing, then decreasing

   B. Increasing

   C. Decreasing

   D. Neither increasing nor decreasing

(Average) (Skill 5.4)

45. Which graph represents the equation of
$y = x^2 + 3x$?

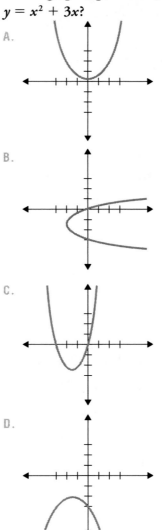

A.

B.

C.

D.

(Rigorous) (Skill 5.4)

46. Find the zeroes of
$f(x) = x^3 + x^2 - 14x - 24$

A. 4, 3, 2

B. 3, –8

C. 7, –2, –1

D. 4, –3, –2

(Rigorous) (Skill 5.4)

47. Which equation corresponds to the logarithmic statement: $\log_x k = m$?

A. $x^m = k$

B. $k^m = x$

C. $x^k = m$

D. $m^x = k$

(Rigorous) (Skill 5.4)

48. Solve for x: $10^{x-3} + 5 = 105$.

A. 3

B. 10

C. 2

D. 5

(Easy) (Skill 6.1)

49. L'Hopital's rule provides a method to evaluate which of the following?

A. Limit of a function

B. Derivative of a function

C. Sum of an arithmetic series

D. Sum of a geometric series

(Average) (Skill 6.7)

50. Find the area under the function $y = x^2 + 4$ from $x = 3$ to $x = 6$.

A. 75

B. 21

C. 96

D. 57

(Average) (Skill 6.7)

51. If the velocity of a body is given by $v = 16 - t^2$, find the distance traveled from $t = 0$ until the body comes to a complete stop.

A. 16

B. 43

C. 48

D. 64

(Average) (Skill 6.1)

52. Find the following limit: $\lim\limits_{x \to 2} \dfrac{x^2 - 4}{x - 2}$

A. 0

B. Infinity

C. 2

D. 4

(Rigorous) (Skill 6.5)

53. Find the first derivative of the function: $f(x) = x^3 + 6x^2 + 5x + 4$?

A. $3x^3 - 12x^2 + 5x$

B. $3x^2 - 12x^2 - 5$

C. $3x^2 - 12x^2 + 9$

D. $3x^2 + 12x + 5$

(Rigorous) (Skill 6.6)

54. Find the absolute maximum obtained by the function $y = 2x^2 + 3x$ on the interval $x = 0$ to $x = 3$.

    A. $-\frac{3}{4}$

    B. $-\frac{4}{3}$

    C. 0

    D. 27

(Rigorous) (Skill 6.8)

55. Find the antiderivative for $4x^3 - 2x + 6 = y$

    A. $x^4 - x^2 + 6x + C$

    B. $x^4 - \frac{2}{3}x^3 + 6x + C$

    C. $12x^2 - 2 + C$

    D. $\frac{4}{3}x^4 - x^2 + 6x + C$

(Rigorous) (Skill 6.8)

56. Find the antiderivative for the function $y = e^{3x}$.

    A. $3x(e^{3x}) + C$

    B. $3(e^{3x}) + C$

    C. $\frac{1}{3}(e^x) + C$

    D. $\frac{1}{3}(e^{3x}) + C$

(Rigorous) (Skill 6.8)

57. Evaluate: $\int_0^2 (x^2 + x - 1)dx$

    A. 11/3

    B. 8/3

    C. −8/3

    D. −11/3

(Rigorous) (Skill 6.1)

58. Find the following limit: $\lim\limits_{x \to 0} \frac{\sin 2x}{5x}$

    A. Infinity

    B. 0

    C. 0.4

    D. 1

(Rigorous) (Skill 7.2)

59. Compute the standard deviation for the following set of temperatures:

    (37, 38, 35, 37, 38, 40, 36, 39)

    A. 37.5

    B. 1.5

    C. 0.5

    D. 2.5

(Easy) (Skill 7.2)

60. Compute the median for the following data set:
    {12, 19, 13, 16, 17, 14}

    A. 14.5

    B. 15.17

    C. 15

    D. 16

(Easy) (Skill 8.1)

61. A jar contains 3 red marbles, 5 white marbles, 1 green marble, and 15 blue marbles. If one marble is picked at random from the jar, what is the probability that it will be red?

    A. $\frac{1}{3}$

    B. $\frac{1}{8}$

    C. $\frac{3}{8}$

    D. $\frac{1}{24}$

(Average) (Skill 7.7)

62. **Which of the following is not a valid method of collecting statistical data?**

    A. Random sampling

    B. Systematic sampling

    C. Cluster sampling

    D. Cylindrical sampling

(Rigorous) (Skill 7.2)

63. **Half the students in a class scored 80% on an exam, and most of the rest scored 85%, except for one student who scored 10%. Which would be the best measure of central tendency for the test scores?**

    A. Mean

    B. Median

    C. Mode

    D. Either the median or the mode because they are equal

(Rigorous) (Skill 7.3)

64. **If the correlation between two variables is given as zero, the association between the two variables is:**

    A. Negative linear

    B. Positive linear

    C. Quadratic

    D. Random

(Rigorous) (Skill 8.2)

65. **A die is rolled several times. What is the probability that a 3 will not appear before the third roll of the die?**

    A. $\frac{1}{3}$

    B. $\frac{25}{216}$

    C. $\frac{25}{36}$

    D. $\frac{1}{216}$

(Rigorous) (Skill 8.2)

66. **If there are three people in a room, what is the probability that at least two of them will share a birthday? (Assume a year has 365 days.)**

    A. 0.67

    B. 0.05

    C. 0.008

    D. 0.33

(Rigorous) (Skill 8.2)

67. **A baseball team has a 60% chance of winning any particular game in a seven-game series. What is the probability that it will win the series by winning games six and seven?**

    A. 8.3%

    B. 36%

    C. 50%

    D. 60%

(Easy) (Skill 7.1)

68. **What conclusion can be drawn from the graph below?**

MLK Elementary School
Student Enrollment

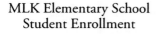

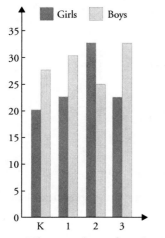

A. The number of students in first grade exceeds the number in second grade

B. There are more boys than girls in the entire school

C. There are more girls than boys in the first grade

D. Third grade has the largest number of students

(Easy) (Skill 7.1)

69. **The pie chart below shows sales at an automobile dealership for the first four months of a year. What percentage of the vehicles were sold in April?**

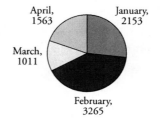

A. More than 50%

B. Less than 25%

C. Between 25% and 50%

D. None

(Easy) (Skill 9.2)

70. **The scalar multiplication of the number 3 with the matrix $\begin{pmatrix} 2 & 1 \\ 3 & 5 \end{pmatrix}$ yields:**

A. 33

B. $\begin{pmatrix} 6 & 1 \\ 9 & 5 \end{pmatrix}$

C. $\begin{pmatrix} 2 & 3 \\ 3 & 15 \end{pmatrix}$

D. $\begin{pmatrix} 6 & 3 \\ 9 & 15 \end{pmatrix}$

(Easy) (Skill 9.2)

71. Find the sum of the following matrices.

$$\begin{pmatrix} 6 & 3 \\ 9 & 15 \end{pmatrix} \begin{pmatrix} 4 & 7 \\ 1 & 0 \end{pmatrix}$$

A. $\begin{pmatrix} 10 & 10 \\ 10 & 15 \end{pmatrix}$

B. $\begin{pmatrix} 13 & 7 \\ 9 & 16 \end{pmatrix}$

C. 45

D. $\begin{pmatrix} 20 \\ 25 \end{pmatrix}$

(Easy) (Skill 9.2)

72. The product of two matrices can be found only if:

A. The number of rows in the first matrix is equal to the number of rows in the second matrix

B. The number of columns in the first matrix is equal to the number of columns in the second matrix

C. The number of columns in the first matrix is equal to the number of rows in the second matrix

D. The number of rows in the first matrix is equal to the number of columns in the second matrix

(Average) (Skill 9.2)

73. Solve the following matrix equation:

$$3x + \begin{pmatrix} 1 & 5 & 2 \\ 0 & 6 & 9 \end{pmatrix} = \begin{pmatrix} 7 & 17 & 5 \\ 3 & 9 & 9 \end{pmatrix}$$

A. $\begin{pmatrix} 2 & 4 & 1 \\ 1 & 1 & 0 \end{pmatrix}$

B. 2

C. $\begin{pmatrix} 8 & 23 & 7 \\ 3 & 15 & 18 \end{pmatrix}$

D. $\begin{pmatrix} 9 \\ 2 \end{pmatrix}$

(Rigorous) (Skill 9.2)

74. Evaluate the following matrix product

$$\begin{pmatrix} 2 & 1 & 3 \\ 2 & 2 & 4 \end{pmatrix} \begin{pmatrix} 6 & 5 \\ 2 & 1 \\ 2 & 7 \end{pmatrix}$$

A. $\begin{pmatrix} 20 & 32 & 24 \\ 24 & 40 & 48 \end{pmatrix}$

B. $\begin{pmatrix} 20 & 32 \\ 40 & 24 \\ 24 & 48 \end{pmatrix}$

C. 116

D. $\begin{pmatrix} 20 & 32 \\ 24 & 40 \end{pmatrix}$

(Average) (Skill 9.4)

75. Find the value of the determinant of the matrix.

$$\begin{vmatrix} 2 & 1 & -1 \\ 4 & -1 & 4 \\ 0 & -3 & 2 \end{vmatrix}$$

A. 0

B. 23

C. 24

D. 40

(Average) (Skill 10.2)

76. Which of the following is a recursive definition of the sequence $\{1, 2, 2, 4, 8, 32, ...\}$?

A. $N_i = 2N_{i-1}$

B. $N_i = 2N_{i-2}$

C. $N_i = N^2_{i-1}$

D. $N_i = N_{i-1}N_{i-2}$

(Average) (Skill 10.4)

77. What is the sum of the first 20 terms of the geometric sequence (2, 4, 8, 16, 32, …)?

    A. 2,097,150

    B. 1,048,575

    C. 524,288

    D. 1,048,576

(Rigorous) (Skill 10.4)

78. Find the sum of the first one hundred terms in the progression.
    (−6, −2, 2, …)

    A. 19,200

    B. 19,400

    C. −604

    D. 604

(Average) (Skill 10.3)

79. On which of the following sets is multiplication not symmetric?

    A. Real numbers

    B. Complex numbers

    C. Polynomials

    D. Matrices

(Average) (Skill 10.4)

80. If an initial deposit of $1,000 is made to a savings account with a continuously compounded annual interest rate of 5%, how much money is in the account after 4.5 years?

    A. $1,200.00

    B. $1,225.00

    C. $1,245.52

    D. $1,252.29

ANSWER KEY								
1. B	10. C	19. B	28. A	37. C	46. D	55. A	64. D	73. A
2. B	11. C	20. B	29. C	38. A	47. A	56. D	65. B	74. D
3. A	12. A	21. A	30. B	39. A	48. D	57. B	66. C	75. C
4. C	13. B	22. C	31. C	40. B	49. A	58. C	67. A	76. D
5. C	14. A	23. B	32. B	41. C	50. A	59. B	68. B	77. A
6. D	15. C	24. C	33. D	42. C	51. B	60. C	69. B	78. A
7. B	16. C	25. A	34. D	43. A	52. D	61. B	70. D	79. D
8. B	17. A	26. D	35. C	44. B	53. D	62. D	71. A	80. D
9. D	18. C	27. C	36. D	45. C	54. D	63. B	72. C	

RIGOR TABLE	
Rigor level	**Questions**
Easy 25%	1, 7, 13, 15, 22, 31, 32, 43, 49, 60, 61, 68, 69, 70, 71, 72
Average Rigor 50%	2, 3, 4, 6, 9, 11, 12, 14, 16, 17, 24, 25, 26, 27, 33, 34, 35, 40, 41, 42, 44, 45, 50, 51, 52, 62, 73, 75, 76, 77, 79, 80
Rigorous 50%	5, 8, 10, 18, 19, 20, 21, 23, 28, 29, 30, 36, 37, 38, 39, 46, 47, 48, 53, 54, 55, 56, 57, 58, 59, 63, 64, 65, 66, 67, 74, 78

Sample Questions with Rationales

(Easy) (Skill 1.3)

1. **Find the LCM of 27, 90, and 84.**

   A. 90

   B. 3,780

   C. 204,120

   D. 1,260

   Answer: B

   To find the LCM of the above numbers, factor each into its prime factors and multiply each common factor the maximum number of times it occurs. Thus, $27 = 3 \times 3 \times 3$; $90 = 2 \times 3 \times 3 \times 5$; $84 = 2 \times 2 \times 3 \times 7$; LCM $= 2 \times 2 \times 3 \times 3 \times 3 \times 5 \times 7 = 3,780$.

(Average) (Skill 1.2)

2. **Which of the following sets is closed under division?**

   I) {½, 1, 2, 4}

   II) {-1, 1}

   III) {-1, 0, 1}

   A. I only

   B. II only

   C. III only

   D. I and II

   Answer: B

   I is not closed because $\frac{4}{0.5} = 8$ and 8 is not in the set. III is not closed because $\frac{1}{0}$ is undefined. II is closed because $\frac{-1}{1} = -1, \frac{1}{-1} = -1, \frac{1}{1} = 1, \frac{-1}{-1} = 1$ are all in the set.

(Average) (Skill 1.4)

3. **What would be the total cost of a suit for $295.99 and a pair of shoes for $69.95 including 6.5% sales tax?**

   A. $389.73

   B. $398.37

   C. $237.86

   D. $315.23

   Answer: A

   Before the tax, the total comes to $365.94. Then .065($365.94) = $23.79. With the tax added on, the total bill is $365.94 + $23.79 = $389.73. (A quicker way is 1.065($365.94) = $389.73.)

(Average) (Skill 1.3)

4. **Which of the following is always composite if x is odd, y is even, and both x and y are greater than or equal to 2?**

   A. $x + y$

   B. $3x + 2y$

   C. $5xy$

   D. $5x + 3y$

   Answer: C

   A composite number is a number that is not prime. The prime number sequence begins 2, 3, 5, 7, 11, 13, 17, … To determine which of the expressions is always composite, experiment with different values of x and y, such as $x = 3$ and $y = 2$, or $x = 5$ and $y = 2$. It turns out that $5xy$ will always be an even number and, therefore, composite if $y = 2$.

(Rigorous) (Skill 1.8)

5. **Find the length of the major axis of $x^2 + 9y^2 = 36$.**

   A. 4

   B. 6

   C. 12

   D. 8

   Answer: C

   Dividing by 36 yields $\frac{x^2}{36} + \frac{y^2}{4} = 1$, which implies that the ellipse intersects the x-axis at 6 and -6. Therefore, the length of the major axis is 12.

(Average) (Skill 1.5)

6. **Which graph represents the solution set for $x^2 - 5x > -6$?**

   A. ⊕———⊕
      -2 0 2

   B. ⊕———————⊕
      -3 0 3

   C. ⊕————⊕
      -2 0 2

   D. ⊕⊕
      0 2 3

   Answer: D

   Rewriting the inequality yields $x^2 - 5x + 6 > 0$. Factoring yields $(x - 2)(x - 3) > 0$. The two cut-off points on the number line are now at $x = 2$ and $x = 3$. Choosing a random number in each of the three parts of the number line, test each one to see if it produces a true statement. If $x = 0$ or $x = 4$, $(x - 2)(x - 3) > 0$ is true. If $x = 2.5$, $(x - 2)(x - 3) > 0$ is false. Therefore, the solution set is all numbers smaller than 2 or greater than 3.

(Easy) (Skill 1.5)

7. **What is the equation of the graph shown below?**

   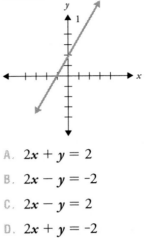

   A. $2x + y = 2$

   B. $2x - y = -2$

   C. $2x - y = 2$

   D. $2x + y = -2$

   Answer: B

   By observation, we see that the graph has a y-intercept of 2 and a slope of $\frac{2}{1} = 2$. Therefore, its equation is $y = mx + b = 2x + 2$. Rearranging the terms yields $2x - y = -2$.

(Rigorous) (Skill 1.8)

8. **Which equation represents a circle with a diameter whose endpoints are (0, 7) and (0, 3)?**

   A. $x^2 + y^2 + 21 = 0$

   B. $x^2 + y^2 - 10y + 21 = 0$

   C. $x^2 + y^2 - 10y + 9 = 0$

   D. $x^2 - y^2 - 10y + 9 = 0$

   Answer: B

   With a diameter going from (0,7) to (0,3), the diameter of the circle must be 4, the radius must be 2, and the center of the circle must be at (0,5). Using the standard form for the equation of a circle, we get $(x - 0)^2 + (y - 5)^2 = 2^2$. Expanding yields $x^2 + y^2 - 10y + 21 = 0$.

(Average) (Skill 1.3)

9. **What is the smallest number that is divisible by 3 and 5 and leaves a remainder of 3 when divided by 7?**

    A. 15

    B. 18

    C. 25

    D. 45

Answer: D

To be divisible by both 3 and 5, the number must be divisible by 15. Inspecting the first few multiples of 15, you will find that 45 is the first of the sequence that is 4 greater than a multiple of 7.

(Rigorous) (Skill 1.5)

10. **Solve for x: $18 = 4 + |2x|$**

    A. {-11, 7}

    B. {-7, 0, 7}

    C. {-7, 7}

    D. {-11, 11}

Answer: C

Using the definition of absolute value, two equations are possible: $18 = 4 + 2x$ or $18 = 4 - 2x$. Solving for x yields $x = 7$ or $x = -7$.

(Average) (Skill 2.1)

11. **The mass of a Chips Ahoy cookie is about:**

    A. 1 kilogram

    B. 1 gram

    C. 15 grams

    D. 15 milligrams

Answer: C

Since an ordinary cookie would not weigh as much as 1 kilogram or as little as 1 gram or 15 milligrams, the only reasonable answer is 15 grams.

(Average) (Skill 2.1)

12. **Given that M is a mass, V is a velocity, A is an acceleration and T is a time, what type of unit corresponds to the overall expression $\frac{AMT}{V}$?**

    A. Mass

    B. Time

    C. Velocity

    D. Acceleration

Answer: A

Use unit analysis to find the simplest expression for the units associated with the expression. Choose any unit system: for example, the metric system.

$$\frac{AMT}{V} - \frac{(\frac{m}{s^2})(kg)(s)}{(\frac{m}{s})}$$

Simplify the units in the expression

$$\frac{AMT}{V} - \frac{(\frac{m}{s})(kg)}{(\frac{m}{s})} = kg$$

Kilograms is a unit of mass, and thus the correct answer is A.

(Easy) (Skill 2.2)

13. **Which word best describes a set of measured values that are all very similar but that all deviate significantly from the expected result?**

    A. Perfect

    B. Precise

    C. Accurate

    D. Appropriate

Answer: B

A set of measurements that are close to the same value are precise. Measurements that are close to the actual (or expected) value are accurate. In this case, the set of measurements described in the question are best summarized as precise.

(Average) (Skill 2.1)

14. The term "cubic feet" indicates which kind of measurement?

    A. Volume

    B. Mass

    C. Length

    D. Distance

Answer: A

The word *cubic* indicates that this is a term describing volume.

(Easy) (Skill 3.6)

15. Find the surface area of a box that is 3 feet wide, 5 feet tall, and 4 feet deep.

    A. 47 sq. ft.

    B. 60 sq. ft.

    C. 94 sq. ft.

    D. 188 sq. ft.

Answer: C

Assume the base of the rectangular solid (box) is 3 by 4, and the height is 5. Then the surface area of the top and bottom together is $2(12) = 24$. The sum of the areas of the front and back are $2(15) = 30$, and the sum of the areas of the sides are $2(20) = 40$. The total surface area is therefore 94 square feet.

(Average) (Skill 3.6)

16. Find the height of a box with surface area of 94 sq. ft. with a width of 3 feet and a depth of 4 feet.

    A. 3 ft.

    B. 4 ft.

    C. 5 ft.

    D. 6 ft.

Answer: C

Use the expression for surface area and solve for the unknown value h.

$94 = 2(3h) + 2(4h) + 2(12)$
$94 = 6h + 8h + 24$
$94 = 14h + 24$
$70 = 14h$
$5 = h$

Thus, the height of the box is 5 feet.

(Average) (Skill 3.6)

17. Given a 30 meter by 60 meter garden with a circular fountain with a 5 meter radius, calculate the area of the portion of the garden not occupied by the fountain.

    A. 1,721 m²

    B. 1,879 m²

    C. 2,585 m²

    D. 1,015 m²

Answer: A

Find the area of the garden and then subtract the area of the fountain:
$30(60) - \pi(5)^2$ or approximately 1,721 square meters.

(Rigorous) (Skill 3.6)

18. **If the area of the base of a cone is tripled, the volume will be**

    A. the same as the original

    B. 9 times the original

    C. 3 times the original

    D. 3 p times the original

Answer: C

The formula for the volume of a cone is $V = \frac{1}{3}Bh$ where B is the area of the circular base and h is the height. If the area of the base is tripled, the volume becomes $V = \frac{1}{3}(3B)h = Bh$, or three times the original volume.

(Rigorous) (Skill 3.6)

19. **Find the area of the figure pictured below.**

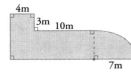

    A. 136.47 m²

    B. 148.48 m²

    C. 293.86 m²

    D. 178.47 m²

Answer: B

Divide the figure into 2 rectangles and one quarter circle. The tall rectangle on the left has dimensions 10 by 4 and area 40. The rectangle in the center has dimensions 7 by 10 and area 70. The quarter circle has area $.25(\pi)7^2 = 38.48$. The total area is therefore approximately 148.48.

(Rigorous) (Skill 3.6)

20. **Compute the area of the shaded region, given a radius of 5 meters. Point O is the center.**

    A. 7.13 cm²

    B. 7.13 m²

    C. 78.5 m²

    D. 19.63 m²

Answer: B

The area of triangle AOB is $.5(5)(5) = 12.5$ square meters. Since $\frac{90}{360} = .25$, the area of sector AOB (the pie-shaped piece) is approximately $.25(\pi)5^2 = 19.63$. Subtracting the triangle area from the sector area to get the area of segment AB yields approximately $19.63 - 12.5 = 7.13$ square meters.

(Rigorous) (Skill 5.4)

21. **The length of a picture frame is 2 inches greater than its width. If the area of the frame is 143 square inches, what is its width?**

    A. 11 inches

    B. 13 inches

    C. 12 inches

    D. 10 inches

Answer: A

First, set up the equation for the problem. If the width of the picture frame is w, then $w(w + 2) = 143$. Next, solve the equation to obtain w. Using the method of completing squares yields $w^2 + 2w + 1 = 144$; $(w + 1)^2 = 144$; $w + 1 = \pm 12$. Thus $w = 11$ or -13. Since the width cannot be negative, the correct answer is 11.

(Easy) (Skill 3.1)

22. **When you begin by assuming that the conclusion of a theorem is false, then show through a sequence of logically correct steps that you contradict an accepted fact, this is known as:**

    A. Inductive reasoning

    B. Direct proof

    C. Indirect proof

    D. Exhaustive proof

Answer: C

By definition, this describes the procedure of an indirect proof.

(Rigorous) (Skill 3.6)

23. **Determine the area of the shaded region of the trapezoid in terms of x and y.**

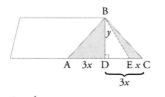

    A. $4xy$

    B. $2xy$

    C. $3x^2y$

    D. There is not enough information given

Answer: B

To find the area of the shaded region, find the area of triangle ABC and then subtract the area of triangle DBE. The area of triangle ABC is $.5(6x)(y) = 3xy$. The area of triangle DBE is $.5(2x)(y) = xy$. The difference is $2xy$.

(Average) (Skill 3.1)

24. **Which theorem can be used to prove $\triangle BAK \cong \triangle MKA$?**

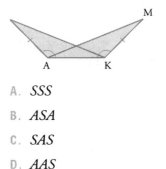

    A. SSS

    B. ASA

    C. SAS

    D. AAS

Answer: C

Since side AK is common to both triangles, the triangles can be proved congruent by using the Side-Angle-Side Postulate.

(Average) (Skill 3.3)

25. **Choose the correct statement concerning the median and altitude in a triangle.**

    A. The median and altitude of a triangle may be the same segment

    B. The median and altitude of a triangle are always different segments

    C. The median and altitude of a right triangle are always the same segment

    D. The median and altitude of an isosceles triangle are always the same segment

Answer: A

The most one can say with certainty is that the median (segment drawn to the midpoint of the opposite side) and the altitude (segment drawn perpendicular to the opposite side) of a triangle <u>may</u> coincide, but they more often do not. In an isosceles triangle, the median and the altitude to the <u>base</u> are the same segment.

(Average) (Skill 3.7)

26. **Compute the distance from (-2, 7) to the line $x = 5$.**

    A. -9

    B. -7

    C. 5

    D. 7

Answer: D

The line $x = 5$ is a vertical line passing through (5, 0) on the Cartesian plane. By observation, the distance along the horizontal line from the point (-2, 7) to the line $x = 5$ is 7 units.

(Average) (Skill 3.2)

27. **Which of the following statements about a trapezoid is incorrect?**

    A. It has one pair of parallel sides

    B. The parallel sides are called bases

    C. If the two bases are the same length, the trapezoid is called isosceles

    D. The median is parallel to the bases

Answer: C

A trapezoid is isosceles if the two legs (not bases) are the same length.

(Rigorous) (Skill 3.7)

28. **Given $K(-4, y)$ and $M(2, -3)$ with midpoint L(x, 1), determine the values of x and y.**

    A. $x = -1, y = 5$

    B. $x = 3, y = 2$

    C. $x = 5, y = -1$

    D. $x = -1, y = -1$

Answer: A

The formula for finding the midpoint (a, b) of a segment passing through the points (x_1, y_1) and (x_2, y_2) is $(a, b) = (\frac{x_1 + x_2}{2}, \frac{y_1 + y_2}{2})$. Setting up the corresponding equations from this information yields $x = \frac{-4 + 2}{2}$ and $1 = \frac{y - 3}{2}$. Solving for x and y yields $x = -1$ and $y = 5$.

(Rigorous) (Skill 3.2)

29. **What is the degree measure of an interior angle of a regular 10-sided polygon?**

    A. 18°

    B. 36°

    C. 144°

    D. 54°

Answer: C

The formula for finding the measure of each interior angle of a regular polygon with n sides is $\frac{(n - 2)180}{n}$. For $n = 10$, $\frac{8(180)}{10} = 144$.

(Rigorous) (Skill 3.4)

30. **What is the measure of minor arc AD, given measure of arc PS is 40° and $m < K = 10°$?**

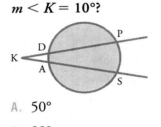

A. 50°

B. 20°

C. 30°

D. 25°

Answer: B

The formula relating the measure of angle K and the two arcs it intercepts is $m\angle K = \frac{1}{2}(mPS - mAD)$ Substituting the known values yields $10 = \frac{1}{2}(40 - mAD)$. Solving for mAD gives an answer of 20 degrees.

(Easy) (Skill 4.1)

31. **The cosine function is equivalent to:**

A. $\frac{1}{sine}$

B. $\frac{1}{tangent}$

C. $\frac{sine}{tangent}$

D. $\frac{cotangent}{sine}$

Answer: C

The cosine function is clearly not the reciprocal of the sine or tangent functions. Simplify answers C or D to determine which is the correct answer. For instance: $\frac{sine}{tangent} = (sine)(cotangent) = sine(\frac{cosine}{sine}) = cosine$

Thus, answer C is correct.

(Easy) (Skill 4.3)

32. **Which of the following is a Pythagorean identity?**

A. $\sin^2 \theta - \cos^2 \theta = 1$

B. $\sin^2 \theta + \cos^2 \theta = 1$

C. $\cos^2 \theta - \sin^2 \theta = 1$

D. $\cos^2 \theta - \tan^2 \theta = 1$

Answer: B

The Pythagorean identity $\sin^2 \theta + \cos^2 \theta = 1$ is derived from the definitions of the sine and cosine functions and Pythagorean Theorem of geometry.

(Average) (Skill 4.1)

33. **Determine the measures of angles A and B.**

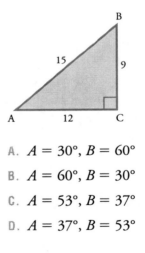

A. $A = 30°, B = 60°$

B. $A = 60°, B = 30°$

C. $A = 53°, B = 37°$

D. $A = 37°, B = 53°$

Answer: D

It is the case that $\tan A = \frac{9}{12} = .75$ and $\tan^{-1} .75 = 37$ degrees. Since angle B is complementary to angle A, the measure of angle B is therefore 53 degrees.

(Average) (Skill 4.3)

34. **Which expression is not identical to sin x?**

    A. $\sqrt{1 - \cos^2 x}$

    B. $\tan x \cos x$

    C. $1/\csc x$

    D. $1/\sec x$

Answer: D

Using the basic definitions of the trigonometric functions and the Pythagorean identity, it can be seen that the first three options are all identical to sin x. $\frac{1}{\sec x} = \cos x$ is not the same as sin x.

(Average) (Skill 4.5)

35. **Determine the rectangular coordinates of the point with polar coordinates (5, 60°).**

    A. (0.5, 0.87)

    B. (−0.5, 0.87)

    C. (2.5, 4.33)

    D. (25, 150°)

Answer: C

Given the polar point $(r, \theta) = (5, 60)$, the rectangular coordinates can be found as follows: $(x, y) = (r\cos\theta, r\sin\theta) = (5 \cos 60, 5 \sin 60) = (2.5, 4.33)$.

(Rigorous) (Skill 4.3)

36. **Which expression is equivalent to $1 - \sin^2 x$?**

    A. $1 - \cos^2 x$

    B. $1 + \cos^2 x$

    C. $1/\sec x$

    D. $1/\sec^2 x$

Answer: D

Using the Pythagorean Identity, it is apparent that $\sin^2 x + \cos^2 x = 1$. Thus, $1 - \sin^2 x = \cos^2 x$, which by definition is equal to $1/\sec^2 x$.

(Rigorous) (Skill 4.1)

37. **For an acute angle x, sin $x = 0.6$. What is cot x?**

    A. $\frac{5}{3}$

    B. 0.75

    C. 1.33

    D. 1

Answer: C

Using the Pythagorean Identity, it is apparent that $\sin^2 x + \cos^2 x = 1$. Thus, $\cos x = \sqrt{1 - \frac{9}{25}} = \frac{4}{5}$ and $\cot x = \frac{\cos x}{\sin x} = \frac{4}{3}$.

(Rigorous) (Skill 5.4)

38. **Which of the following is a factor of the expression $9x^2 + 6x - 35$?**

    A. $3x - 5$

    B. $3x - 7$

    C. $x + 3$

    D. $x - 2$

Answer: A

Recognize that the given expression can be written as the sum of two squares and use the formula $a^2 - b^2 = (a + b)(a - b)$.

$9x^2 + 6x - 35 = (3x + 1)^2 - 36 = (3x + 1 + 6)(3x + 1 - 6) = (3x + 7)(3x - 5)$

(Rigorous) (Skill 5.4)

39. Which of the following is a factor of $6 + 48m^3$?

   A. $(1 + 2m)$

   B. $(1 - 8m)$

   C. $(1 + m - 2m)$

   D. $(1 - m + 2m)$

Answer: A

Removing the common factor of 6 and then factoring the sum of two cubes yields $6 + 48m^3 = 6(1 + 8m^3) = 6(1 + 2m)(1^2 - 2m + (2m)^2)$.

(Average) (Skill 5.4)

40. State the domain of the function $f(x) = \frac{3x - 6}{x^2 - 25}$.

   A. $x \neq 2$

   B. $x \neq 5, -5$

   C. $x \neq 2, -2$

   D. $x \neq 5$

Answer: B

The values 5 and -5 must be omitted from the domain because if x took on either of those values, the denominator of the fraction would have a value of 0. Therefore the fraction would be undefined. Thus, the domain of the function is all real numbers x not equal to 5 and -5.

(Average) (Skill 5.4)

41. Solve for x by factoring: $2x^2 - 3x - 2 = 0$

   A. $x = (-1, 2)$

   B. $x = (0.5, -2)$

   C. $x = (-0.5, 2)$

   D. $x = (1, -2)$

Answer: C

Because $2x^2 - 3x - 2 = 2x^2 - 4x + x - 2 = 2x(x - 2) + (x - 2) = (2x + 1)(x - 2) = 0$, then $x = -0.5$ or 2.

(Average) (Skill 5.5)

42. Given $f(x) = 3x - 2$ and $g(x) = x^2$, determine $g(f(x))$.

   A. $3x^2 - 2$

   B. $9x^2 + 4$

   C. $9x^2 - 12x + 4$

   D. $3x^3 - 2$

Answer: C

The composite function $g(f(x))$ is $(3x - 2)^2 = 9x^2 - 12x + 4$.

(Easy) (Skill 5.4)

43. Which of the following is equivalent to $\sqrt[b]{x^a}$?

   A. $x^{a/b}$

   B. $x^{b/a}$

   C. $a^{x/b}$

   D. $b^{x/a}$

Answer: A

The bth root, expressed in the form 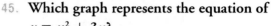, can also be written as an exponential, $1/b$. Writing the expression in this form, $(x^a)^{1/b}$, and then multiplying exponents yields $x^{a/b}$.

(Average) (Skill 5.4)

44. **How does the function $y = x^3 + x^2 + 4$ behave from $x = 1$ to $x = 3$?**

    A. Increasing, then decreasing

    B. Increasing

    C. Decreasing

    D. Neither increasing nor decreasing

Answer: B

To find critical points, take the derivative of the function and set it equal to 0, and solve for x.

$$f'(x) = 3x^2 + 2x = x(3x + 2)$$

The critical points are at $x = 0$ and $x = -\frac{2}{3}$. Neither of these is on the interval from $x = 1$ to $x = 3$. Test the endpoints: at $x = 1$, $y = 6$, and at $x = 3$, $y = 38$. Since the derivative is positive for all values of x from $x = 1$ to $x = 3$, the curve is increasing on the entire interval.

(Average) (Skill 5.4)

45. **Which graph represents the equation of $y = x^2 + 3x$?**

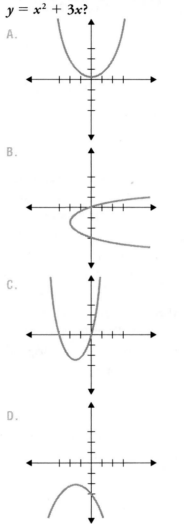

A.

B.

C.

D.

Answer: C

Answer B is not the graph of a function. Answer D is the graph of a parabola, where the coefficient of x^2 is negative. Answer A appears to be the graph of $y = x^2$. To find the x-intercepts of $y = x^2 + 3x$, set $y = 0$ and solve for x: $0 = x^2 + 3x = x(x + 3)$. This gives the solution $x = 0$ or $x = -3$. Therefore, the graph of the function intersects the x-axis at $x = 0$ and $x = -3$.

(Rigorous) (Skill 5.4)

46. **Find the zeroes of**
    $$f(x) = x^3 + 3x^2 - 14x - 24$$

    A. 4, 3, 2

    B. 3, –8

    C. 7, –2, –1

    D. 4, –3, –2

    Answer: D

    Possible rational roots of the equation $0 = x^3 + x^2 - 14x - 24$ are all the positive and negative factors of 24. By substituting into the equation, we find that –2 is a root, and therefore that $x + 2$ is a factor. By performing the long division $\frac{(x^3 + x^2 - 14x - 24)}{(x + 2)}$, we can find that another factor of the original equation is $x^2 - x - 12$ or $(x - 4)(x + 3)$. Therefore the zeros of the original function are –2, –3 and 4.

(Rigorous) (Skill 5.4)

47. **Which equation corresponds to the logarithmic statement: $\log_x k = m$?**

    A. $x^m = k$

    B. $k^m = x$

    C. $x^k = m$

    D. $m^x = k$

    Answer: A

    By definition of log form and exponential form, $\log_x k = m$ corresponds to $x^m = k$.

(Rigorous) (Skill 5.4)

48. **Solve for x: $10^{x-3} + 5 = 105$.**

    A. 3

    B. 10

    C. 2

    D. 5

    Answer: D

    Simplify: $10^{x-3} = 100$. Taking the logarithm to base 10 of both sides yields $(x - 3)\log_{10} 10 = \log_{10} 100$. Thus, $x - 3 = 2$ and $x = 5$.

(Easy) (Skill 6.1)

49. **L'Hopital's rule provides a method to evaluate which of the following?**

    A. Limit of a function

    B. Derivative of a function

    C. Sum of an arithmetic series

    D. Sum of a geometric series

    Answer: A

    L'Hopital's rule is used to find the limit of a function by taking the derivatives of the numerator and denominator. Since the primary purpose of the rule is to find the limit, A is the correct answer.

(Average) (Skill 6.7)

50. **Find the area under the function $y = x^2 + 4$ from $x = 3$ to $x = 6$.**

    A. 75

    B. 21

    C. 96

    D. 57

Answer: A

To find the area, set up the definite integral: $\int_{3}^{6}(x^2 + 4)dx = (\frac{x^3}{3} + 4x)$. Evaluate the expression at $x = 6$ and $x = 3$, and then subtract to get $(72 + 24) - (9 + 12) = 75$.

(Average) (Skill 6.7)

51. **If the velocity of a body is given by $v = 16 - t^2$, find the distance traveled from $t = 0$ until the body comes to a complete stop.**

    A. 16

    B. 43

    C. 48

    D. 64

Answer: B

Recall that the derivative of the distance function is the velocity function. Conversely, the integral of the velocity function is the distance function. To find the time needed for the body to come to a stop when $v = 0$, solve for t: $v = 16 - t^2 = 0$. The result is $t = 4$ seconds. The distance function is $s = 16t - \frac{t^3}{3}$. Evaluating the function at the limits $t = 0$ and $t = 4$, we get $s = 0$ at $t = 0$ and $s = 64 - 64/3$ at $t = 4$. So the value of the definite integral is $(64 - 63/3) - 0$ or approximately 43 units.

(Average) (Skill 6.1)

52. **Find the following limit:** $\lim_{x\to 2} \frac{x^2 - 4}{x - 2}$

    A. 0

    B. Infinity

    C. 2

    D. 4

Answer: D

First, factor the numerator and cancel the common factor to get the limit.

$\lim_{x\to 2} \frac{x^2 - 4}{x - 2} = \lim_{x\to 2} \frac{(x - 2)(x + 2)}{(x - 2)} = \lim_{x\to 2} (x + 2) = 4$

(Rigorous) (Skill 6.5)

53. **Find the first derivative of the function: $f(x) = x^3 + 6x^2 + 5x + 4$?**

    A. $3x^3 - 12x^2 + 5x$

    B. $3x^2 - 12x^2 - 5$

    C. $3x^2 - 12x^2 + 9$

    D. $3x^2 + 12x + 5$

Answer: D

Use the Power Rule for polynomial differentiation: if $y = ax^n$, then $y' = nax^{n-1}$. Apply this rule to each term in the polynomial to yield the result in answer D.

(Rigorous) (Skill 6.6)

54. **Find the absolute maximum obtained by the function $y = 2x^2 + 3x$ on the interval $x = 0$ to $x = 3$.**

    A. $-\frac{3}{4}$

    B. $-\frac{4}{3}$

    C. 0

    D. 27

Answer: D

Find the critical point at $x = -.75$ as done in #44. Since the critical point is not in the interval from $x = 0$ to $x = 3$, simply find the values of the function at the endpoints. The endpoints are $x = 0$, $y = 0$, and $x = 3$, $y = 27$. Therefore, 27 is the absolute maximum on the given interval.

(Rigorous) (Skill 6.8)

55. **Find the antiderivative for $4x^3 - 2x + 6 = y$**

    A. $x^4 - x^2 + 6x + C$

    B. $x^4 - \frac{2}{3}x^3 + 6x + C$

    C. $12x^2 - 2 + C$

    D. $\frac{4}{3}x^4 - x^2 + 6x + C$

Answer: A

Use the rule for polynomial integration: given ax^n, the antiderivative is $\frac{ax^{n+1}}{n+1}$. Apply this rule to each term in the polynomial to get the result in answer A.

(Rigorous) (Skill 6.8)

56. **Find the antiderivative for the function $y = e^{3x}$.**

    A. $3x(e^{3x}) + C$

    B. $3(e^{3x}) + C$

    C. $\frac{1}{3}(e^x) + C$

    D. $\frac{1}{3}(e^{3x}) + C$

Answer: D

Use the rule for integration of functions of e $(\int e^x dx = e^x + C)$ along with definition of a new variable $u = 3x$. The result is answer D.

(Rigorous) (Skill 6.8)

57. **Evaluate: $\int_0^2 (x^2 + x - 1)dx$**

    A. 11/3

    B. 8/3

    C. −8/3

    D. −11/3

Answer: B

Use the fundamental theorem of calculus to find the definite integral: given a continuous function f on an interval $[a, b]$, then $\int_a^b f(x)dx = F(b) - F(a)$, where F is an antiderivative of f.

$\int_0^2 (x^2 + x - 1)dx = (\frac{x^3}{3} + \frac{x^2}{2} - x)$

Evaluate the expression at $x = 2$, at $x = 0$, and then subtract to get $\frac{8}{3} + \frac{4}{2} - 2 - 0 = \frac{8}{3}$.

(Rigorous) (Skill 6.1)

58. **Find the following limit: $\lim\limits_{x \to 0} \frac{\sin 2x}{5x}$**

    A. Infinity

    B. 0

    C. 0.4

    D. 1

Answer: C

Since substituting $x = 0$ will give an undefined answer, we can use L'Hopital's rule and take derivatives of both the numerator and denominator to find the limit.

$\lim\limits_{x \to 0} \frac{\sin 2x}{5x} = \lim\limits_{x \to 0} \frac{2\cos 2x}{5} = \frac{2}{5} = 0.4$

(Rigorous) (Skill 7.2)

59. **Compute the standard deviation for the following set of temperatures:**
    (37, 38, 35, 37, 38, 40, 36, 39)

    A. 37.5

    B. 1.5

    C. 0.5

    D. 2.5

Answer: B

First find the mean: 300/8 = 37.5. Then, using the formula for standard deviation yields

$$\sqrt{\frac{2(37.5-37)^2+2(37.5-38)^2+(37.5-35)^2+(37.5-40)^2+(37.5-36)^2+(37.5-39)^2}{8}}$$

This expression has a value of 1.5.

(Easy) (Skill 7.2)

60. **Compute the median for the following data set:**

    {12, 19, 13, 16, 17, 14}

    A. 14.5

    B. 15.17

    C. 15

    D. 16

    Answer: C

    Arrange the data in ascending order: 12, 13, 14, 16, 17, 19. The median is the middle value in a list with an odd number of entries. When there is an even number of entries, the median is the mean of the two center entries. Here the average of 14 and 16 is 15.

(Easy) (Skill 8.1)

61. **A jar contains 3 red marbles, 5 white marbles, 1 green marble, and 15 blue marbles. If one marble is picked at random from the jar, what is the probability that it will be red?**

    A. $\frac{1}{3}$

    B. $\frac{1}{8}$

    C. $\frac{3}{8}$

    D. $\frac{1}{24}$

    Answer: B

    The total number of marbles is 24 and the number of red marbles is 3. Thus the probability of picking a red marble from the jar is $\frac{3}{24} = \frac{1}{8}$.

(Average) (Skill 7.7)

62. **Which of the following is not a valid method of collecting statistical data?**

    A. Random sampling

    B. Systematic sampling

    C. Cluster sampling

    D. Cylindrical sampling

    Answer: D

    There is no such method as cylindrical sampling.

(Rigorous) (Skill 7.2)

63. Half the students in a class scored 80% on an exam, and most of the rest scored 85%, except for one student who scored 10%. Which would be the best measure of central tendency for the test scores?

   A. Mean

   B. Median

   C. Mode

   D. Either the median or the mode because they are equal

Answer: B

In this set of data, the median is the most representative measure of central tendency because the median is independent of extreme values. Because of the 10% outlier, the mean (average) would be disproportionately skewed. In this data set, it is true that the median and the mode (number which occurs most often) are the same, but the median remains the best choice because of its special properties.

(Rigorous) (Skill 7.3)

64. If the correlation between two variables is given as zero, the association between the two variables is:

   A. Negative linear

   B. Positive linear

   C. Quadratic

   D. Random

Answer: D

A correlation of 1 indicates a perfect positive linear association, a correlation of -1 indicates a perfect negative linear association, and a correlation of zero indicates a random relationship between the variables.

(Rigorous) (Skill 8.2)

65. A die is rolled several times. What is the probability that a 3 will not appear before the third roll of the die?

   A. $\frac{1}{3}$

   B. $\frac{25}{216}$

   C. $\frac{25}{36}$

   D. $\frac{1}{216}$

Answer: B

The probability that a 3 will not appear before the third roll is the same as the probability that the first two rolls will consist of numbers other than 3. Since the probability of any one roll resulting in a number other than 3 is $\frac{5}{6}$, the probability of the first two rolls resulting in a number other than 3 is $\left(\frac{5}{6}\right) \times \left(\frac{5}{6}\right) = \frac{25}{36}$.

(Rigorous) (Skill 8.2)

66. If there are three people in a room, what is the probability that at least two of them will share a birthday? (Assume a year has 365 days.)

   A. 0.67

   B. 0.05

   C. 0.008

   D. 0.33

Answer: C

The best way to approach this problem is to use the fact that the probability of an event plus the probability of the event not happening is unity. First, find the probability that no two people will share a birthday, and then subtract that value from 1. The probability that two of the people will not share a birthday is $\frac{364}{365}$ (since the second person's birthday can be one of the 364 days other than the birthday of the first person). The probability that the third person will also not share either of the first two birthdays is $\left(\frac{364}{365}\right)\left(\frac{363}{365}\right) = 0.992$. Therefore, the probability that at least two people will share a birthday is $1 - 0.992 = 0.008$.

(Rigorous) (Skill 8.2)

67. **A baseball team has a 60% chance of winning any particular game in a seven-game series. What is the probability that it will win the series by winning games six and seven?**

    A. 8.3%

    B. 36%

    C. 50%

    D. 60%

Answer: A

The team needs to win four games to win a seven-game series. Thus, if the team needs to win games six and seven to win the series, it can only win two of the first five games. There are 10 different ways in which the team can win two of the first five games (where W represents a win and L represents a loss): WWLLL, WLLLW, WLLWL, WLWLL, LWWLL, LWLWL, LWLLW, LLWLW, LLWWL and LLLWW. This is also the same as the number of combinations of 5 taken 2 at a time. In each case, the probability that the team will win two games and lose three is the following:

P(2 wins and 3 losses) = $(0.6)^2(0.4)^3$ = 0.02304

Since there are ten ways this can occur, the probability of two wins out of five consecutive games is

P(2 wins out of 5 games) = $10(0.6)^2(0.4)^3 = 0.2304$

The probability of the team winning the last two consecutive games is simply 0.6^2, or 0.36. Then, the probability that the team will win the series by winning games six and seven is the following:

P(Series win with wins in games 6 and 7) = $(0.2304)(0.36) = 0.082944$

(Easy) (Skill 7.1)

68. **What conclusion can be drawn from the graph below?**

MLK Elementary School
Student Enrollment

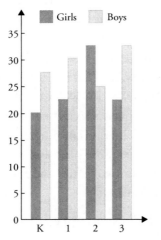

A. The number of students in first grade exceeds the number in second grade

B. There are more boys than girls in the entire school

C. There are more girls than boys in the first grade

D. Third grade has the largest number of students

Answer: B

In Kindergarten, first grade and third grade, there are more boys than girls. The number of extra girls in grade two is more than compensated by the extra boys in all the other grades put together.

(Easy) (Skill 7.1)

69. **The pie chart below shows sales at an automobile dealership for the first four months of a year. What percentage of the vehicles were sold in April?**

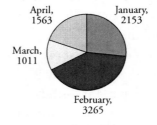

A. More than 50%

B. Less than 25%

C. Between 25% and 50%

D. None

Answer: B

It is clear from the chart that the April segment covers less than a quarter of the pie.

(Easy) (Skill 9.2)

70. **The scalar multiplication of the number 3 with the matrix $\begin{pmatrix} 2 & 1 \\ 3 & 5 \end{pmatrix}$ yields:**

A. 33

B. $\begin{pmatrix} 6 & 1 \\ 9 & 5 \end{pmatrix}$

C. $\begin{pmatrix} 2 & 3 \\ 3 & 15 \end{pmatrix}$

D. $\begin{pmatrix} 6 & 3 \\ 9 & 15 \end{pmatrix}$

Answer: D

In scalar multiplication of a matrix by a number, each element of the matrix is multiplied by that number.

(Easy) (Skill 9.2)

71. **Find the sum of the following matrices.**

$$\begin{pmatrix} 6 & 3 \\ 9 & 15 \end{pmatrix} \begin{pmatrix} 4 & 7 \\ 1 & 0 \end{pmatrix}$$

  A. $\begin{pmatrix} 10 & 10 \\ 10 & 15 \end{pmatrix}$

  B. $\begin{pmatrix} 13 & 7 \\ 9 & 16 \end{pmatrix}$

  C. 45

  D. $\begin{pmatrix} 20 \\ 25 \end{pmatrix}$

Answer: A

Two matrices with the same dimensions are added by adding the corresponding elements. In this case, element 1,1 (i.e. row 1, column 1) of the first matrix is added to element 1,1 of the second matrix; element 2,1 of the first matrix is added to element 2,1 of the second matrix; and so on for all four elements.

(Easy) (Skill 9.2)

72. **The product of two matrices can be found only if:**

  A. The number of rows in the first matrix is equal to the number of rows in the second matrix

  B. The number of columns in the first matrix is equal to the number of columns in the second matrix

  C. The number of columns in the first matrix is equal to the number of rows in the second matrix

  D. The number of rows in the first matrix is equal to the number of columns in the second matrix

Answer: C

The number of columns in the first matrix must equal the number of rows in the second matrix because the process of multiplication involves multiplying the elements of every row of the first matrix with corresponding elements of every column of the second matrix.

(Average) (Skill 9.2)

73. **Solve the following matrix equation:**

$$3x + \begin{pmatrix} 1 & 5 & 2 \\ 0 & 6 & 9 \end{pmatrix} = \begin{pmatrix} 7 & 17 & 5 \\ 3 & 9 & 9 \end{pmatrix}$$

  A. $\begin{pmatrix} 2 & 4 & 1 \\ 1 & 1 & 0 \end{pmatrix}$

  B. 2

  C. $\begin{pmatrix} 8 & 23 & 7 \\ 3 & 15 & 18 \end{pmatrix}$

  D. $\begin{pmatrix} 9 \\ 2 \end{pmatrix}$

Answer: A

Use the basic rules of algebra and matrices.

$$3x = \begin{pmatrix} 7 & 17 & 5 \\ 3 & 9 & 9 \end{pmatrix} - \begin{pmatrix} 1 & 5 & 2 \\ 0 & 6 & 9 \end{pmatrix} = \begin{pmatrix} 6 & 12 & 3 \\ 3 & 3 & 0 \end{pmatrix}$$

$$x = \frac{1}{3} \begin{pmatrix} 6 & 12 & 3 \\ 3 & 9 & 0 \end{pmatrix} = \begin{pmatrix} 2 & 4 & 1 \\ 1 & 1 & 0 \end{pmatrix}$$

(Rigorous) (Skill 9.2)

74. **Evaluate the following matrix product**

$$\begin{pmatrix} 2 & 1 & 3 \\ 2 & 2 & 4 \end{pmatrix} \begin{pmatrix} 6 & 5 \\ 2 & 1 \\ 2 & 7 \end{pmatrix}$$

A. $\begin{pmatrix} 20 & 32 & 24 \\ 24 & 40 & 48 \end{pmatrix}$

B. $\begin{pmatrix} 20 & 32 \\ 40 & 24 \\ 24 & 48 \end{pmatrix}$

C. 116

D. $\begin{pmatrix} 20 & 32 \\ 24 & 40 \end{pmatrix}$

Answer: D

The product of a 2 × 3 matrix with a 3 × 2 matrix is a 2 × 2 matrix. This alone should be enough to identify the correct answer. Each term in the 2 × 2 matrix is calculated as described below.

Matrix 1, row 1 multiplied by matrix 2, column 1 yields entry 1, 1: $2 \times 6 + 1 \times 2 + 3 \times 2 = 12 + 2 + 6 = 20$.

Matrix 1, row 1 multiplied by matrix 2, column 2 yields entry 1, 2: $2 \times 5 + 1 \times 1 + 3 \times 7 = 10 + 1 + 21 = 32$.

Matrix 1, row 2 multiplied by matrix 2, column 1 yields entry 2, 1: $2 \times 6 + 2 \times 2 + 4 \times 2 = 12 + 4 + 8 = 24$.

Matrix 1, row 2 multiplied by matrix 2, column 2 yields entry 2, 2: $2 \times 5 + 2 \times 1 + 4 \times 7 = 10 + 2 + 28 = 40$.

(Average) (Skill 9.4)

75. **Find the value of the determinant of the matrix.**

$$\begin{vmatrix} 2 & 1 & -1 \\ 4 & -1 & 4 \\ 0 & -3 & 2 \end{vmatrix}$$

A. 0

B. 23

C. 24

D. 40

Answer: C

To find the determinant of a matrix without the use of a graphing calculator, repeat the first two columns as shown,

```
2   1  -1   2   1
4  -1   4   4  -1
0  -3   2   0  -3
```

Starting with the top left-most entry (2), multiply the three numbers in the diagonal going down to the right: $2(-1)(2) = -4$. Do the same starting with 1: $1(4)(0) = 0$. Repeat starting with -1: $-1(4)(-3) = 12$. Adding these three numbers yields 8. Repeat the same process starting with the top right-most entry, 1. That is, multiply the three numbers in the diagonal going down to the left: $1(4)(2) = 8$. Do the same starting with 2: $2(4)(-3) = -24$. Repeat starting with -1: $-1(-1)(0) = 0$. Add these together to get -16. To find the determinant, subtract the second result from the first: $8 - (-16) = 24$.

(Average) (Skill 10.2)

76. **Which of the following is a recursive definition of the sequence {1, 2, 2, 4, 8, 32, ...}?**

    A. $N_i = 2N_{i-1}$

    B. $N_i = 2N_{i-2}$

    C. $N_i = N^2_{i-1}$

    D. $N_i = N_{i-1}N_{i-2}$

Answer: D

Test each answer, or look at the pattern of the numbers in the sequence. Note that each number (with the exception of the first two) is the product of the preceding two numbers. In recursive form using index i, the expression is $N_i = N_{i-1} N_{i-2}$ and the correct answer is D.

(Average) (Skill 10.4)

77. **What is the sum of the first 20 terms of the geometric sequence (2, 4, 8, 16, 32, ...)?**

    A. 2,097,150

    B. 1,048,575

    C. 524,288

    D. 1,048,576

Answer: A

For a geometric sequence $a, ar, ar^2, ..., ar^n$, the sum of the first n terms is given by $\frac{a(r^n - 1)}{r - 1}$. In this case, $a = 2$ and $r = 2$. Thus, the sum of the first 20 terms of the sequence is $\frac{2(2^{20} - 1)}{2 - 1} = 2,097,150$.

(Rigorous) (Skill 10.4)

78. **Find the sum of the first one hundred terms in the progression.**

    (–6, –2, 2, …)

    A. 19,200

    B. 19,400

    C. –604

    D. 604

Answer: A

Examine the pattern of the sequence. To find the 100th term, use the following expression:

$t100 = -6 + 99(4) = 390$

To find the sum of the first 100 terms, use

$S = \frac{100}{2}(-6 + 390) = 19200$

(Average) (Skill 10.3)

79. **On which of the following sets is multiplication not symmetric?**

    A. Real numbers

    B. Complex numbers

    C. Polynomials

    D. Matrices

Answer: D

A binary relation R is symmetric on a set if, for all a and b in a set, both aRb and bRa have the same truth value. For real numbers, complex numbers and polynomials with members a and b in each case, ab is always equal to ba. For matrices, however, ab is not always equal to ba for given matrices a and b. Thus, the correct answer is D.

(Average) (Skill 10.4)

80. **If an initial deposit of $1,000 is made to a savings account with a continuously compounded annual interest rate of 5%, how much money is in the account after 4.5 years?**

   A. $1,200.00

   B. $1,225.00

   C. $1,245.52

   D. $1,252.29

Answer: D

Use the formula for continually compounded interest: $A = Pe^{rt}$, where A is the amount in an account with a principal of P and annual interest rate r compounded continually for t years. Then:

$A = \$1000e^{(0.05)(4.5)}$

$\quad = \$1000e^{(0.225)}$

$\quad = \$1,252.29$

CPSIA information can be obtained at www.ICGtesting.com
Printed in the USA
LVOW031617200412

278500LV00002B/88/P